The Politic ...ought of African Independence

An Anthology of Sources

The Political Thought of African Independence

An Anthology of Sources

Edited by
Gregory R. Smulewicz-Zucker

With the Assistance of
Chelsea Schields

Hackett Publishing Company, Inc.
Indianapolis/Cambridge

Copyright © 2017 by Hackett Publishing Company, Inc.

All rights reserved
Printed in the United States of America

20 19 18 17   1 2 3 4 5 6 7

For further information, please address
    Hackett Publishing Company, Inc.
    P.O. Box 44937
    Indianapolis, Indiana 46244-0937

    www.hackettpublishing.com

Cover design by Rick Todhunter
Composition by Aptara, Inc.

Though every reasonable effort has been made to trace the owners of the copyrighted materials included in this book, in some instances this has proven impossible. Hackett Publishing will be glad to receive information leading to a more complete understanding of the permissions required for this book and in the meantime extends its apologies for any omissions.

Library of Congress Cataloging-in-Publication Data

Names: Smulewicz-Zucker, Gregory R., 1983– editor. | Schields, Chelsea, editor.
Title: The political thought of African independence : an anthology of
    sources / edited by Gregory Smulewicz-Zucker with the assistance of
    Chelsea Schields.
Description: Indianapolis ; Cambridge : Hackett Publishing Company, Inc.,
    2017. | Includes bibliographical references and index.
Identifiers: LCCN 2016035840 | ISBN 9781624665400 (pbk.) |
    ISBN 9781624665417 (cloth)
Subjects: LCSH: Decolonization—Africa. | Africa—History—Autonomy
    and independence movements. | Africa—Politics and government—19th
    century. | Africa–Politics and government—20th century.
Classification: LCC DT31 .P59 2017 | DDC 320.96—dc23
LC record available at https://lccn.loc.gov/2016035840

The paper used in this publication meets the minimum requirements of American National Standard for Information Sciences—Permanence of Paper for Printed Library Materials, ANSI Z39.48–1984.

∞

CONTENTS

ACKNOWLEDGMENTS

This volume has been almost a decade in the making and I have incurred many debts in the process. I am incredibly grateful to Rick Toddhunter and the entire team at Hackett. Rick has been committed to this project from its inception. It has been an unusually rewarding experience working with such an intellectually engaged editor. One of the great hurdles of this project and the cause of many delays has been securing rights to republish the many texts included in this volume. Many of these texts were first published during turbulent historical moments and it took time to determine who owned the rights to them. This necessitated an ongoing rethinking of the collection's design and contents. Christina Kowalewski and Frederick Courtright did a remarkable job locating the rights holders. They went far beyond what any author could expect from a publisher. Laura Clark has been a rigorous production editor whose work has ensured that the manuscript turned into a much better book than it was when she first received it. Hackett sent the manuscript to two anonymous reviewers who helpfully provided recommendations for its improvement.

Over the years, Michael J. Thompson and Frank Kirkland have consistently provided valuable counsel. In all my undertakings, I have been fortunate to have their guidance. It is also important to highlight the contributions of Timothy Scott Johnson. He readily came to my aid at several critical moments and his expertise has rescued me from several errors. I have also benefited greatly from discussions with numerous friends, colleagues, and scholars. Some may be entirely unaware of their impact on this project, but I would be remiss if I did not take this opportunity to acknowledge my appreciation for their help. They have included Linda Alcoff, Stanley Aronowitz, the late Martin Atangana, Uche Azikiwe (the wife of the late Nnamdi Azikiwe), Dennis Bathory, Herman Bennett, Jim Block, Stephen Eric Bronner, Anthony Browne, the late Dennis Brutus, Alan Court, Katie Davison, Cynthia De Windt, Howard Dodson, John Dunn, Jonathon Earle, Steven Feierman, Kyle Francis, Carol Gould, Dagmar Herzog, the late Istvan Hont, Candice Jenkins, Robert Kaufman, Michael Luther, Michael MacDonald, Giovanni Menegalle, Charles Mills, Andrew Murphy, Immanuel Ness, Paulette Nichols, Moses Ochonu, Katherine Pence, Frances Fox Piven, Gerald Press, Clifford Rosenberg, Helena Rosenblatt, Timothy Scarnecchia, Sibyl Schwarzenbach, Sophie Smith, Michael Sonenscher, Brett Stoudt, Megan Vaughan, Cornel West,

Gary Wilder, Ian Williams, and Richard Wolin. Whether our conversations lasted minutes or hours, all these people offered sage wisdom that, in some significant way, influenced my work on this book.

I was honored to correspond with the late Vesta Sithole (the wife of Rev. Ndabaningi Sithole). She was generous with her time while battling the illness that would eventually take her from this world. I know she was pleased that her husband's writings would become more readily available to students of African history, thought, and politics through this book. I hoped she would live to hold a copy of this book. I can only wish that the final product might meet the expectations she had for it.

My family has—as always—been an incredible source of support. My mother, Hedda Smulewicz, has been a tireless cheerleader and genuinely invested in this project. Though they did not live to see this volume appear in print, my grandmother, Renate Smulewicz, and my uncle, Daniel Smulewicz, were always eager to hear about its progress. It has been a pleasure to discuss this project with my sister, Alexa Zucker, and find where it intersects with her interests. The part played by Romy and Mitya goes without saying.

Though she is listed as an assistant editor, Chelsea Schields' contributions extend far beyond that title. This book would never have appeared were it not for the fact that Chelsea helped to revive it during a particularly frustrating period. It is impossible to overstate how much Chelsea has done for this book. In the course of working together, Chelsea continually challenged my thinking about this volume's content and structure. She assiduously pored over the text with the keen eye that is characteristic of her erudition. I have learned much from her. It is a joy to have such a friend and colleague.

This book has its origins in J. Michael Turner's course in Modern West African History at Hunter College, CUNY. J. Michael was an inspiring mentor and friend. His dedication to Africa's past and future came from a sincere passion for the many cultures of the continent. Through his work as scholar, consultant to UNICEF, co-director of Hunter College's Global Afro Latino and Caribbean Initiative, and activist, he acquired a breadth of knowledge and experience that left his students in awe. He may have been a born-and-bred Harlem man, but he was as much at home in Ghana, Benin, Nigeria, Mozambique, and Angola. J. Michael was a true cosmopolitan intellectual and a mensch. This collection is lovingly dedicated to his memory. It is my hope that its contents will excite the interest of future students of African history, thought, and politics much as the time I spent with Prof. Turner did for me.

While this book has benefitted from the assistance and insights of all the people I have mentioned, its shortcomings are attributable to me alone.

GENERAL INTRODUCTION

Between the mid-1950s and 1960s, European colonial rule in Africa began to come to an end. The independence of the former colonies and their transition to sovereign nation-states captivated global attention. Initially, observers of this transformation of the global order focused on the political figures who seemed to play a pivotal role in overseeing the paths to independence of Africa's newly established states. Their books were widely published and their writings were included in anthologies. Students and scholars alike sought to comprehend the process of African independence through the study of the political thought of Africa's new political elites. Much has changed both in Africa and the study of Africa since the rise of these figures. Increasingly, analysts called into question the policies of the new regimes as some of Africa's new leaders silenced their opponents and tried to turn their countries into one-party states. In part, this was a consequence of Africa's central role in the competition between Western Bloc and Eastern Bloc countries for spheres of influence during the Cold War. Moreover, the economic crisis of the 1970s contributed to the failure of the aspirations for the economic development of these new states, placing these states into spirals of economic debt. The political visions of Africa's elite leaders were viewed as failures, either because of the antidemocratic regimes that emerged or because of the challenges that African states faced in a changing global context. Since that time, greater scholarly attention has turned to the complexity of Africa's colonial and postcolonial history and politics for answers. In turn, interest in the political thought of Africa's political leaders has dwindled.

Among historians, there have been important advances in the study of Africa's history. Their work, along with that of anthropologists, has drawn attention to Africa's social and environmental history. These scholars have shown that it is impossible to understand twentieth-century African history apart from the study of the lives and experiences of Africa's populations. The role of women and Africa's peasant populations in the lead-up to and achievement of independence is no longer ignored. Furthermore, historians have shown that the decline of empires was not inevitable, and that the formation of independent nation-states was not the natural outcome of Africa's independence movements.

Among political scientists, the analysis of the African state, the status
of minority ethnic groups, internal political conflicts and civil wars,
and the inherent problems of sustaining sovereign borders have become
pressing concerns. Yet, amidst these changes in the focus of scholars,
the political thought of the first generation of African political leaders,
which attracted so much interest in the early years of independence,
has receded into the background. The purpose of this reader in African
political thought is not to challenge the remarkable advances that have
occurred in the study of Africa over the last three decades. Rather, it is
motivated by the idea that we can further deepen our understanding of
Africa's pre- and post-independence history and politics by making the
political writings of Africa's leading politicians once again readily available to students and scholars.

By turning our attention to the political debates and discourses surrounding African independence that took place among African political
elites, we can begin to evaluate the political visions that these leaders
had for Africa's future. Many of these intellectuals were first politicized
by local political problems. They joined local organizations that were
focused on the particular problems that colonial policies posed for
their regions and ethnic groups, became labor organizers, and served
on the staffs of newspapers. Throughout Africa, these local organizations focused on a wide range of European efforts to transform Africa.
Colonial authorities imposed economic policies that sought to reshape
agrarian economies to produce goods to satisfy the demands of European
markets. They attempted to create migrant labor forces to encourage
the growth of a proletarian class of African laborers, while also trying
to ensure that these laborers did not become radicalized. They forged
new structures of authority, implanting systems of governance overseen
by local African leaders whose ties to colonial governments were stronger than to those they governed. Consequently, the legitimacy of these
leaders implanted by colonial authorities was often questioned. Corruption was a common problem among these local African authorities, and
local organizations tried to circumvent them by voicing their grievances
directly to colonial governors. The restructuring of African economic
and political life destabilized everyday life, and it was in response to
such issues that Africans mobilized to begin to form social movements,
unions, and parties. While the specific issues that galvanized Africans to
organize varied across the continent and in radically different colonial
contexts, it was these broad sets of concerns that formed the context

in which many of Africa's future political class received their early education in politics.

To further their educations, many of Africa's future leaders traveled abroad. Both in the United States and in European metropoles, these leaders received western-style educations. Yet they were also exposed to a wide range of political ideas. These ranged from more moderate forms of political liberalism to radical Marxist organizations. They encountered both African-American and Afro-Caribbean intellectuals who further shaped their political ideologies. In this respect, they were members of what the social and cultural theorist Paul Gilroy has termed the "Black Atlantic." They were at the center of robust debates that raged over the conflicts between liberalism, democratic socialism, and communism. They also forged their own organizations among fellow African students and European-based diasporic intellectuals to debate the issues, such as the future of the relationship between metropole and colony, the prospects for decolonization, and the possibilities for Pan-African collaboration. They were inspired by the examples set by diasporic intellectuals who were battling racism in the United States and Europe, as well as the ideas of earlier generations of African thinkers. These young intellectuals were just as frequently in conflict with each other as they were in agreement. The Second World War, the struggle against fascism, and the open question of how colonialism might be affected by the outcome of the war provided much of the context for these discussions. The distinct realities on the ground in Africa often divided African intellectuals whose homelands were under different forms of colonial rule. Indeed, the many different trajectories taken by Africa's leaders when they came into power bespeaks the uniqueness of the questions and problems with which they were confronted.

Despite the many differences among Africa's leaders, one of the remarkable features of each of Africa's political leaders is the ways they synthesized the political ideas they encountered as young activists, party leaders, and heads of state. They drew freely from indigenous political ideas, strands of Christianity and Islam, liberalism, socialism, Pan-Africanism, and communism. African intellectuals of the past served as a fount for rich intellectual resources upon which leaders of the independence period could draw. They melded the lessons they learned from their own participation in political and social movements with those they encountered abroad. They would also look to the struggles against colonialism in other parts of the colonized world. There was no single source for their ideas. Africa's intellectuals were cosmopolitan thinkers who searched for answers in an array of intellectual traditions without feeling solely bound to their native political traditions.

While attuned to and critical of the problem of Eurocentrism, Africa's intellectuals would frequently appropriate and refashion many European intellectual ideas to serve their own purposes. This fact calls into question the claims of postcolonial theorists over the last thirty years that colonialism not only manifested in outright political control of the colonized, but also that racism and justifications for colonialism and imperialism are embedded in European intellectual traditions. Africa's intellectuals were in dialogue with these ideas even if they did not embrace all of their assumptions. They extracted those features of ideas that were useful to them. They consulted many resources because they recognized that the complexities of Africa's future depended on novel ways of thinking. By blending ideas, they would, ultimately, forge a unique and highly diverse tradition of political thought that centered on the question of African independence. This book is concerned with providing students with a sense of the variegated ways the idea of independence was discussed and envisioned prior to, during, and after independence became realized as a political and global reality.

With the gradual collapse of colonialism and the formation of new nation-states, Africa's new political elites were confronted by an array of pragmatic questions and concerns. They had to determine how to address the ethnic diversity of the states they now led. The conflicting demands of different ethnic groups and classes had to be reconciled. Divisions between peasant and proletarian, men and women, and rural and urban populations remained deeply ensconced. Many segments of the population of these new states continued to favor traditional local and ethnic political authorities over the new leaders who emerged to take the reins of government. The possibility of secessionist movements posed a particular challenge to many of Africa's new political elites. The emerging political regimes had to legitimize themselves. New national boundaries had to be drawn. Constitutions had to be written. In some cases, political leaders worked hard to develop federal systems to maintain political unity. Africa's new leaders had to consider the extent to which they wished to maintain their ties to former colonial powers, as well as whether or not they would develop ties with other African states. Debates over how to imagine ties to former colonial powers, and the results of meetings to define African unity, are included in this collection. Each of Africa's leaders took different stances on these questions. Although the contexts differed, these African political thinkers were connected by the fact that they all felt compelled to resolve these problems.

This collection hones in on the political thought of African independence as expressed in the writings of Africa's educated elites, the statements of parties and nationalist organizations, and the recollections of influential activists. It is impossible to fully understand the trajectory of Africa's history since independence without reference to the political ideologies that were promoted by leaders and organizations, the political decisions that they made, or the ways that they wielded their new-found power. The leading figures of Africa's independence movements were theorists, activists, and politicians. Unlike the study of European political thought, in which many of the most prominent political theorists seldom took on the additional role of heads of state or government officials, Africa's political intellectuals of the independence period often had the power to implement their ideas as members of government. In making their political decisions they were also forced to respond to the decisions of international political organizations, as well as the positions of European heads of states who had formerly colonized Africa. Some African leaders were more amenable to finding ways of cooperating with former colonial powers, while others rejected ties to the metropole entirely. They not only faced external challenges, but internal ones as well. In some cases, European settlers determined to retain positions of power competed with African leaders. Moreover, African politicians and intellectuals often questioned the policies of the newly elected heads of state. At times, these debates led heads of state to engage in persecution of their opponents, brought new states to the brink of civil war, or, as in the case of Nigeria, erupted into outright conflict. This collection includes readings from many different perspectives to give the reader a stronger sense of the complexities of independence.

This volume is organized into four parts that explore different themes in African political thought on independence. A brief introduction prefaces each part, introducing the reader to the connective threads between the selections and important historical points of reference. Each document is also prefaced by a short biography of the author or history of the organization that issued the statement. The first part examines the changing meanings of independence from the mid-nineteenth to the early twentieth centuries, when a transatlantic political discourse around the idea of African independence emerged and developed. This discourse encompassed numerous—often weakly allied or fundamentally opposed—ideological positions and strands of thought. Nevertheless, the authors of these texts are loosely connected by their engagement with the question of the meaning of independence. The second part covers the period from the mid-1940s to the 1960s, during which time independence became a political reality. This part explores the predominant realization of independence in the form of the nation-state alongside responses to the political manifestation of self-determination by African leaders, the political leadership of the white settlers, and the international community. The third part deals with the broader issue of resistance and examines the relationship between the language of independence and varied forms of resistance. The fourth and final part deals with the issue of development, a prominent theme in postcolonial analyses of Africa. The selections in this part, however, focus on how African political leaders in the 1950s and 1960s at once understood the troubling legacies of foreign development and sought to recast plans of development as part of the realization of independence.

The parts of this volume can be read independently of each other, and each provides a different thematic take on a common historical moment. At the core of this collection is the second part, which details the narrowing of independence in Africa premised on the nation-state. The purpose in using this as the volume's pivot point is not to suggest that nation-statism was the inexorable outcome of the discourses included in the preceding part. Quite the opposite, reading the second part in light of the first allows readers to critically reflect on why, amidst the many understandings of independence presented in the run-up to decolonization, the African nation-state is part of our political reality today. Similarly, the third part, on varied forms of resistance, begs the question as to why certain political formations emerged and succeeded through certain forms of resistance. Yet European colonialism was not always the target of resistance. Some Africans resisted versions of the African nation-state. Violent conflict, secessionism, and social movements contested its legitimacy. Finally, the fourth part demonstrates the urgency with which leaders of newly independent nation-states struggled to legitimize their political projects, consolidate power, create a political base, and their efforts to deal with the legacy of social upheaval.

This collection seeks to complement the work of contemporary scholars who are transforming the methods and approaches for studying the history and politics of African independence. By making these texts available, it opens them to renewed scrutiny. The influence of these texts and of these figures in Africa's history cannot be denied. For the many flaws of Africa's political leaders, which often only became apparent after they assumed power, their writings are fascinating for their insightfulness as well as their naiveté. The reader is drawn into a world of high political stakes and, at times, noble as well as ignoble ambitions. These writings bespeak the stark complexities of the process of building new states in societies where the political order was rapidly transformed if not entirely uprooted. Much can be learned about the broader problems of state-building through a study of these texts. The authors of these writings engaged very practical and common political problems, such as the opposition to oppression, the formation of movements and parties, and the establishment of political legitimacy. The student and scholar can only benefit by engaging with their thought.

PART ONE: EARLY VISIONS OF INDEPENDENCE

Introduction

The decolonization of Africa in the 1950s and 1960s was preceded by over a century of discourse about and political agitation on behalf of African independence. This question engaged men and women both within Africa and throughout the African diaspora in the United States, the Caribbean, and Europe. They drew on multiple intellectual traditions, ranging from indigenous ideas and Christianity to elements of European political thought and philosophy. Given the multiplicity of ideas employed and debated, in many cases, it is difficult to distinguish the "African" features of the ideas in circulation from the "Western" ones. Thinkers concerned with the question of Africa's independence refashioned the meaning of concepts to suit specific concerns and struggles, which had implications beyond the continent as well. Frequently, anti-colonial intellectuals turned to the discourses on race and racism, which had developed in the late nineteenth and early twentieth centuries, to confront and understand the problems of peoples of color. However, it was not always obvious that African problems could sufficiently be addressed by having the problem of colonialism understood via the problems of racism alone. The problems that Africans faced as colonized subjects were not necessarily reducible to the problem of racism, but, rather, entailed more specific issues, such as confronting the distinct manifestations of colonialism, developing strategies for opposition, and articulating alternative visions of African autonomy, as well as class and gender divisions and rural and urban differences and conflicts.

This part offers a sampling of the discussions on forms of African independence that occurred from the mid-nineteenth to the early twentieth centuries. These included such diverse approaches as strengthening the African church, peasant resistance, appeals to the international community, and the development of Pan-Africanism. Each played a formative role in fomenting debate around questions of independence. Participants in this debate not only included Africans from across the continent, but also African Americans and Afro-Caribbeans, who played a key part in the cultivation of ideas and political organizations. Their interest in forging bonds of association across linguistic, national, or ethnic divides provides insight into the intensely innovative century of political thought that preceded decolonization. Their ideas thus became part of the evolving political languages and strategies for achieving African independence. At times, these ideas were reconciled or synthesized. Perhaps just as frequently, these ideas remained bitterly opposed to one another. The ideas Africans and peoples of the African diaspora developed about the meaning of independence and the methods for achieving it were as complex as colonialism itself. The readings collected here attempt to convey, albeit not exhaustively, the climate of spirited debate and the extraordinary diversity and creativity of anti-colonial discourse and activism. These ideas, disparate though they often were, helped to mold the terms of debate and action for the generation who witnessed and urgently sought to realize Africa's independence.

1

Letter to the Secretaries of the Church Missionary Society, 1841[1]

Samuel Crowther

Samuel Ajayi Crowther (1809–1891) was an African missionary and the first African to be ordained as an Anglican bishop. Born in modern-day Nigeria, Crowther's village was raided and he was sold to Portuguese slave traders in 1821. The traders were, however, intercepted by the British Navy. The British government had abolished the slave trade in 1807, and British warships were active in preventing the continuation of the trade. As a young man, Crowther was educated by the Anglican Missionary Society and converted to Christianity in 1825. Crowther received further education in England. He became actively involved in missionary work, which he saw as essential to bringing an end to the slave trade. In 1841, he accompanied James Frederick Schön on an expedition along the Niger River. The following excerpt comes from an introductory letter to his journals from the expedition. The expedition, in addition to its aims of helping abolish slavery and promote conversion, also set out to promote commerce and trade with native populations. Crowther had an extensive education in the study of languages, and part of his task in the mission was to learn Yoruba. Later, Crowther would translate Christian texts into Yoruba, as well as write grammar books and dictionaries for Igbo and Nupe. In 1864, Crowther was ordained as an Anglican bishop. He was a strong advocate of creating autonomous African churches that could undertake missionary work themselves by means of training and educating Africans. This early text expresses Crowther's belief that the spread of Christianity and the creation of strong churches throughout Africa could reinvigorate a continent ravaged by the slave trade.

---

1. Samuel Crowther, "Letter to the Secretaries of the Church Missionary Society," *Journals of the Rev. James Frederick Schön and Mr. Samuel Crowther* (London: Hatchard and Son, 1842).

The Expedition has met with success, as far as it has been able to go on with its grand object—the abolition of the Slave-trade. Obi, king of Aboh, and the Attah of Eggarra, have very readily entered into treaties to that effect; and sold, or promised, land for settlements of Europeans or Natives among their people, and are very desirous to be led in a better way. A Model Farm is commenced at the foot of Stirling Hill, at the Confluence. Many of the Natives begin to look up to that place as an asylum from the oppressions of their voracious enemies, the Fulatahs; though they do not as yet see that, if it prospers, they will derive other benefits from it. As far as I can recollect, we have met with no opposition from any of the Chiefs to whom we came; but, on the contrary, all were ready to receive the White Men, and were happy to see them their friends.

. . . .

As regards Missionary labours on the banks of the Niger and in the Interior of Africa, I think the Committee will see, from the condition of the Expedition, that very little can be done by European Missionaries except by such as have, before ascending the river, become inured to the climate of Africa. We hope that there will be some communication between England and Africa, by which a European Missionary may have an opportunity, when sickness should render it necessary, to leave the river for the benefit of his health; for if there should be no such communication, he would be left in a helpless state. However, I do not limit the power of the Lord of the Vineyard, who has commanded, *Go ye into all the world, and preach the Gospel to every creature*: neither do I distrust His promise, *Lo! I am with you always, even unto the end of the world.* Still, I am reluctantly led to adopt the opinion, that Africa can chiefly be benefitted by her own Children.

I have read, in Sir T. F. Buxton's[2] work on the "Slave-Trade and Its Remedies," that some promising Youths among the Children of Africa should be sent to England for education; who would afterward hold situations in their countries, and whose conduct would have a beneficial influence upon their country-people. If such a plan be in contemplation for other employments, could it not be adopted for preparing

2. Thomas Fowell Buxton (1786–1845) was a Member of Parliament and a prominent abolitionist.

Missionaries, too, from the Coast of Africa, who might become useful among their countrymen? . . .

But at the same time, I still hope and pray that European Missionaries may be able to bestow their valuable labours upon the Nations of the interior, and lay the foundation of the Church of Christ. I always feel that myself and my Brethren of the Natives are not sufficiently qualified for so great a work; and I cannot but express a wish that the means of improvement should be afforded to some of us, to make us fit instruments in the service of God.

At the same time, I am fully aware that human learning will be of very little avail, if the heart is not inspired by the Holy Spirit from above, with love for the salvation of souls, and the extension of Christ's Kingdom on earth.

2

Advice to the Rising Generation in West Africa, 1868[3]

James Africanus Horton

James Africanus Horton (1835–1883) was born James Beale Horton in Sierra Leone. In 1853, Horton traveled to Britain on a scholarship from the War Office to study medicine. Horton studied at King's College London and Edinburgh University. He received his medical degree in 1859. In Edinburgh, Horton registered his name as James Africanus Beale Horton. His major book, West African Countries and Peoples, British and Native *and* A Vindication of the African Race, *was largely a critique of the scientific racism prevalent in the nineteenth century. It also outlined a vision for the formation of African nations. In the following concluding remarks of the book, Horton addresses the younger generation of West Africans. He encourages education as a means of racial uplift to enable Africans to govern themselves and their independent nations.*

CONCLUDING REMARKS.—ADVICE TO THE RISING GENERATION IN WEST AFRICA.

In 1846, Mr. Hilary Teage, a Liberian, delivered a most graphic, eloquent, and touching speech in Monrovia to the citizens of Liberia, in which we find the following passage: 'Upon you [fellow-citizens], rely upon it, depends, in a measure you can hardly conceive, the future destiny of your race. You are to give the answer whether the African race is doomed to interminable degradation—a hideous blot on the fair face of creation, a libel upon the dignity of human nature; or whether they are capable to take an honourable rank amongst the great family of nations.'

3. James Africanus Horton, "Advice to the Rising Generation in West Africa," *West African Countries and Peoples, British and Native and A Vindication of the African Race* (Cambridge: Cambridge University Press, 2011; original 1868).

This is a most valuable admonition, which should be treasured up by every one in Western Africa, but especially the rising generation, bearing in mind that they have a special mission to fulfill on earth; that they are not exclusively their own property, but that by industry and perseverance they might so better their circumstances and position as to give material aid to those less favoured than themselves. It must also be remembered by them that Western Africa in literature and science is among the least of nations. It has been so destined that, with the exception of the aboriginals, no other nation has been able to plant a sure footing in her, and consequently that from her sons, and her sons alone, must her complete regeneration be looked for. The initiative cannot be expected to come from within—it must come from without; and it is certain that 'genius, talent, and virtue will be honoured, whether clad in rags or in broadcloth, and the nobility of a manly nature will not always continue to be estimated according to the colour of the skin.'

Let the younger portion of the population, who are so susceptible and ready to take offence and retort at the least occasion, remember that all Europeans who enter their country, by the higher degree of intellectual and moral cultivation which they, as a race, have received, are entitled to a certain degree of respect as the harbingers of civilization, imitating the good and virtuous, whilst shunning those whose actions are a disgrace to civilization—waiting patiently whilst maintaining an upright and dignified course, for the time when they will see the necessity of modifying their opinions and acting up to them with ideas of loftier and holier order. In the mean time, however, let them be uniformly courteous, cultivate their minds, and strive zealously for substantial worth. Let them seek independence without bravado, manliness without subserviency; and let them put their shoulders to the work, and 'prove by the effort they themselves make that they, too, desire, and are striving, and will strive for the Christian and industrial regeneration of Africa; and do this with the modesty not at all incompatible with manly self-reliance, and a due sense of the innate dignity which should characterize men who have been helped out of their degradation, and brought at once into the ranks of a Christian civilization which has taken eighteen centuries to be developed.'

It must be remembered that there is no royal road to greatness—that it cannot be said that this or that man possesses a heaven-born reputation, greatness, or talent. It must be bought by severe perseverance, by an undaunted courage and industry, by real hard work and application, with a love for the undertaking we have in hand, by an uncompro-mising, disinterested adhesion to the truth. These, and these alone, will be the keystone for every one to ascend to the altitude of material and honourable success—success that will produce in us primarily real improvement, for real and extensive usefulness to our country hereafter, when the time is ripe. What, may be asked, are the passports to this honourable success? Dr. Rivington, in an admirable address delivered at the opening of one of the London Medical Schools, stated them to be ability, labour, and character—these three are the passports to an hon-ourable fame. 'Ability,' says he, 'is the capacity for acquiring and using knowledge and skill; labour, the means of acquirement and use; char-acter, the direction and control of acquirement and usefulness. Ability without labour is the talent wrapped up in a napkin; ability without virtue will work not for the true end of all talents, all knowledge, and all effort—the use and advantage of men—but for the gratification of a selfish vanity, which would tarnish its laurel wreaths.' That the African race possesses undoubtedly this ability may be further proved by the result of competitive examination in Europe between those who are educated there and their more favoured schoolmates, by the progress they make in different undertakings in their native climate; and it behoves them, therefore, to labour steadfastly for the regeneration of their country, and to dissipate from the minds of those indisposed to the advancement of their race, the false theory always advanced, that they are incapable of advancement.

. . . .

Let the rising generation, therefore, study to exert themselves to obtain the combined attractive influence of knowledge and wisdom, wealth and honesty, great place and charity, fame and happiness, book-learning and virtue, so that they may be made to bring their happy influences to bear on the regeneration of their country; and then there will be the real exercise of those qualities which will gradually lead to the attainment of the power of self-government, and the contemplated improvement of the House of Commons Committee will go on *tuto, cito, et jucunde.**

*Safely, quietly, and with ease.

3

The Fanti Confederation Constitution, 1871[4]

The Fanti Confederation was founded in 1868 by the Fanti peoples of the Gold Coast (modern-day Ghana). It was conceived as a federal grouping that would protect the Fanti from the threat of both European settlers and the neighboring Asante. The Confederation was weakened by a failed effort to reclaim land from the Dutch, as well as a prohibition by the British to collect taxes. It collapsed in 1874. Nonetheless, the Confederation is an important example of an African attempt to maintain self-rule in a climate of increasing colonial incursion and power. The following articles are excerpted from the constitution that the Confederacy submitted for approval to the governor-in-chief and emphasize autonomous rule.

Whereas we, the undersigned kings and chiefs of Fanti, have taken into consideration the deplorable state of our peoples and subjects in the interior of the Gold Coast, and whereas we are of opinion that unity and concord among ourselves would conduce to our mutual well-being, and promote and advance the social and political condition of our peoples and subjects, who are in a state of degradation, without the means of education and of carrying on proper industry; we, the said kings and chiefs, after having fully discussed and considered the subject at meetings held at Mankessim on the 16th day of October last and following days, have unanimously resolved and agreed upon the articles hereinafter named.

Article I. That we, the kings and chiefs of Fanti here present, form ourselves into a committee with the view of effecting unity of purpose and of action between the kings and chiefs of the Fanti territory.

    2. That we, the kings and chiefs here assembled, now form ourselves into a compact body for the purpose of more effectually

---

4. "The Constitution of the Fanti Confederacy," *Origins of West-African Nationalism*, edited by Henry S. Wilson (New York: St. Martin's, 1969).

bringing about certain improvements (hereinafter to be considered) in the country.

3. That this compact body shall be recognized under the title and designation of the 'Fanti Confederation'.

4. That there shall be elected a president, vice-president, secretary, under-secretary, treasurer and assistant-treasurer.

5. That the president be elected from the body of kings, and be proclaimed king-president of the Fanti Confederation.

6. That the vice-president, secretary and under-secretary, treasurer and assistant-treasurer, who shall constitute the ministry, be men of education and position.

7. That it be competent to the Fanti Confederation thus constituted to receive into its body politic any other king or kings, chief or chiefs, who may not now be present.

8. That it be the object of the Confederation:

   i. To promote friendly intercourse between all the kings and chiefs of Fanti, and to unite them for offensive and defensive purposes against their common enemy.

   ii. To direct the labours of the Confederation towards the improvement of the country at large.

   iii. To make good and substantial roads throughout all the interior districts included in the Confederation.

   iv. To erect school-houses and establish schools for the education of all children within the Confederation, and to obtain the service of efficient school-masters.

   v. To promote agricultural and industrial pursuits, and to endeavour to introduce such new plants as may hereafter become sources of profitable commerce to the country.

   vi. To develop and facilitate the working of the mineral and other resources of the country.

4

The Origin and Purpose of Colonization, 1881[5]

Edward Blyden

Born in St. Thomas, Danish West Indies, Edward Wilmot Blyden (1832–1912) is regarded as one of the founding intellectuals of Pan-Africanism. Blyden attempted to pursue a career in the clergy, reflecting the many religious themes found in his writings, but was rejected admission to Rutgers' Theological College because of his race. In 1851, Blyden traveled to the recently formed Republic of Liberia (established in 1847) to begin work as an educator. In 1821, the American Colonization Society (ACS) founded Liberia as a colony for free African Americans. Following his trip to Liberia, Blyden became a noted spokesperson for African development via recolonization by peoples of African descent. The following excerpt, which summarizes Blyden's views, is from a speech Blyden delivered at the sixty-sixth anniversary of the ACS. Here, Blyden appeals for support for African development programs and the return of peoples of color to Africa.

No natural impulses bring the European hither—artificial or external causes move him to emigrate. The Negro is drawn to Africa by the necessities of his nature.

We do not ask that all the colored people should leave the United States and go to Africa. If such a result were possible it is not, for the present at least, desirable, certainly it is not indispensable. For the work to be accomplished much less than one-tenth of the six millions would be necessary. "In a return from exile, in the restoration of a people," says George Eliot, "the question is not whether certain rich men will choose to remain behind, but whether there will be found worthy men who will choose to lead the return. Plenty of prosperous Jews remained in Babylon when Ezra marshalled his band of forty thousand, and began

5. Edward Wilmot Blyden, *The Origin and Purpose of African Colonization* (Washington, DC: The American Colonization Society, 1883).

a new glorious epoch in the history of his race, making the preparation for that epoch in the history of the world, which has been held glorious enough to be dated from forevermore."

There are Negroes enough in this country to join in the return—descendants of Africa enough, who are faithful to the instincts of the race, and who realize their duty to their fatherland. I rejoice to know that here where the teachings of generations have been to disparage the race, there are many who are faithful, there are men and women who will go, who have a restless sense of homelessness which will never be appeased until they stand in the great land where their forefathers lived; until they catch glimpses of the old sun, and moon and stars, which still shine in their pristine brilliancy upon that vast domain; until from the deck of the ship which bears them back home they see visions of the hills rising from the white margin of the continent, and listen to the breaking music of the waves—the exhilarating laughter of the sea as it dashes against the beach. These are the elements of the great restoration. It may come in our own life time. It may be our happiness to see those rise up who will formulate progress for Africa—embody the ideas which will reduce our social and political life to order; and we may, before we die, thank God that we have seen His salvation; that the Negro has grasped with a clear knowledge his meaning in the world's vast life—in politics—in science—in religion.

I say it is gratifying to know that there are Negroes of this country who will go to do this great work—cheerfully go and brave the hardships and perils necessary to be endured in its accomplishment. These will be among the redeemers of Africa. If they suffer they will suffer devotedly, and if they die, they will die well. And what is death for the redemption of a people? History is full of examples of men who have sacrificed themselves for the advancement of a great cause—for the good of their country. Every man who dies for Africa—if it is necessary to die—adds to Africa a new element of salvation, and hastens the day of her redemption. And when God lets men suffer and gives them to pain and death, it is not the abandoned, it is not the worst or the guiltiest, but the best and the purest, whom He often chooses for His work, for they will do it best. Spectators weep and wonder; but the sufferers themselves accept the pain in the joy of doing redemptive work, and rise out of lower levels to the elevated regions of those nobler spirits—the glorious army of martyrs—who rejoice that they are counted worthy to die for men.

The nation now being reared in Africa by the returning exiles from this country will not be a reproduction of this. The restoration of the Negro to the land of his fathers, will be the restoration of a race to its original integrity, to itself; and working by itself, for itself and from itself, it will discover the methods of its own development, and they will not be the same as the Anglo-Saxon methods.

In Africa there are no physical problems to be confronted upon the solution of which human comfort and even human existence depend. In the temperate regions of the earth there are ever recurring problems, first physical or material, and then intellectual, which press for solution and cannot be deferred without peril.

It is this constant pressure which has developed the scientific intellect and the thoughtfulness of the European. Africa can afford to hand over the solution of these problems to those who, driven by the exigencies of their circumstances, must solve them or perish. And when they are solved we shall apply the results to our purposes, leaving us leisure and taste for the metaphysical and spiritual. Africa will be largely an agricultural country. The people, when assisted by proper impulse from without—and they need this help just as all other races have needed impulse from without—will live largely in contact with nature. The Northern races will take the raw materials from Africa and bring them back in such forms as shall contribute to the comfort and even elegance of life in that country; while the African, in the simplicity and purity of rural enterprises, will be able to cultivate those spiritual elements in humanity which are suppressed, silent and inactive under the pressure and exigencies of material progress. He will find out, not under pressure but in an entirely normal and natural way, what his work is to be.

There is evidently, at this moment, no philanthropic institution before the American public that has more just and reasonable claims upon private and official benevolence than the American Colonization Society. And the Christian sentiment of the country, as I gather it from the east and from the west, from the north and from the south, is largely in favor of giving substantial and generous aid to that struggling Christian Republic in West Africa, the power of which, it is conceded, it should be the pride of this nation, as it is its commercial interest, to increase and perpetuate.

5

To the Nations of the World, 1900[6]

W. E. B. Du Bois

William Edward Burghardt (W. E. B.) Du Bois (1868–1963) is perhaps the most celebrated African-American intellectual of the twentieth century. His major works include the sociological study The Philadelphia Negro *(1899), the collected essays* The Souls of Black Folk *(1903), and the historical study* Black Reconstruction in America *(1935). The first African American to receive a doctorate from Harvard, Du Bois later co-founded the National Association for the Advancement of Colored People (NAACP) and became editor of the association's magazine,* The Crisis. *Throughout his life, Du Bois was an engaged scholar-activist who intervened in many of the major political debates of the first half of the twentieth century. In 1961, at the age of ninety-three, Du Bois settled in Ghana at the invitation of Kwame Nkrumah to begin work on the* Encyclopedia Africana. *The work was incomplete at the time of his death in Accra, Ghana.*

The following speech was given at the 1900 Pan-African Conference in London. The Trinidadian lawyer, Henry Sylvester Williams, organized the conference, which advocated the right of colonies to self-government. In this speech, given at the conference's closing session, Du Bois made his influential declaration that "the problem of the twentieth century is the problem of the colour line," and appealed to the international community to address racial disparities and inequities both in their home countries and in the colonies.

In the metropolis of the modern world, in this the closing year of the nineteenth century, there has been assembled a congress of men and women of African blood, to deliberate solemnly upon the present situation and outlook of the darker races of mankind. The problem of the twentieth century is the problem of the colour line, the question as to

---

6. W. E. B. Du Bois, "To the Nations of the World." Reprinted with the permission of The Permissions Company, Inc., on behalf of the David Graham Du Bois Trust.

how differences of race, which show themselves chiefly in the colour of the skin and the texture of the hair, are going to be made, hereafter, the basis of denying to over half the world the right of sharing to their utmost ability the opportunities and privileges of modern civilisation.

To be sure, the darker races are today the least advanced in culture according to European standards. This has not, however, always been the case in the past, and certainly the world's history, both ancient and modern, has given many instances of no despicable ability and capacity among the blackest races of men.

In any case, the modern world must needs remember that in this age, when the ends of the world are being brought so near together, the millions of black men in Africa, America, and the Islands of the Sea, not to speak of the brown and yellow myriads elsewhere, are bound to have great influence upon the world in the future, by reason of sheer numbers and physical contact. If now the world of culture bends itself towards giving Negroes and other dark men the largest and broadest opportunity for education and self-development, then this contact and influence is found to have a beneficial effect upon the world and hasten human progress. But if, by reason of carelessness, prejudice, greed and injustice, the black world is to be exploited and ravished and degraded, the results must be deplorable, if not fatal, not simply to them, but to the high ideals of justice, freedom, and culture which a thousand years of Christian civilisation have held before Europe.

And now, therefore, to these ideals of civilisation, to the broader humanity of the followers of the Prince of Peace, we, the men and women of Africa in world congress assembled, do now solemnly appeal:—

Let the world take no backward step in that slow but sure progress which has successively refused to let the spirit of class, of caste, of privilege, or of birth, debar from like liberty and the pursuit of happiness a striving human soul.

Let not mere colour or race be a feature of distinction drawn between white and black men, regardless of worth or ability.

Let not the natives of Africa be sacrificed to the greed of gold, their liberties taken away, their family life debauched, their just aspirations repressed, and avenues of advancement and culture taken from them.

Let not the cloak of Christian missionary enterprise be allowed in the future, as so often in the past, to hide the ruthless economic exploitation and political downfall of less developed nations, whose chief fault has been reliance on the plighted faith of the Christian church.

Let the British nation, the first modern champion of Negro freedom, hasten to crown the work of Wilberforce, and Clarkson, and Buxton, and Sharpe, Bishop Colenso, and Livingstone, and give, as soon as practicable, the rights of responsible government to the black colonies of Africa and the West Indies.

Let not the spirit of Garrison, Phillips, and Douglass wholly die out in America; may the conscience of a great nation rise and rebuke all dishonesty and unrighteous oppression toward the American Negro, and grant to him the right of franchise, security of person and property, and generous recognition of the great work he has accomplished in a generation toward raising nine millions of human beings from slavery to manhood.

Let the German Empire, and the French Republic, true to their great past, remember that the true worth of colonies lies in their prosperity and progress, and that justice, impartial alike to black and white, is the first element of prosperity.

Let the Congo Free State become a great central Negro State of the world, and let its prosperity be counted not simply in cash and commerce, but in the happiness and true advancement of its black people.

Let the nations of the World respect the integrity and independence of the free Negro States of Abyssinia, Liberia, Hayti, etc., and let the inhabitants of these States, the independent tribes of Africa, the Negroes of the West Indies and America, and the black subjects of all nations take courage, strive ceaselessly, and fight bravely, that they may prove to the world their incontestable right to be counted among the great brotherhood of mankind.

Thus we appeal with boldness and confidence to the Great Powers of the civilized world, trusting in the wide spirit of humanity, and the deep sense of justice of our age, for a generous recognition of the righteousness of our cause.

6

The West African Problem, 1911[7]

Mojola Agbebi

Mojola Agbebi (1860–1917) was a Yoruba Baptist minister. He advo-
cated the formation of an African-led church that would not rely on
European missionaries or European guidance. In 1888, Agbebi helped
to establish the Native Baptist Church in Lagos, the first indigenous
West African church. He also served as director of the Niger Delta
Mission and president of the Baptist Union of West Africa. Agbebi was
a key figure among the early generation of African nationalists who
promoted the idea of nationalism through the creation of independent
churches. In the following piece, Agbebi focuses on the lack of knowl-
edge and respect for African traditions and institutions on the part of
Europeans. He condemns Europe's paternalistic attitude toward Africa.

The appropriation of the tropical parts of Africa by the European nations
has added one more to the race problems confronting Europe. From the
African standpoint the African problem presents a twofold aspect—one
relating to the question involved as affecting the European; another
as affecting the African himself. The problem for the European obviously involves the objects he has in view in assuming the government
of Tropical West Africa, and the means for attaining that object. Such
objects resolve themselves into ends political and economic, embodying
political sway and a process of commercial or industrial development
designed to benefit both the ruler and the ruled. On the African side
the problem chiefly relates to the effect which the close contact and
dominating influence of Europe will exert upon the African living under
primitive conditions, whose mode of life is entirely dissimilar to that
of the European, if not actually opposed to it. The resultant effect of
bringing two dissimilar life-problems into contact and collision must
necessarily be far-reaching, and disturb not a little the morals and the

7. Mojola Agbebi, "The West African Problem," *Papers on Inter-Racial Problems*
Communicated to the First Universal Races Congress Held at the University of London,
edited by G. Spiller (London: P. S. King, 1911).

social arrangements of a people whose simple lives and indigenous characteristics render them liable to be easily affected. It is this effect upon his morals, his idea of society, and his view of an All-Father which vests the expropriation of Tropical Africa by the nations of Europe with a problem for the African. The problem is accentuated by the fact that it is the foundation and vital part of African life that is thus affected.

The problem, however, with its many complexities and complications, offers an easy way of being solved successfully if only a measure of sincerity, earnestness, and particularly sympathy is brought to bear on the solution. The tractable character of the African, and his having lived under political systems different from the European organized systems of rule on a large scale, combined with a possible indifference here and there to formal governments, ought to make the political object of the European nations easy of attainment. The one essential feature in the premises would be to make the political yoke as light as possible, in order that it might not bear too heavily upon a people quite unaccustomed to it. The difference between the social laws and institutions of Africa as contrasted with those of Europe, and exemplified in the absence from the former of policemen and detectives, bolts and bars, ought to suggest the prudence of modifying social methods, which carry such factors as accessories. The absence of any arrangement for enforcing compulsory restraint denotes emphatically order and right living on the part of the people sought to be governed. It would seem that the simplicity of the political part of the problem for the European is really what has rendered it complex and bewildering for him. Accustomed to a *régime* of government altogether different, which calls for the exercise of restraint as its chief controlling factor, the European finds it difficult to divest himself of prejudice to European ways in his dealing with the African. And this prejudice is sustained, as it were, by reason of the fact that European rule over the African is based upon the principle of might, from which the idea of force is inseparable. Circumstances alter cases, however, in every domain of human energy and activity, and if this idea were prominently kept in view the solution of the political problem to which Europe is committed in regard to Tropical Africa would be rendered much more easy. If Europe could realize that its political role in Tropical Africa entailed dealing with a new and altogether different set of circumstances which chiefly called for the exercise of sympathy and patience to study and understand, and the readiness to deal with them upon the basis of the knowledge gained of them, there can be no doubt that the problem would be solved in its political and economic aspects to the advantage of both European and African.

The exercise of sympathy and patience would avail to bring the European and African closer together, thus promoting that unity and co-operation which are essential and indispensable, imparting consolidation to European rule, and communicating stimulus and progress to economic development.

The cardinal essential in both cases is the cultivation of knowledge of the African; such knowledge as is calculated to engender respect and consideration for him and his institutions. Where such knowledge is acquired, it will reveal the effects, which the complex and artificial systems of European life are calculated to produce upon the moral and other conditions of a people addicted to simple living. The lack of knowledge of the effects wrought, and the unremitting help lent them in consequence, have invested the African problem with grave consequences for the African. The introduction of the usages and institutions of European life into the African social system has resulted in a disordering and a dislocation of the latter which threatens to overthrow the system altogether and produce a state of social anarchy. Dire evidence of the resultant social chaos is to be found in the total breakdown of parental control, and the advent of a life of wild license mistakenly taken to mean the exercise of the rights and prerogatives of individual liberty, as defined and permitted under the customs and usages of European life. This fatal mistake, with the fundamental fallacy it involves of abnegating African social laws on the part of Europeanised Africans, growing out of the dislike and contempt for which unfamiliarity with African customs on the part of the European is largely responsible, comprises a phase of the African problem which calls urgently for attention and consideration. Social organizations are the outgrowth of a people's life, and, founded more or less upon innate racial characteristics, are incapable of being transferred from one people of a certain type to another of a different type and condition. The phrase "state of transition" is usually applied to people who are supposed to be affected by passing social conditions, but who really are in the unfortunate dilemma of having their social order of life dislocated by the introduction of a foreign order, really implies a state of transition from a regular order of life ingrained in a people and practiced by them, to a social whirlpool of confusion and disorder, where there is not sufficient material for, or the materials which exist do not contribute to, social reconstruction. On the other hand, there is the powerful and irresistible current of man's wild will and passions arrayed against reconstruction and social regulation. It is conceivable what a state of social anarchy means in the sense of moral deterioration, with its concomitant of physical impairment. By most positive and impressive evidences the African has come to feel that this is the heritage which the African problem entails for him, a heritage due to lack of knowledge of and contempt for his institutions and customs, and also for the life-problems founded upon these customs and institutions.

7

Race Emancipation: Particular Considerations: African Nationality, 1911[8]

J. E. Casely Hayford

J. E. Casely Hayford (1866–1930) was a pan-African nationalist from the Gold Coast (modern-day Ghana). While a law student in Sierra Leone, he became strongly influenced by the work of Edward Blyden. In 1919, after continuing his legal education in England, Casely Hayford formed the National Congress of British West Africa. The group advocated the related issues of African nationalism, colonial emancipation, and racial equality. His novel Ethiopia Unbound *was published in 1911. In the following excerpt, Casely Hayford defends the cultural and political heritage of Africans, which he suggests are shared by all peoples of African descent, particularly those living in the United States. In this respect, the excerpt argues for the recovery of African history and culture by both Africans and peoples of African descent living outside of Africa.*

A two-fold danger threatens the African everywhere. It is the outcome of certain economic conditions whose method is the exploitation of the Ethiopian for all he is worth. He is said to be pressed into the service of man, in reality, the service of the Caucasian. That being so, he never reaps the full meed of his work as a *man*. He materially contributes to the building of pavements on which he may not walk—take it as a metaphor, or as a fact, which you please. He helps to work up revenues and to fill up exchequers over which, in most cases, he has no effective control, if any at all. In brief, he is labeled as belonging to a class apart among the races, and any attempt to rise above his station is terribly resented by the aristocracy of the races. Indeed, he is reminded at every turn that he is only intended to be a hewer of wood and drawer of water. And so it happens that those among the favoured sons of men who occasionally consider the lot of the Ethiopian are met with jeers

8. J. E. Casely Hayford, *Ethiopia Unbound: Studies in Race Emancipation*, 2nd ed. (London: Frank Cass, 1969).

and taunts. Is it any wonder, then, that even in the Twentieth Century, the African finds it terribly difficult to make headway even in his own country? The African may turn socialist, may preach and cry for reform until the day of judgment; but the experience of mankind shows this, that reform never comes to a class or a people unless and until those concerned have worked out their own salvation. And the lesson we have yet to learn is that we cannot depart from Nature's way and hope for real success.

And yet, it would seem as if in some notable instances the black man is bent upon following the line of greatest resistance in coping with the difficulties before him. Knowledge is the common property of mankind, and the philosophy which seeks for the Ethiopian the highest culture and efficiency in industrial and technical training is a sound one. It is well to arrest in favour of the race public opinion as to its capability in this direction. But that is not all, since there are certain distinctive qualities of race, of country, and of peoples which cannot be ignored without detriment to the particular race, country, or people. Knowledge, deprived of the assimilating element which makes it natural to the one taught, renders that person but a bare imitator. The Japanese, adopting and assimilating Western culture, of necessity commands the respect of Western nations, because there is something distinctly Eastern about him. He commands, to begin with, the uses of his native tongue, and has a literature of his own, enriched by translations from standard authors of other lands. He respects the institutions and customs of his ancestors, and there is an intelligent past which inspires him. He does not discard his national costume, and if, now and again, he dons Western attire, he does so as a matter of convenience, much as the Scotch, across the border, puts away, when the occasion demands it, his Highland costume. It is not the fault of the black man in America, for example, that he suffers today from the effects of a wrong that was inflicted upon him years ago by the forefathers of the very ones who now despise him. But he can see to it that as the years go by it becomes a matter of necessity for the American whites to respect and admire his manhood; and the surest way to the one or the other lies not so much in imitation as in originality and natural initiative. Not only must the Ethiopian acquire proficiency in the arts and sciences, in technical and industrial training, but he must pursue a course of scientific enquiry which would reveal to him the good things of the treasure house of his own nationality. . . .

[T]he average Afro-American citizen of the United States has lost absolute touch with the past of his race, and is helplessly and hopelessly groping in the dark for affinities that are not natural, and for effects for which there are neither national nor natural causes. That being so, the African in America is in a worse plight than the Hebrew in Egypt. The one preserved his language, his manners and customs, his religion and household gods; the other has committed national suicide, and at present it seems as if the dry bones of the vision have no life in them. Looking at the matter closely, it is not so much *Afro-Americans* that we want as *Africans* or *Ethiopians*, sojourning in a strange land, who, out of a full heart and a full knowledge can say: If I forget thee, Ethiopia, let my right hand forget its cunning! Let us look at the other side of the picture. How extraordinary would be the spectacle of this huge Ethiopian race—some millions of men—having imbibed all that is best in Western culture in the land of their oppressors, yet remaining true to racial instincts and inspiration, customs and institutions, much as did the Israelites of old in captivity! When this more pleasant picture will have become possible of realisation, then, and only then, will it be possible for our people in bondage "metaphorically to walk out of Egypt in the near future with a great and real spoil."

Someone may say, but, surely, you don't mean to suggest that questions of dress and habits of life matter in the least. I reply emphatically, they do. They go to the root of the Ethiopian's self-respect. Without servile imitation of our teachers in their get-up and manner of life, it stands to reason that the average white man would regard the average black man far more seriously than he does at present. The adoption of a distinctive dress for the cultured African, therefore, would be a distinct step forward, and a gain to the cause of Ethiopian progress and advancement. Pray listen to the greatest authority on national life upon this matter, "Behold, I have taught you statutes and judgments even as the Lord God commanded me that ye should do in the land whither ye go to possess it. Keep, therefore, and do them: for this is your wisdom and your understanding in the sight of the nations which shall hear these statutes and say, surely, this great nation is a wise and understanding people." Yes, my people are pursuing knowledge as for a hidden treasure, and have neglected wisdom and true understanding, and hence are they daily a laughing stock in the sight of the nations.

Here, then, is work for cultured West Africans to start a reform which will be world-wide in its effects among Ethiopians, remembering as a basis that we, as a people, have our own statues, the customs and institutions of our fore-fathers, which we cannot neglect and live. We on the Gold Coast are making a huge effort in this direction, and though European habits will die hard with some of our people, the effort is worth making; and, if we don't succeed quite with this generation, we shall succeed with the next.

8

Explanation of the Objectives of the Universal Negro Improvement Association, 1921[9]

Marcus Garvey

Although Pan-Africanist ideas had been discussed by a variety of intellectuals, the early movement remains most closely associated with the Jamaican-born Marcus Garvey (1887–1940). In 1914, Garvey founded the Universal Negro Improvement Association (UNIA) to promote political unity between Africans and the peoples of the African diaspora. During his tour of the United States, Garvey established a UNIA chapter in New York. The success of the UNIA in the United States led to the founding of a weekly newspaper, The Negro World. In 1919, Garvey founded Black Star Line, Inc., a shipping line that brought goods and people of African descent to Africa. This was followed by the Negro Factories Corporation, which sought to promote the business ventures of peoples of African descent. Garvey's activities came under the scrutiny of J. Edgar Hoover, the head of intelligence at the Bureau of Investigation (BOI). The UNIA was politically weakened when the BOI charged Garvey with mail fraud. Garvey was ultimately deported to Jamaica in 1927 where he remained politically active. The following is a transcription of a recording Garvey made on a 78-rpm record in 1921, explaining the aims of the UNIA.

Fellow citizens of Africa, I greet you in the name of the Universal Negro Improvement Association and African Communities League of the World. You may ask, "what organization is that?" It is for me to inform you that the Universal Negro Improvement Association is an organization that seeks to unite, into one solid body, the four hundred million Negroes in the world, to link up the fifty million Negroes in the

9.   Marcus Garvey, "If You Believe the Negro Has a Soul" (1921), transcript. Courtesy of the Marcus Garvey and the Universal Negro Improvement Association (UNIA) Papers Project at the University of California, Los Angeles: http://history matters.gmu.edu/d/5124/ (accessed September 10, 2016). Recording courtesy of Michigan State University, G. Robert Vincent Voice Library.

United States of America, with the twenty million Negroes of the West Indies, the forty million Negroes of South and Central America, with the two hundred and eighty million Negroes of Africa, for the purpose of bettering our industrial, commercial, educational, social, and political conditions.

As you are aware, the world in which we live today is divided into separate race groups and distinct nationalities. Each race and each nationality is endeavoring to work out its own destiny, to the exclusion of other races and other nationalities. We hear the cry of "England for the Englishman," of "France for the Frenchman," of "Germany for the German," of "Ireland for the Irish," of "Palestine for the Jew," of "Japan for the Japanese," of "China for the Chinese." We of the Universal Negro Improvement Association are raising the cry of "Africa for the Africans," those at home and those abroad. There are four hundred million Africans in the world who have Negro blood coursing through their veins, and we believe that the time has come to unite these 400 million people toward the one common purpose of bettering their condition.

The great problem of the Negro for the last five hundred years has been that of disunity. No one or no organization ever succeeded in uniting the Negro race. But within the last four years, the Universal Negro Improvement Association has worked wonders. It is bringing together in one fold four million organized Negroes who are scattered in all parts of the world, here in the forty-eight States of the American Union, all the West Indies islands, and the countries of South and Central America and Africa. These four million people are working to convert the rest of the four hundred million that are all over the world, and it is for this purpose, that we are asking you to join our land and to do the best you can to help us to bring about an emancipated race.

If anything stateworthy is to be done, it must be done through unity, and it is for that reason that the Universal Negro Improvement Association calls upon every Negro in the United States to rally to this standard. We want to unite the Negro race in this country. We want every Negro to work for one common object, that of building a nation of his own on the great continent of Africa. That all Negroes all over the world are working for the establishment of a government in Africa, means that it will be realized in another few years. We want the moral and financial support of every Negro to make this dream a possibility. Our race, this organization, has established itself in Nigeria, West Africa, and it endeavors to do all possible to develop that Negro country to become a great industrial and commercial commonwealth. Pioneers have been sent by this organization to Nigeria, and they are now laying the foundations upon which the four hundred million Negroes of the world will build.

If you believe that the Negro has a soul, if you believe that the Negro is a man, if you believe the Negro was endowed with the senses commonly given to other men by the Creator, then you must acknowledge that what other men have done, Negroes can do. We want to build up cities, nations, governments, industries of our own in Africa, so that we will be able to have a chance to rise from the lowest to the highest position in the African Commonwealth.

PART TWO: PATHS TO INDEPENDENCE

Introduction

In 1960, heralded as the "Year of Africa," seventeen African countries gained independence. These new states joined ten other African countries that achieved their independence at earlier dates, each of them following a unique path to national sovereignty. The state of Liberia had been independent since the country's founding in 1847 as a homeland for former slaves from North America. South Africa, though technically independent since 1910, was a British dominion until 1931 and became a Republic in 1961. Yet independence from Britain did not bring about the liberation of the majority black Africans living there, further entrenching white minority rule until the official abolition of the apartheid system in 1990. Egypt had revolted against British rule in 1922. Ethiopia had been independent throughout much of its history, with the exception of Italy's occupation from 1895 to 1896 and again from 1935 to 1940. Certainly in Sub-Saharan Africa, two of the most significant moves toward independence came when the Gold Coast (modern-day Ghana) declared independence from Britain in 1957 and French Guinea (modern-day Guinea) declared independence from France in 1958.

As the primary sources in this part display, African states achieved independence in a multitude of ways. After the Second World War, African troops who fought to liberate their colonizers from fascism anticipated that their efforts would be rewarded with the expansion of rights and freedoms. The idea of independence was discussed at meetings, such as the Fifth Pan-African Congress (see Document 9), where African intellectuals and students demanded immediate decolonization. These young Africans would return to their homelands and begin to agitate for independence. At the same time, the leaders and publics of war-torn European states began to consider the inevitable future of imperial reform—though how quickly this future would arrive and precisely what it might look like took many by surprise. Indeed, European powers were not looking to abandon the colonial project so much as to find ways to refashion it. The British adopted the language of gradually preparing Africans for self-rule. For Africans living in the

British Empire, 1960 was certainly not the "Year of Africa." Only Nigeria and Somalia achieved independence that year. Ghana's independence therefore emerges as an outlier. The Ghanaian people had rallied around the leadership of Kwame Nkrumah and his demand for "self-government now"—an outright rejection of Britain's plans to gradually transition to self-rule. By 1968—much sooner than most British anticipated—all former British colonies in Africa realized self-rule.

In the histories of decolonization in Francophone Africa, the Algerian War looms large. The event resounded in the metropole and throughout the colonial world. Algeria had been so central to the French colonial project—indeed, since 1848 the colony was formally considered a part of France—that the escalating anti-colonial violence led to the fall of the Fourth Republic. A new constitution in 1958 returned the French General Charles de Gaulle to power, and the first years of France's Fifth Republic developed with plans to keep as much of the empire intact as possible. The reformed multinational state, known as the French Community, would maintain commercial and military ties between France and its former colonies while extending citizenship rights under a federal government. Although Algeria rejected continued ties with the metropole, gaining its independence after an eight-year war in 1962, the territories of French West Africa experimented with forms of federation under the French Community until Guinea's exit hastened the independence of many African states during the "Year of Africa."

Not all empires fell apart in the 1960s, and many resisted what now appeared as an inevitable tidal wave of liberation movements. Portugal fought to halt independence movements in its colonies and battled rebel groups, while colonists in Algeria, Rhodesia, and South Africa sought to create systems of white rule (see Part Three: Fighting for Independence). The actions of white settler populations hint at the complexity surrounding the meaning of independence. For many of these people, too, independence from the metropole offered greater opportunities for expanding local white minority rule, as was the case with the Pieds-Noirs of Algeria (Algerians of European descent), the white minority of Rhodesia, and white South Africans.

The purpose of the readings in this part is to give an indication of the various ways independence occurred, and was fought over, and negotiated on the ground. It looks to the activities of African political parties and movements, colonial governments, and international bodies from the late 1950s to the late 1960s. Within this period, most colonies under British and French dominion achieved independence after lengthy and often violent negotiations about how empires should break apart and sovereignty should be transferred. They are focused entirely on the period in which the most colonies achieved independence (primarily from the late 1950s to the late 1960s), as well as on the terms under which independence occurred. Hence, this part attempts to tell the story of how independence occurred in parts of Anglophone and Francophone Africa through the sometimes cooperative, sometimes conflict-ridden relationships between and among the British and French metropoles and the British and French colonies. It focuses on the period during which the majority of African states achieved independence and sheds light on the multiple meanings that African independence had for peoples both inside and outside of Africa.

9

Resolutions, 1945[10]

The Fifth Pan-African Congress

The Fifth Pan-African Congress was held in Manchester, England, in 1945. While the Congress was presented as a successor to the four preceding Pan-African Congresses, it had little direct relation to the original Congresses. It was organized by the Trinidadian journalist and former Communist, George Padmore, and Ghana's future president, Kwame Nkrumah (see Documents 11 and 37, respectively). In the aftermath of the Second World War, the Congress pushed to make the issue of decolonization a central issue of the postwar settlement. It was distinct from the previous Congresses in the overwhelming presence of young African intellectuals who would later become leading figures in their countries' respective independence movements. While older intellectuals, particularly W. E. B. Du Bois and Padmore, presided over the sessions, young African intellectuals, such as Nkrumah and Kenya's future president Jomo Kenyatta, and union leaders took on a greater leadership role in the Congress than Africans had had at previous Congresses.

Though the Congress was advertised as an event that would represent the interests of the entire African continent, all the attendees came from British Africa. Further, though attendees traveled from other British colonies and protectorates, the Congress' focus was on African and Afro-Caribbean affairs. Delegates from each region proposed their own separate set of resolutions to address the particular concerns of their region. The following selection consists of the Congress' Resolutions, which addresses the particular dilemmas and aims of the different national struggles. The Congress also passed resolutions pertaining to other colonial holdings, such as the West Indies and Jamaica, as well as to racism within Britain. These resolutions have been excised because they fall outside of the scope of this volume.

10. "The Fifth Pan-African Congress: Resolutions," *History of the Pan-African Congress* (1947), edited by George Padmore. Reprinted in *The 1945 Manchester Pan-African Congress Revisited* by Hakim Adi and Marika Sherwood (London: New Beacon Books, 1995).

Congress Resolutions.

West Africa.

1. Political.

(a) That since the advent of British, French, Belgian and other European nations in West Africa, there has been regression instead of progress as a result of systematic exploitation by these alien imperialist Powers. The claims of "partnership," "trusteeship," "guardianship," and the "mandate system," do not serve the political wishes of the people of West Africa.

(b) That the democratic nature of the indigenous institutions of the peoples of West Africa has been crushed by obnoxious and oppressive laws and regulations, and replaced by autocratic systems of Government which are inimical to the political wishes of the peoples of West Africa.

(c) That the introduction of pretentious constitutional reforms into the West African Territories are nothing but spurious attempts on the part of alien imperialist Powers to continue the political enslavement of the peoples.

(d) That the introduction of Indirect Rule is not only an instrument of oppression but also an encroachment on the rights of the West African natural rulers.

(e) That the artificial divisions and territorial boundaries created by the Imperialist Powers are deliberate steps to obstruct the political unity of the West African peoples.

2. Economic.

(a) That there has been a systematic exploitation of the economic resources of the West African territories by imperialist Powers to the detriment of the inhabitants.

(b) That the industrialisation of West Africa by the indigenes has been discouraged and obstructed by the imperialist rulers, with the result that the standard of living has fallen below subsistence level.

(c) That the land, the rightful property of West Africans is gradually passing into the hands of foreign governments and other agencies through various devices and ordinances.

(d) That the workers and farmers of West Africa have not been allowed independent trades unions and cooperative movements without official interference.

(e) That the mining industries are in the hands of foreign monopolies of finance capital, with the result that wherever a mining industry has developed there has been a tendency to deprive the people of their land holding (e.g., mineral rights in Nigeria and Sierra Leone are now the property of the British Government).

(f) That the British Government in West Africa is virtually controlled by a merchants' united front, whose main objective is the exploitation of the people, thus rendering the indigenous population economically helpless.

(g) That when a country is compelled to rely on one crop (e.g., cocoa) for a single monopolistic market, and is obliged to cultivate only for export while at the same time its farmers and workers find themselves in the grip of finance capital, then it is evident that the government of that country is incompetent to assume economic responsibility for it.

3. Social.

(a) That the democratic organisations and institutions of the West African peoples have been interfered with; that alien rule has not improved education, health or the nutrition of the West African peoples but on the contrary tolerates mass illiteracy, ill-health, malnutrition, prostitution, and many other social evils.

(b) That organised Christianity in West Africa is identified with the political and economic exploitation of the West African peoples by alien Powers.

In view of these conditions, the Congress unanimously supports the members of the West African delegation in declaring:

That complete and absolute Independence for the Peoples of West Africa is the only solution to the existing problems.

The Congo and North Africa.

1. This Congress views with great concern the deplorable conditions imposed upon the Africans by French and Belgian Imperialisms in the Congo and Equatorial Africa, and demands that immediate steps be taken to remedy conditions in these territories.

2. That the demand of Egypt for the removal of British armed forces be conceded without delay, and that the Condominium over Sudan be abolished and the Sudanese granted complete independence from British and Egyptian rule.

3. That the demands of the indigenous peoples of Tunis, Algeria, Morocco and Libya for democratic rights and independence from French and Italian rule be recognised.

East Africa.

That this Congress of African peoples demands democratic rights and self-government for the people of Kenya, Uganda, Tanganyika, Nyasaland, Somaliland and Zanzibar.

That this Congress calls upon the Secretary of State for the Colonies to implement the following immediate demands of the people of East African territories.

1. The principles of the Four Freedoms and the Atlantic Charter be put into practice at once.

2. The abolition of land laws which allow Europeans to take land from the Africans. Immediate cessation of any further settlement by Europeans in Kenya or in any other territory in East Africa. All available land to be distributed to the landless Africans.

3. The right of Africans to develop the economic resources of their country without hindrance.

4. The immediate abolition of all racial and other discriminatory laws at once (Kipandi system in particular), and the system of equal citizenship to be introduced forthwith.

5. Freedom of speech, press, association and assembly.

6. Revision of the system of taxation and of the civil and criminal code.

7. Compulsory free and uniform education for all children up to the age of 16, with free meals, free books and school equipment.

8. Granting of the franchise, i.e., the right of every man and woman over the age of 21 to elect and be elected to Legislative Council, Provincial Council and all other Divisional and Municipal Councils.

9. A state Medical Service, Health and Welfare Service to be made available to all.

10. Abolition of forced labour, and the introduction of the principle of EQUAL PAY FOR EQUAL WORK.

Union of South Africa.

This Fifth Pan-African Congress, representing millions of Africans and peoples of African descent throughout the world, condemns with all its power the policy towards Africans and other non-Europeans carried out by the Union of South Africa which, although representing itself abroad as a democracy with a system of parliamentary government, manifests essentially the same characteristics as Fascism:

(a) the Herrenvolk[11] ideology which has transformed itself into a mania;

(b) the ruthless trampling underfoot of all human rights;

(c) the erection of one system of law and of morality for the "Aryans" and a different system of law and of morality for the non-white "non-Aryans."

This Congress demands for the non-European citizens of South Africa the immediate practical application of the following ten fundamental democratic rights.

1. The franchise, i.e., the right of every man and woman over the age of 21 to elect and be elected to Parliament, Provincial Council, and all other Divisional and Municipal Councils.

2. Compulsory free and uniform education for all children up to the age of 6, with free meals, free books and school equipment for the needy.

3. Inviolability of person, of one's house and privacy.

4. Freedom of speech, press, meeting, and association.

5. Freedom of movement and occupation.

6. Full equality of rights for all citizens, without distinction of race, culture and sex.

7. Revision of the land question in accordance with the needs of the Africans.

---

11. Political system in which one ethnic group dominates government.

8. Revision of the civil and criminal codes to accord with the foregoing demands.

9. Revision of the system of taxation to bring it into line with the above.

10. Revision of labour legislation and its application to the mines and agriculture.

This Congress pledges itself to work unceasingly with and on behalf of its non-European brothers in South Africa until they achieve the status of freedom and human dignity. This Congress regards the struggle of our brothers in South Africa as an integral part of the common struggle for national liberation throughout Africa.

MAYI BUYE I AFRICA![12]

The Protectorates of Bechuanaland, Basutoland, and Swaziland.

1. Since the Union of South Africa became a Dominion there has been developed an insistent urge to gain possession of the Native Protectorates of Bechuanaland, Basutoland and Swaziland, covering a total area of 293,420 square miles, with a population of over 1,000,000. Control of these territories is desired in order to (1) exploit the minerals, (2) secure more land for agriculture and farming purposes, and (3) obtain additional supplies of cheap labour by taxing the natives.

2. In recent years this desire for expansion has assumed an aggressive form and has created great alarm among the natives of the Protectorates for they are the last remaining Africans in the southern part of the continent who own land and enjoy a nominal independence.

3. The Government of the Union of South Africa is demanding the immediate transfer of the Protectorates to the Union and is in correspondence with the Imperial Government on the subject. The Colonial Office has already set up a Joint Advisory Commission of South African and British officials to examine the question and propose ways and means of effecting transfer if and when Parliament agrees.

---

12. South African slogan meaning "bring back Africa" in the Xhosa language.

4. The African people object bitterly to being used as pawns in bargains between different member states of the British Commonwealth as a means of settling imperialist adjustments. Africans are not chattels to be bartered like cattle in the markets of white nations, where statesmen and diplomats, like brokers, do their trade in the name of Democracy and Peace.

5. The natives of the Protectorates look with horror upon such a proposal for they know of the slave conditions under which 8 million Africans in the Union live, who bear the brunt of taxation and other burdens but have no representation in Government. Eighty per cent of their lands have been taken away from them. They are denied the most elementary democratic rights—freedom of speech, press, assembly and movement. They are debarred from Trade Unions and excluded from skilled occupations by the Colour Bar. They are saddled with Pass Laws and other forms of repressive legislation. Recording their opposition to transfer, the Chiefs of Bechuanaland have adopted the following resolution: "This meeting of Chiefs and Councillors present on behalf of their respective tribes of Bechuanaland Protectorates records its protest and objection to the incorporation of the territory in the Union of South Africa."

6. The natives of the Protectorates demand that the British Labour Government honour the promise of Protection made to their Chiefs by Her Majesty Queen Victoria's Government during the latter part of the last century in return for their allegiance to the British Crown.

Ethiopia, Liberia, Haiti.

This Fifth Pan-African Congress sends fraternal greetings to the Governments and peoples of Ethiopia, Liberia and Haiti, and pledges its support in mobilising world public opinion among Africans and peoples of African descent in defence of their Sovereign independence. We assure the Governments and peoples of these States that we shall ever be vigilant against any manifestation of Imperial encroachment which may threaten their independence.

We take this opportunity to inform the Imperial powers that we look with jealous pride upon these nations and regard them as symbols of the realisation of the political hopes and aspirations of African peoples still under Imperialist domination.

Additional Resolution on Ethiopia.

This Fifth Pan-African Congress sends its warmest greetings to the Emperor and peoples of Ethiopia, one of the three free states in the world that are controlled by African people. It pledges itself to guard with jealousy the interests of Ethiopia.

1. This Congress condemns the suggestion that parts of Massawa and Asmara should be put under international control. It further condemns most strongly the attempts of the European Powers to impose conditions of Trusteeship which suggest that Ethiopia cannot be fully trusted to look after her own affairs.

2. In the interest of justice as well as of economic geography this Congress supports most heartily the claims of the Somalis and Eritreans to be returned to their Motherland instead of being parcelled out to foreign powers.

3. This Congress demands the immediate withdrawal of the British Military Administration from Ethiopian soil.

4. This Congress calls upon the United Nations Relief Organisation to extend to Ethiopia the same aid as being afforded to the other victims of aggression.

. . . .

Resolution to U.N.O. on South-West Africa.

In order to register their protest against South Africa's demand for the abolition of the Mandate over South West Africa and the incorporation of the territory into the Union, the League of Coloured Peoples, the Pan-African Federation, the West African National Secretariat, and other coloured organisations in Britain, sent the following Resolution to the Trusteeship Committee of the United Nations:

(a) To reject categorically the claim of the Government of the Union of South Africa to incorporate the mandated territory of South-West Africa, (b) To request the surrender of the mandate of the territory of South-West Africa to the Trusteeship Council of the United Nations

Organisation by the European peoples of the Union of South Africa, (c) To investigate the conditions of life and work, the political rights and civil liberties of the non-European peoples of the Union of South Africa, and (d) To require of the Union of South Africa an undertaking to respect and abide by the principles of the United Nations Charter in the treatment of all peoples within the jurisdiction on pain of expulsion from membership of the United Nations Organisation.

As is generally known, the policy pursued by the Government of South Africa towards its subjects of non-European race is a direct negation of the principles of racial tolerance, justice and freedom. Since the year 1920 when the mandated territory of South-West Africa was placed under the Trusteeship of the Union of South Africa the Native Policy of the Union Government has steadily deteriorated. As the native in South Africa has become, in spite of Legislative and Administrative restrictions, more efficient in the field of industrial labour and more advanced in knowledge, so have the repressive measures directed against him been extended and intensified. The whole purpose of these measures is to make of the African nothing more than an "indentured labourer," a being in perpetual enslavement to the Mining and Agricultural enterprises of the country.

In 1936 the passing of the Native Franchise Act, the Native Land Act and the Urban Areas Act deprived the natives of the Cape Province of the right to buy, hire or occupy land wherever they chose and confined them to restricted areas; the right to be on the Common Voters Roll, their representation being limited to three appointed European members in a House of Assembly consisting of one hundred and fifty-three members; their right to sell their labour where they chose by restricting their movements. The Industrial Conciliation Act No. 36 of 1937 excludes from the definition of "Employee" over ninety per cent of the African workers merely because they are natives. The result of this Act is that the Minister of Labour refuses to recognize African Trade Unions or to implement any agreement negotiated between White employer and black employee under the terms of the Act. Under the covenant of the League of Nations the Mandatory Power was entitled to apply to the mandated territory the same law as those in force in its own territory. Thus by means of proclamations some of the restrictive laws of the Union have been extended to South-West Africa. For instance, The Native Administration Proclamation No. 11 of 1924 and The Urban Areas Proclamation No. 34 of 1924 followed closely the lines of Urban

Legislation and enforced segregation of the African peoples. In 1927 Proclamation No. 11 placed a restriction on the number of native squatters on farms and by the introduction of a system of "passes" restricted all movement including travel by rail.

There is little doubt that in its attitude to the territory of South-West Africa the Union Government has assumed a position which is not in keeping with that of a trustee but, on the contrary, in accord with that of a conqueror bent upon territorial aggrandisment and the spoliation and humiliation of the vanquished. The question arises whether the Union Government is one that should reasonably be entrusted with the care of subject and helpless peoples. The racial policy of this Government is a direct affront to the express determination of the United Nations "to re-affirm faith in fundamental human rights, in the dignity and worth of the human person, in the equal rights of men and women of nations large and small."

Africans are not the only victims of this racialism, for the Indians, who number a bare quarter of a million, suffer discrimination in a similar manner. Incidentally, the latest manifestation of anti-Indian Legislation, the Asiatic Land Tenure and Indian Representation Act forms the subject of a complaint to the United Nations Organisation by the Government of India.

We demand justice and social equality for the Indian community in South Africa.

10

Speech at the Kenya African Union Meeting at Nyeri, 1952[13]

Jomo Kenyatta

Jomo Kenyatta (1893–1978) was one of the leading figures in the Kenyan independence movement and served as the first prime minister of Kenya from 1963 to 1964 and the country's first president from 1964 to 1978. A member of Kenya's Kikuyu ethnic group, Kenyatta first became involved in Kikuyu politics regarding land disputes with colonial authorities and British settlers. In 1935, Kenyatta chose to pursue his education in England after having first visited the country as a representative of the Kikuyu Central Association. He studied anthropology at the London School of Economics (LSE) under the famed anthropologist Bronisław Malinowski, which led to Kenyatta's important study of the Kikuyu, Facing Mount Kenya *(published in 1938). After his return to Kenya in 1946, Kenyatta became president of the Kenyan African Union (KAU).*

In 1951, the Mau Mau Rebellion broke out. A state of emergency was declared, which was used as a pretext for banning the KAU and arresting its leadership. After Kenyan independence in 1963, Kenyatta's terms as prime minister and president were marked by the creation of a single-party state in which opposition leaders were persecuted. He was often accused of favoring Kikuyu over other ethnic groups. In the following speech, recorded with notes in parentheses by the Assistant Superintendent of Police, Kenyatta outlines the KAU's position on the Mau Mau Rebellion. He asserts that the KAU's tactics are primarily peaceful and democratic. Kenyatta's comments about the peaceful purpose of the KAU are directed as much to his supporters as to the police who were recording the event.

13. Jomo Kenyatta, "Speech at the Kenya African Union Meeting at Nyeri" (July 26, 1952), *Historical Survey of the Origins and Growth of Mau Mau*, presented to Parliament by the Secretary of State for the Colonies by Command of Her Majesty, May 1960 (London: Her Majesty's Stationary Office).

Time is limited and I am now starting. I want you to know the purpose of K.A.U. It is the biggest purpose the African has. It involves every African in Kenya and it is their mouthpiece which asks for freedom. (Applause.) K.A.U. is you and you are the K.A.U. If we unite now, each and every one of us, and each tribe to another, we will cause the implementation in this country of that which the European calls democracy. True democracy has no colour distinction. It does not choose between black and white. We are here in this tremendous gathering under the K.A.U. flag to find which road leads us from darkness into democracy. In order to find it we Africans must first achieve the right to elect our own representatives. That is surely the first principle of democracy. We are the only race in Kenya which does not elect its own representatives in the Legislature and we are going to set about to rectify this situation. (Applause. Jesse Kariuki[14] is working the crowd up by translating Kenyatta's speech in such a way that he is conveying to the people an inference that Jomo Kenyatta does not convey.) We feel we are dominated by a handful of others who refuse to be just. God said this is our land. Land in which we are to flourish as a people. We are not worried that other races are here with us in our country, but we insist that we are the leaders here, and what we want we insist we get. We want our cattle to get fat on our land so that our children grow up in prosperity; we do not want that fat removed to feed others. (Applause.) He who has ears should now hear that K.A.U. claims this land as its own gift from God and I wish those who are black, white or brown at this meeting to know this. K.A.U. speaks in daylight. He who calls us the *Mau Mau* is not truthful. We do not know this thing *Mau Mau*. (Jeers and applause.) We want to prosper as a nation, and as a nation we demand equality, that is equal pay for equal work. Whether it is a chief, headman or labourer he needs in these days increased salary. He needs a salary that compares with a salary of a European who does equal work. We will never get our freedom unless we succeed in this issue. We do not want equal pay for equal work tomorrow—we want it right now. Those who profess to be just must realize that this is the foundation of justice. It has never been known in history that a country prospers without equality. We despise bribery and corruption, those two words that the European repeatedly refers to. Bribery and corruption is prevalent in this country, but I am

14. Kariuki was a leader of the Kikuyu Central Association, which was banned in 1940. Many of the Association's leaders helped to form the KAU.

not surprised. As long as a people are held down, corruption is sure to rise and the only answer to this is a policy of equality. If we work together as one, we must succeed.

Our country today is in a bad state for its land is full of fools—and fools in a country delay the independence of its people. K.A.U. seeks to remedy this situation and I tell you now it despises thieving, robbery and murder, for these practices ruin our country. I say this because if one man steals, or two men steal, there are people sitting close by lapping up information, who say the whole tribe is bad because a theft has been committed. Those people are wrecking our chances of advancement. They will prevent us getting freedom. If I have my own way, let me tell you I would butcher the criminal, and there are more criminals than one in more senses than one. The policeman must arrest an offender, a man who is purely an offender, but he must not go about picking up people with a small horn of liquor in their hands and march them in procession with his fellow policemen to Government and say he has got a *Mau Mau* amongst the Kikuyu people. (Applause.) The plain clothes man who hides in the hedges must, I demand, get the truth of our words before he flies to Government to present them with false information. I ask this of them who are in the meeting to take heed of my words and do their work properly and justly. (Applause.) We are black people and when we achieve our freedom, we will also have police and plain clothes men.

. . . .

K.A.U. is a good union and we do not want divided people. I think *Mau Mau* is a new word. Elders do not know it. K.A.U. is not a fighting union that uses fists and weapons. If any of you here think that force is good, I do not agree with you: remember the old saying that he who is hit with a *rungu* returns, but he who is hit with justice never comes back. I do not want people to accuse us falsely—that we steal and that we are *Mau Mau*. (Tremendous applause.) I pray to you that we join hands for freedom and freedom means abolishing criminality. Beer harms us and those who drink it do us harm and they may be the so-called *Mau Mau*. (Tremendous applause. It is obvious that Jomo is sidestepping denouncing *Mau Mau*.) Whatever grievances we have, let us air them here in the open. The criminal does not want freedom and land—he wants to line his own pocket. Let us therefore demand our rights justly. The British Government has discussed the land problem in Kenya and we hope to have a Royal Commission to this country to look into the land problem very shortly. When this Royal Commission comes, let us show it that we are a good peaceful people and not thieves and robbers.

11

Communism and Black Nationalism, 1955[15]

George Padmore

George Padmore (1903–1959) was a former Communist who became a leading Pan-Africanist intellectual and advisor to Ghana's Kwame Nkrumah. Born in British-controlled Trinidad, Padmore studied in the United States where he became involved in the Communist Party. In 1929, Padmore attended the Communist International in Moscow as a representative of the Negro Bureau of the Red International of Labour Unions (also known as the Profintern). In 1930, he formed the International Trade Union Committee of Negro Workers (ITUCNW). Increasingly disappointed by the Communist movement's lack of support for colonized people, Padmore left the organization three years later. He was expelled from the Communist movement in 1934. Thereafter, he embraced Pan-Africanist politics and, in 1945, helped organize the Fifth Pan-African Congress with Nkrumah (see Document 9).

In the following excerpt from his book Pan-Africanism or Communism, *Padmore argues that aid from the Western bloc would help to turn Africans away from communism. In keeping with his Pan-Africanist principles, Padmore asserts that African states should be allowed to develop along a "self-help" program and with minimal Western interference. He closes by explaining why Pan-Africanism provides the correct political principles for an independent Africa.*

. . . [W]hite folk who want to help Africa must be prepared to work *with* Africans on the basis of complete racial equality. For racial arrogance and colour bars are greater obstacles to peace and co-operation in Africa than Communism.

15. George Padmore, "Communism and Black Nationalism" from *African Socialism*, edited by William H. Friedland and Carl G. Rosberg, Jr. Copyright © 1964 by the Board of Trustees of the Leland Stanford Jr. University; renewed 1992. All rights reserved. Reprinted with the permission of Stanford University Press.

In this connection of aid to Africa, if America, the 'foremost champion and defender of the free world' is really worried about Communism taking root in Africa and wants to prevent such a calamity from taking place, I can offer an insurance against it. This insurance will not only forestall Communism, but endear the people of the great North American Republic for ever to the Africans. Instead of underwriting the discredited system of Colonialism by bolstering up the European regimes, especially in North, Central and South Africa, with military and financial aid, let American statesmen make a bold gesture to the Africans in the spirit of the anti-Colonialist tradition of 1776.

This gesture should take the form of a Marshall Aid programme for Africa. Having regard, moreover, to the fact that millions of Africans were taken from the Guinea coast during the period of the Slave Trade and their labour used to lay the foundations of the fabulous wealth of the Republic, what could be a finer way of making restitution for past wrongs inflicted upon Africa than for the U.S. Congress to construct the Volta River project in the Gold Coast—the first African country to achieve independence in the twentieth century, the 'Century of the Common Man'? Such a free national gift without strings from America would achieve more than all the propaganda in the world to cement the bonds of eternal friendship between a grateful African people and a generous American nation. Already Russia is offering such aid to Egypt and Sudan; India and Burma.

Africans have lived so long on promises. What they want to see are a few concrete deeds. They are tired of listening to pious sermons about 'democracy' and 'freedom' while the chains of servitude still hang around their necks. Africans, too, want to live as human beings and enjoy with white folk some of the material benefits of modern civilization.

. . . .

Once confidence, trust and mutual respect is established between African leaders and their European advisers, there is nothing to prevent the rapid economic and social advancement of Africa. It is a continent of great potentialities. In planning its welfare and development certain basic principles should be observed. For example, the main sector of the national economy should be State controlled, since there is not enough local capital available to undertake large scale enterprises. But the rest should be left to private initiative. The Africans must be encouraged to do things for themselves and not just sit back and expect Government to do everything for them. The emphasis must be upon *Self-Help*. In undertakings sponsored by the Government, they must not be managed by civil servants, but should be operated through statutory bodies which must enjoy the maximum amount of freedom from bureaucratic control. History is moving fast and Africa can no longer afford to remain what the French call *le musée vivant*. Land should be controlled and made available to the rural populations engaged in agriculture. Africans must never surrender their communal land tenure system in favour of landlordism—the great curse of Asia. The co-operative movement must be encouraged, strengthened and extended to embrace the greatest number of primary producers. Measures must also be taken to develop the consumers' co-operative movement among the wage-workers and lower paid salaried employees. Trade Unionism and the Four Freedoms— freedom of assembly, press, speech and worship—must be guaranteed by law. And last but not least, African leaders must encourage social discipline, civic responsibility and honesty among themselves and the people, who must be made to realize that democracy can only succeed to the extent that the voters elect honest and incorruptible rulers. Much of the Communists' strength in Asia lies in the fact that they have been able to offer the people honest government in China and Viet-minh— even if it is sometimes oppressive.

Old-fashioned paternalistic government planning will make no appeal to politically-awakened Africans. They must be able to take a part in the control of the plans by representation on the various committees and boards. To win the trust and confidence of Africans, the Colonial Office must push on with constitutional advance even at the risk of temporary set-backs. At present there is too much hesitation and doubletalk in official quarters. For example, while the Colonial Office pays lip service to the principle that Uganda is to be regarded as 'primarily an African State', the Governor has proceeded to draft a constitution that will introduce the menace of communalism into the body politic by giving a few thousand Europeans and Indian immigrants who do not consider themselves citizens of Uganda, communal representation in the Legislative Assembly and Executive Council that no community of African immigrants in Britain or India would dare to demand. Is this how the confidence of Ugandans is to be won? If so, the Colonial Office is going to be faced with constitutional crises and political deadlocks for a long time to come. Africans are no longer asleep. They are becoming increasingly conscious of their fights to be rulers of their own countries. So Britain may as well face up to the problem and not wait until it has to be solved by violence. That is the great mistake that France is making throughout her empire, and losing the friendship of her subjects as a consequence. The French bourgeoisie, like the Bourbons, 'learn nothing and forget nothing'. They will only leave Africa when they suffer a series of disasters there like Dien-Bien-Phu.[16]

. . . .

In our struggle for national freedom, human dignity and social redemption, Pan-Africanism offers an ideological alternative to Communism on the one side and Tribalism on the other. It rejects both white racialism and black chauvinism. It stands for racial coexistence on the basis of absolute equality and respect for human personality.

Pan-Africanism looks above the narrow confines of class, race, tribe and religion. In other words, it wants equal opportunity for all. Talent to be rewarded on the basis of merit. Its vision stretches beyond the limited frontiers of the nation-state. Its perspective embraces the federation of regional self-governing countries and their ultimate amalgamation into a *United States of Africa*.

In such a Commonwealth, all men, regardless of tribe, race, colour or creed, shall be free and equal. And all the national units comprising the regional federations shall be autonomous in all matters regional, yet united in all matters of common interest to the African Union. This is our vision of the Africa of Tomorrow—the goal of Pan-Africanism.

16. A major battle held from March to May 1954 where the forces of the French Union were defeated by the Viet Minh during the First Indochina War.

12

French Africa and the French Union, 1957[17]

Félix Houphouët-Boigny

Félix Houphouët-Boigny (1905–1993) was Côte d'Ivoire's first president after declaring independence in 1960. A political moderate, Houphouët-Boigny maintained close political ties with France throughout his life and chose to distance himself from radicals in the decolonization movements. As a member of the National Assembly in France, he presented a bill abolishing forced labor. Known as the Loi Houphouët-Boigny, the Assembly adopted the bill in 1946. That same year Houphouët-Boigny formed the African Democratic Rally (RDA), a radical party with ties to the French Communist Party (PCF). However, Houphouët-Boigny's politics became increasingly conservative and, in 1951, he severed ties with the PCF. When de Gaulle proposed the formation of the French Community, Houphouët-Boigny was one of its most vocal supporters. He opposed calls for immediate territorial sovereignty advocated by African independence leaders, such as Kwame Nkrumah, and is suspected of supporting coups against several African politicians with Marxist leanings, including Nkrumah, Mathieu Kérékou of Benin, and Thomas Sankara of Burkina Faso. As president, he maintained an ardent anti-communist foreign and domestic policy. In the following excerpt from his speech to the Fourth Committee of the United Nations General Assembly on January 7, 1957, Houphouët-Boigny argues that France's African colonies should sustain ties with France. Notably, Houphouët-Boigny heralds the end of French racial discrimination and claims that Africans had benefited from some aspects of French colonialism.

The Atlantic Charter has made the right of peoples to self determination a universal principle. The dependent peoples of Black Africa also must, therefore, move toward the constitution of new nations.

17. Félix Houphouët-Boigny, "French Africa and the French Union," *The Political Awakening of Africa*, edited by Rupert Emerson and Martin Kilson (Englewood Cliffs: Prentice Hall, 1965).

But we Black Africans are just becoming acquainted with political life at a time when the very notion of the absolute independence of nations is undergoing a remarkable development.

In this century, each nation feels more and more cramped within its boundaries. The nations, even the largest, the most powerful or the most prosperous, can no longer complacently enjoy the deceptive luxury of isolation. Thus the world is tending to become organized in large economic and political units.

On the morrow of the last world war, France conceived a very beautiful and grand design: to free and emancipate her former colonies scattered on the five continents of the world and to associate them with her destiny.

She undertook, by the very act of setting up the French Union, to lead the peoples for whom she is responsible toward the freedom to administer their own affairs democratically.

France renounced force as a means of domination: she knows that the same is true of the force of men as of that of nations; it is born, grows and dies. That which endures is work done together in equality and justice; that which endures is brotherhood. She wants to construct a new community, based on confidence and friendship.

"Watch out," we were then advised from various quarters. "Don't let yourselves be taken in by the voice of the Sirens; the association offered you is that of the horse and the horseman."

The conscientious and responsible men of French Black Africa, those who have fought colonialism the hardest and are still fighting colonialism in all its forms, want, while remaining extremely vigilant, to do away with paralyzing distrust, to rise above all feelings of bitterness, even the most legitimate, and to grasp the brotherly hand that is held out to them.

We do not have any complexes. We are a young and proud people. The brothers, sons, and grandsons of all those magnificent infantrymen who, during the two world wars when France's independence and the freedom of the world were jeopardized, vied in bravery by the side of the French and of their allies, will know how to give proof of the same courage and the same abnegation, in the peaceful struggle now beginning for their human and social emancipation.

Would France want to deceive us? But her whole tradition of progress, all her generous and emancipating inclinations deny this, as well as her humane ideals and her most obvious self-interest.

She knows that if we need her in order to succeed in our struggle for emancipation, we are indispensable to her if she is to play in the world, and first of all in Europe, that great role of rapprochement between men and peoples which is in her best tradition.

France is a light which must not be extinguished.

Simple justice demands that after having denounced and condemned all the discriminatory laws of French colonialism, we recognize in all honesty the positive side of colonization, colonization which, in itself, is not an isolated fact, peculiar to France, but has been a universal process of history.

France has not exterminated the races placed under her domination; on the contrary, the indigenous populations have grown everywhere.

She has not imposed her regime on those for whom she has assumed responsibility. Here, thrones have been preserved and protected; there, the individual character of the territory and the customs have been respected—all while paving the way for democracy.

Is it not an edifying spectacle to see before you today a Minister of the French Republic, member of a Government under Socialist leadership, an African who follows the customs of matriarchy, a plain middle class African, leader of the largest democratic popular movement in French Black Africa?

Finally, gentlemen, France has never known racial segregation. Who can prove to me the contrary? Certain individuals, in her name, may have shown themselves to be narrow-minded racists, that is true, but the French people as a whole condemn, *de jure* as well as *de facto*, racism in all its forms. . . .

What it is therefore essential to determine, and one must express an opinion on this point, is whether—in Black Africa's present state of development, and bearing in mind the twofold fact that the world trend is toward large economic and political units and that Black Africa is not directly affected by the ideological conflict which divides the world— whether Black Africa's interest lies within the framework of absolute independence or within that of a larger unit.

In West Africa and Equatorial Africa, over 60 million Africans—I wish to speak only of those Africans who are the most advanced politically—were divided, by the accident of colonization in the last century, into two groups of different cultures: English culture and French culture.

The first group, English speaking, is moving toward independence within the framework of the Commonwealth, with ties that are more economical than political.

The second is moving toward self-government within a federal community which remains to be defined juridically but whose ties, within the community, are of a sentimental, economic and political nature.

We, Africans of French culture, are following the bold experiment of our English-speaking brothers with much interest and much sympathy.

Yes, Kwame Nkrumah and the leaders of Nigeria and Sierra Leone have our affectionate sympathy.

They wish to show what the black people of Africa can accomplish on their own initiative. We cannot be indifferent to their experiment. We wish them prompt and complete success.

But we wish, in a spirit of healthy emulation, to conduct our own experiment. The future will decide which of our methods is better.

In this venture without precedent in the long history of the peoples of the world, the French and ourselves—a community of men of different races, religions and degrees of civilization, engaged in the same struggle for happiness, with freedom and fraternity—the French and ourselves are going to shoulder heavy responsibilities with regard to Africa.

It would be unforgivable for us, the responsible African statesmen of today, to betray Africa when it places its confidence in us.

We are fully aware of our obligations. And so is France who knows that she would betray, not only her own interests, but also all that which has constituted her greatness, her traditional generosity, her cherished and proud motto: Liberty, Equality, Fraternity.

The community we want to achieve, together with her, will be humane, equalitarian and fraternal or it will not be at all. But we are confident that it will be. . . .

The United Nations Organization will not attain its goal if it is satisfied with merely facilitating the birth of new nations.

It must help to ensure within nations, or groups of nations, peace, justice, rising living standards and the social progress of their citizens. There are no happy men in an unhappy country. There cannot be happy nations in an unhappy world. To live an oppressed and miserable life in a politically independent country does not make man truly independent.

To be independent means not only to enjoy political rights and basic freedoms, but beyond that to have the standard of living, health, and education required to exercise fully such rights and freedoms. I have no intention, gentlemen, of inveighing against any particular person or nation. I am only asking you to be fair and to consider the facts. Is there a single country in the world which would offer to an African of my color, race, and stage of civilization, the liberty, equality, fraternity we can find within the French community?

We must therefore help nations, such as France, which are doing their utmost to make the human element prevail, for, gentlemen, the centuries-old dream of peoples and men is not stupendous technical progress, proud though men may be of such achievements, nor is it the conquest of interstellar space or the disintegration of matter; the great dream of humanity is brotherhood.

Some have said that I am a mystic.

Yes, I am a mystic fervently devoted to brotherhood. And because I believe in brotherhood, I believe in the final triumph of the French-African community, inasmuch as we want to be humane, equalitarian and fraternal.

13

The Franco-African Community, 1958[18]

Charles de Gaulle

In 1958, the Fourth French Republic collapsed due to the government's inability to address the growing crisis in Algeria, including threats posed by pro-French Algerian generals. General Charles de Gaulle (1890–1970) came out of retirement to lead the transitional government in writing a new constitution and establishing the Fifth Republic. As part of de Gaulle's efforts to maintain political relationships with France's former colonies, the French Community replaced the French Union, which had included France and its overseas territories and departments. Each member of the Community would become an autonomous state (excluding those territories that were departments of the Republic, like Algeria). The Community's jurisdiction would apply to foreign policy, transportation between the member states, and economic policies.

On September 28, 1958, a referendum was held to adopt the new constitution and all of the Fifth Republic's proposed institutions, including the Community. The overseas territories were given the option of declaring complete independence or of becoming an autonomously governing member state of the newly formed Community. Those overseas territories that voted in favor of the constitution were allowed until February 4, 1959, to decide either to retain their status as overseas territory, become a member state, or become an overseas department of France. Of the overseas territories, only Guinea, under the leadership of Sekou Touré, selected full independence. In this speech given in Conakry prior to the referendum, de Gaulle appeals to the people of Guinea to vote on September 28 in favor of the new constitution.

The question between us, Africans and Metropolitans, is uniquely to know whether we want, the former and the latter, to put a Community into practice together for a duration that I have not determined, which will permit the development of what must be developed from

18. Charles de Gaulle, "The Franco-African Community" (1958), *African History: Texts and Readings*, edited by Robert O. Collins (New York: Random House, 1971).

the economic, social, moral, cultural points of view, and, if necessary, to defend our common liberties against whoever would attack them.

This community is proposed by France; no one is forced to adhere to it. Independence has been spoken of, I say here louder than elsewhere that independence is at the disposition of Guinea. She can have it, she can take it on the 28th of September by saying "No" to the proposition made to her, and in that case I guarantee that the Metropole will set up no obstacles. Of course, she will take the consequences, but there will be no obstacles and your territory can do as it wants and under the conditions it wants, follow the road it wants.

If Guinea answers "Yes," it will be because freely, on its own, spontaneously, she accepts the Community proposed to her by France, and if France, on her side, says "Yes," for she too must say it, then the territories of Africa and Metropole will be able to carry out this new work together, which will be made by the efforts of both, for the profit of the men who live there.

To this work, France will not refuse, I am sure of it in advance, on the condition, of course, that in other places, that understanding, that call, that are necessary to a people when there are efforts required, I might even say sacrifices, particularly when that people is France, that is to say, a country that gladly responds to friendship and feelings and that responds in an opposite sense to the ill will that could oppose her.

This France, I am sure, will participate in the Community with the means that she has and despite the burdens she carries, and these burdens are heavy—the whole world knows it. They are heavy in the Metropole because of the great destruction she has suffered in two world wars for the salvation of liberty and the world and in particular for the salvation of the liberty of Africans. Then she has burdens in Europe, for she wants to make Europe, she wants to do it in the interest of those who live there and also, I think, in the interest of the continent in which I now find myself. France has burdens from a world point of view; she has them in North Africa. She must develop, for the common good, the wealth contained in the Sahara.

All these burdens are considerable, but nevertheless, I believe that, on her side, the Metropole will say "Yes" to the Franco-African Community on the conditions that I indicated a while ago. If we do it together, Africans and Metropolitans, it will be an act of faith in a communal and humane destiny and it will also be, I believe very much, the way, the only way to establish a practical collaboration for the good of the men who are our responsibility. I believe that Guinea will say "Yes" to France, and then I believe the way will be open for us, where we can walk together. The way will not be easy; there will be many obstacles in the road of men of today and words will not change anything.

These obstacles must be surmounted, the obstacle of poverty must be overcome. You have spoken of the obstacle of indignation, yes, it is already largely overcome, it is necessary to completely overcome it; dignity from all points of view, notably from the internal, national point of view. There are yet other obstacles that come from our own human nature, our passions, our prejudices, our exaggeration. These obstacles I think we will be able to surmount.

It is in this spirit that I have come to talk to you in this Assembly, and I have done it confidently, I have done it confidently because in short, I believe in the future made by the ensemble of free men who are capable of extracting from the soil and from human nature what is needed for men to be better and happier. And then I believe that an example must be set for the world, for if we disperse, all that there is of imperialism in the world will be upon us. Of course there will be ideologies like a screen, like a flag to go before it; it would not be the first time in the history of the world that ethnic and national interests march behind signs. We must be ready together for that also; it is our human duty.

I have spoken. You will think it over. I carry away from my visit to Conakry the impression of a popular sentiment that is entirely turned in the direction I would desire. I make the wish that the élites of this country take the direction that I have indicated and that I think responds to the deepest intentions of our masses, and having said that, I will interrupt myself, awaiting perhaps, if the event ever takes place, the supreme occasion to see you, in a few months, when things will be settled and when we will together publicly manifest the establishment of our Community. And if I do not see you again, know that the memory of my stay in this great, beautiful, noble city, working city of the future, this memory I will never lose.

Long live Guinea!
Long live the Republic!
Long live France!

14

Resolution on Imperialism and Colonialism, 1958[19]

The All-African People's Conference

The All-African People's Conference of 1958 was the first of three conferences that aimed to forge solidarity among newly independent African states. Held in Accra, Ghana, December 5–13, just over a year after Ghana's independence in 1957, the All-African People's Conference was comprised of delegates from the independent states of Ethiopia, Ghana, Guinea, Liberia, Libya, Morocco, Tunisia, and the United Arab Republic, as well as delegates from African countries still under European rule. The resolution published by the first conference offered a powerful condemnation of European imperialism and asserted support for the ongoing process of decolonization and independence in Africa. Though it stated that independence should be pursued by nonviolent means, the resolution defended the use of violence when independence movements were forcibly repressed. Hosted by Kwame Nkrumah, the conference should be understood as part of Nkrumah's effort to perpetuate the Pan-Africanism he had first been exposed to as a student in Britain.

CONFERENCE RESOLUTION ON IMPERIALISM AND COLONIALISM

Whereas the great bulk of the African continent has been carved out arbitrarily to the detriment of the indigenous African peoples by European Imperialists, namely: Britain, France, Belgium, Spain, Italy and Portugal.

---

19. "All-African People's Conference: Resolution on Imperialism and Colonialism," Accra, December 5–13, 1958, *All-African People's Conference News Bulletin*, Vol. I, No. 4 (Accra, 1959).

(2) Whereas in this process of colonisation, two groups of colonial territories have emerged, to wit:

   (a) Those territories where indigenous Africans are dominated by foreigners who have their seats of authority in foreign lands, for example, French West Africa, French Equatorial Africa, Nigeria, Sierra Leone, Gambia, Belgian Congo, Portuguese Guinea, Basutoland, Swaziland and Bechuanaland.

   (b) Those where indigenous Africans are dominated and oppressed by foreigners who have settled permanently in Africa and who regard the position of Africa under their sway as belonging more to them than to the Africa, e.g., Kenya, Union of South Africa, Algeria, Rhodesia, Angola and Mozambique.

(3) Whereas world opinion unequivocally condemns oppression and subjugation of one race by another in whatever shape or form.

(4) Whereas all African peoples everywhere strongly deplore the economic exploitation of African peoples by imperialist countries thus reducing Africans to poverty in the midst of plenty.

(5) Whereas all African peoples vehemently resent the militarisation of Africans and the use of African soldiers in a nefarious global game against their brethren as in Algeria, Kenya, South Africa, Cameroons, Ivory Coast, Rhodesia and in the Suez Canal invasion.

(6) Whereas fundamental human rights, freedom of speech, freedom of association, freedom of movement, freedom of worship, freedom to live a full and abundant life, as approved by the All-African People's Conference on 13th December, 1958, are denied to Africans through the activities of imperialists.

(7) Whereas denial of the franchise to Africans on the basis of race or sex has been one of the principal instruments of colonial policy by imperialists and their agents, thus making it feasible for a few white settlers to lord it over millions of indigenous Africans as in the proposed Central African Federation, Kenya, Union of South Africa, Algeria, Angola, Mozambique and the Cameroons.

(8) Whereas imperialists are now coordinating their activities by forming military and economic pacts such as NATO, European Common Market, Free Trade Area, Organisation for European Economic Co-operation, Common Organisation in

Sahara for the purpose of strengthening their imperialist activities in Africa and elsewhere.

Be it resolved and it is hereby resolved by; the All-African People's Conference meeting in Accra 5th to 13th December, 1958, and comprising over 300 delegates representing over 200 million Africans from all parts of Africa as follows:

1. That the All-African People's Conference vehemently condemns colonialism and imperialism in whatever shape or form these evils are perpetuated.

2. That the political and economic exploitation of Africans by imperialist Europeans should cease forthwith.

3. That the use of African manpower in the nefarious game of power politics by imperialists should be a thing of the past.

4. That independent African States should pursue in their international policy principles which will expedite and accelerate the independence and sovereignty of all dependent and colonial African territories.

5. That fundamental human rights be extended to all men and women in Africa and that the rights of indigenous Africans to the fullest use of their lands be respected and preserved.

6. That universal adult franchise be extended to all persons in Africa regardless of race or sex.

7. That independent African states ensure that fundamental human rights and universal adult franchise are fully extended to everyone within their states as an example to imperial nations who abuse and ignore the extension of those rights to Africans.

8. That a permanent secretariat of the All-African People's Conference be set up to organise the All-African Conference on a firm basis.

9. That a human rights committee of the Conference be formed to examine complaints of abuse of human rights in every part of Africa and to take appropriate steps to ensure the enjoyment of the rights by everyone.

10. That the All-African People's Conference in Accra declares its full support to all fighters for freedom in Africa, to all those who resort to peaceful means of non-violence and civil

disobedience, as well as to all those who are compelled to retaliate against violence to attain national independence and freedom for the people. Where such retaliation becomes necessary, the Conference condemns all legislations which consider those who fight for their independence and freedom as ordinary criminals.

15

"Travel for TANU," 1958[20]

Bibi Titi Mohammed

Bibi Titi Mohammed (1926–2000) was—along with Tanzania's future president, Julius Nyerere—one of the founding members of the Tanganyika African National Union (TANU). TANU had been formed in 1954 and helped lead Tanganyika to independence from Britain in 1961 (the country was renamed Tanzania in 1964). Mohammed traveled throughout the country to promote independence, and she was instrumental in organizing women. Special women's sections of TANU branches helped to place women's issues like education, literacy, and childcare on the nationalist agenda. With the consent of their husbands, married women could participate in TANU, distinct from other women's organizations because of its nationalist platform and diverse class makeup. Mohammed played a singular role in strengthening TANU and worked closely with TANU leaders, like Nyerere. However, in 1969, Mohammed was arrested on charges of plotting to overthrow the Tanzanian government. She was pardoned in 1972 by Nyerere and, subsequently, heralded as a national hero. Yet she gradually receded from politics. In this selection from interviews conducted by the historian Susan Geiger in 1984 and 1988, Mohammed discusses her participation in TANU politics in the late 1950s and the unique problems faced by women.

Fortunately, God gave me a talent [for making powerful speeches]. Outside of Dar es Salaam I used to be very impressive. These were very strong speeches and men were very much moved to see a woman traveling for the struggle in their country. It really motivated them—impressed them, my courage to travel up country for the struggle. Especially when the DCs and CID [government intelligence] were there. I got really wild!

20. Bibi Titi Mohammed, "Travel for TANU," in Susan Geiger, *TANU Women: Gender and Culture in the Making of Tangayikan Nationalism, 1955–1965* (Oxford: James Currey, 1997).

[As for the people who called TANU women prostitutes], we thought they were just ignorant. People were doing things without knowing what they were doing. We felt that the time would come when they would realize the gain to be obtained when we won the battle. Then they would regret what they did in the past. [As for me, when I joined TANU] I didn't expect anything [personal gain]. Even my friends were asking me, "Are you going to be the queen of the country?" I didn't want to be queen, I wanted to be free. I didn't expect anything else. That's why I didn't hesitate for a long time—because I didn't expect anything.

I was interested in building my country—to make our lives better. Education for our children; to have land. Some European capitalists had many farms, earning a lot of profit. And we were simply used as workers in our own country. Why? Why should we do that in our own country? That's what I didn't like. I didn't expect to become a minister one day. I didn't even understand the meaning of being a minister or member of parliament. I came to know it only when I was in parliament. I wanted progress for the people.

At that time, women's problems didn't vary much from province to province; the differences were between rural women and women from the town. Women in the rural areas had one main problem: they were subjected to both agricultural labor and housework—a lot of work. Men and women had different problems. Men were regarded as superior to women before independence. Women were always disregarded, even if they had knowledge. A woman was treated as if she knew nothing. That was the first problem. Few men would agree with what their women suggested. Some men also just used women as tools for the house. But independence has given freedom to the woman to exchange ideas in the house with her husband. And the man realized there was someone to share with in the house. But before, the woman had no say and was kept in the house like a package and the man had control of everything. Whether good or bad, you had to follow.

Women had no opportunity before independence. This was the habit of African men. TANU changed this because women themselves volunteered to struggle for independence and were ahead of the men. They were not afraid.

What about the time I gave my first TANU speech in Bagarnoyo? It is true that at that meeting, I said that the cloth barrier [*shiraa*, in Swahili] shielding women from men should be pulled down. It was usual to put a barrier between men and women in meetings. This was outside, not inside. Stretching such a barrier was common practice along the coast, even in Mafia, Mbwera, [it was] the same. I asked [the people of Bagamoyo] why:

Now if you put a barrier, if she [a woman] is bad, do you think the barrier will change this? The behavior of a person is an internal thing. [Regardless of] how bad a woman is, even if you put her under cover, if she wants to do something she will. Because she has brains. Even if you see a woman as useless, she can be of some help. You might not know, and she won't tell you. She is keeping it a secret.

. . . .

Women's education, especially, was minimal before independence. We used to discuss these problems in the Women's Section, and we explained in meetings and this was taken to the TANU Central Committee. Up to the Annual Conferences these things were discussed. TANU helped a lot, and went on doing so. Women's lack of education was the main problem we were fighting. Women should have education equal to men. It should depend on a person's ability. A woman should be equal to a man. She could be a doctor, head teacher, professor of any type, eeehh? And get the education she is capable of.

16

The Political Leader Considered as the Representative of a Culture, 1959[21]

Sekou Touré

> *Guinea's first president, Sekou Touré (1922–1984), became politically active via his participation in the labor movement, helping in 1945 to found the Postal Workers Union. In 1952, he became the leader of the Guinean Democratic Party (PDG), a branch of the Pan-Africanist African Democratic Rally, at the time led by Félix Houphouët-Boigny (see Document 12 by Houphouët-Boigny). Touré utilized his experience in the labor movement to form a common trade union for French West Africa, the General Workers Union of Black Africa (UGTAN). Unlike other francophone African leaders, Touré rejected de Gaulle's proposal for former French African colonies to join the French Community. Consequently, his contemporaries perceived him as a radical. After leading Guinea to independence, Touré forged closer ties with the Soviet Union. He also developed a close relationship with another of West Africa's most radical political leaders, Ghana's Kwame Nkrumah. When Touré became president in 1960, he declared the PDG the only legal political party. He remained in office until his death.*
>
> *In this excerpt from a speech at the Second Congress of Negro Writers and Artists held from March 26 to April 1, 1959, Touré explains the role of the political leader in helping to promote African culture. Accordingly, Touré elaborates on the connection between culture and politics, stressing that independence is both a political and cultural concern.*

It is at this point that the cultural value of a people must be identified with the contributory value which it may represent in the development of universal civilization in establishing between human beings concrete relations of equality, solidarity, unity and fraternity.

---

21.   Sekou Touré, "The Political Leader Considered as the Representative of a Culture," in *Ideologies of Liberation in Black Africa, 1856–1970* by J. Ayo Langley (London: Rex Collings, 1979).

Thus, the true political leaders of Africa, whose thought and attitude tend towards the national liberation of their peoples can only be committed men, fundamentally committed against all the forms and forces of depersonalization of African culture. They represent, by the anti-colonialist nature and the national content of their struggle, the cultural values of their society mobilized against colonization.

It is as representatives of these cultural values that they lead the struggle for the decolonization of all the structures of their country.

But *decolonization* does not consist merely in liberating oneself from the presence of the colonizers: it must necessarily be completed by total liberation from the spirit of the 'colonized', that is to say, from all the evil consequences, moral, intellectual and cultural, of the colonial system.

Colonization, in order to enjoy a certain security, always needs to create and maintain a psychological climate favourable to its justification: hence the negation of the cultural, moral and intellectual values of the subjected people; that is why the struggle for national liberation is only complete when, once disengaged from the colonial apparatus, the country becomes conscious of the negative values deliberately injected into its life, thought and traditions . . . in order to extirpate them in the conditions of its evolution and flourishing This science of depersonalizing the colonized people is sometimes so subtle in its methods that it progressively succeeds in falsifying our natural psychic behaviour and devaluing our own original virtues and qualities with a view to our assimilation. It is no mere chance that French colonialism reached its height at the period of the famous and now exploded theory of 'primitive' and 'pre-logical mentality' of Lévy-Bruhl.[22] In modifying certain forms of its manifestations, although it apparently tries to adapt itself to the inevitable evolution of the oppressed peoples, colonization has never engendered, under the most diverse and subtle aspects, anything but a moral, intellectual and cultural superiority complex towards the colonized peoples. And this policy of depersonalization is all the more successful since the nature of the degree of evolution of the colonized and the colonizer is different. It is all the more deeply rooted where domination is long-lasting.

In the most varied forms, the 'colonized complex' taints evolution and imprints itself on our very reflexes. Thus the wearing of a cap and

22. Lucien Lévy-Bruhl (1857–1939) was a French anthropologist.

sun-glasses, regarded as a sign of western civilization, bears witness to this depersonalization which runs counter to the current of our evolution.

. . . .

Colonialism, through its diverse manifestations, by boasting of having taught our elite in its schools science, technique, mechanics and electricity, succeeds in influencing a number of our intellectuals to such an extent that they end up by finding in this the justification for colonial domination. Some go so far as to believe that, in order to acquire the true universal knowledge of science, they must necessarily disregard the moral, intellectual and cultural values of their own country in order to subject themselves to and assimilate a culture which is often foreign to them in a thousand respects.

And yet, is not the knowledge which leads to the practice of surgery taught in the same way in London, Prague, Belgrade and Bordeaux? Is the procedure for calculating the volume of a body not identical in New York, Budapest and Berlin? Is the principle of Archimedes not the same in China and in Holland? There is no Russian chemistry or Japanese chemistry, there is only chemistry pure and simple.

The science which results from all universal knowledge has no nationality. The ridiculous conflicts which rage about the origin of this or that discovery do not interest us, because they add nothing to the value of the discovery.

But, however much it may dissemble, colonialism betrays its intentions in the organization and nature of the education which it claims to dispense in the name of some humanism or other, I know not what. The truth is that, to start with, it had to satisfy its needs for junior staff, clerks, book-keepers, typists, messengers, etc. The elementary character of the education dispensed bears sufficiently eloquent witness to the object in view, for the colonial power took great care, for example, not to set up real administrative colleges for young Africans which might have trained genuine executives, or to teach the real history of Africa and so forth.

What would have happened on the morrow of the Independence of Guinea, if we had not ourselves created, during the period of the Outline Law, our own administrative college? The administrative life of the Republic of Guinea would have faced us at Government level with a multitude of problems which we could only have solved in empirical fashion.

This determination to keep the populations in a constant state of inferiority marks both the programmes and the nature of colonial education. It was desired that the African teacher should be and should remain a teacher of inferior quality, in order to keep the quality of teaching in Africa at an inferior level. . . .

There is no indictment to be drawn up against intellectualism but it is important to demonstrate the depersonalization of the African intellectual, a depersonalization for which nobody can hold him responsible, because it is the price which the colonial system demands for teaching him the universal knowledge which enables him to be an engineer, a doctor, an architect or an accountant. That is why decolonization at the individual level must operate more profoundly upon those who have been trained by the colonial system.

It is in relation to this decolonization that the African intellectual will afford effective and invaluable aid to Africa. The more he realizes the need to free himself intellectually from the colonized complex, the more he will discover our original virtues and the more he will serve the African cause.

Our incessant efforts will be directed towards finding our own ways of development if we wish our emancipation and our evolution to take place without our personality being changed thereby. Every time we adopt a solution which is authentically African in its nature and its conception, we shall solve our problems easily, because all those who take part will not be disorientated or surprised by what they have to achieve; they will realize without difficulty the manner in which they must work, act, and think. Our specific qualities will be used to the full and, in the long run, we shall speed up our historic evolution.

How many young men and young girls have lost the taste for our traditional dances and the cultural value of our popular songs; they have all become enthusiasts for the tango or the waltz or for some singer of charm or realism. This unconsciousness of our characteristic values inevitably leads to our isolation from our own social background, whose slightest human qualities escape us. In this way we finish by disregarding the real significance of the things which surround us, our own significance.

In contrast, the African peasants and craftsmen are in no way complicated by the colonial system, whose culture, habits and values they do not know.

Is it necessary to emphasize that, in spite of their good will, their discipline and their fidelity to the ideal of freedom and democracy, in spite of their faith in the destiny of their country, the colonized who have been educated by the colonizer have their thought more tainted by the colonial imprint than the rural masses who have evolved in their original context.

Africa is essentially a country of community government. Collective life and social solidarity give its habits a fund of humanism which many peoples might envy. It is also because of these human qualities that a human being in Africa cannot conceive the organization of his life outside that of the family, village or clan society. The voice of the African peoples has no features, no name, no individual ring. But in the circles which have been contaminated by the spirit of the colonizers, who has not observed the progress of personal egoism?

Who has not heard the defence of the theory of art for art's sake, the theory of poetry for poetry's sake, the theory of every man for himself?

Whereas our anonymous artists are the wonder of the world, and everywhere we are asked for our dances, our music, our songs, our statuettes, in order that their profound significance may be better known, some of our young intellectuals think that it is enough to know Prévert, Rimbaud, Picasso or Renoir to be cultivated and to be able to carry our culture, our art and our personality on to a higher plane. These people only appreciate the appearances of things, they only judge through the medium of their complexes and mentality of the 'colonized'. For them, our popular songs are only of value so far as they fit harmoniously into the western modes which are foreign to their social significance.

Our painters! they would like them to be more classical; our masks and our statuettes! purely aesthetic; without realizing that African art is essentially utilitarian and social.

Mechanized and reduced to a certain restrictive form of thought, habituated to judge in the light of values which they have not been allowed to determine for themselves, educated to appreciate according to the spirit, thought, conditions and will of the colonial system, they are stupefied every time we denounce the nefarious character of their behaviour. But if they interrogated themselves, in the light, not of their theoretical knowledge of the world, but by attaining to selfconsciousness, about the true values of their people and their motherland, if they asked themselves what their conduct contributes to all Africa turned towards its objectives of liberation and progress, of peace and dignity, they would judge and appreciate our problems.

. . . .

Intellectuals or artists, thinkers or researchers, their capacities have no values unless they really concur with the life of the people, unless they are integrated in fundamental manner with the action, thought and aspirations of the populations.

If they isolate themselves from their own surroundings by their special mentality of the colonized, they can have no influence, they will be of no value to the revolutionary action which the African populations have undertaken to liberate themselves from colonialism, they will be outcasts and strangers in their own country.

This intellectual decolonization, this decolonization of thoughts and concepts may seem infinitely difficult. There is, in effect, a sum of acquired habits, of uncontrolled behaviour, a way of living, a manner of thinking, the combination of which constitutes a sort of second nature which certainly seems to have destroyed the original personality of the colonized.

It is not intellectual approaches, nor even a sustained and patient labour of readapting the will which will achieve the purpose. It will only be enough if there is reintegration in the social background, a return to Africa by the daily practice of African life so as to readapt oneself to its basic values, its proper activities, its special mentality.

The official, who lives constantly among other officials, will not give up his bad colonial habits, because they represent a daily practice for himself and the circles in which he lives. He will not succeed in defining himself in relation to the African revolution, he will continue to define himself in relation to himself as an official living in administrative circles. He will have reduced his human objectives solely to an administrative career.

The artist who is proudly convinced that it is enough for him to be known in order to express the African personality in his works, will remain a colonized intelligence, an intelligence enslaved by colonial thought.

. . . .

It is not enough to write a revolutionary hymn to take part in the African revolution; it is necessary to act in the revolution with the people—with the people and the hymns will come of their own accord.

In order to exercise authentic action, it is necessary to be oneself a living part of Africa and its thought, an element in that popular energy which is totally mobilized for the Liberation, progress and happiness of Africa. There is no place outside this one combat either for the artist or the intellectual who is not himself committed and totally mobilized with the people in the great struggle of Africa and of suffering humanity.

17

The Philosophy of the Revolution, 1959[23]

Gamal Abdel Nasser

Gamal Abdel Nasser (1918–1970) was a former president of Egypt and a pivotal participant in the 1952 coup that overthrew the Egyptian monarchy. Shortly after he became the second president of Egypt in 1956, Nasser nationalized the Suez Canal Company, leading to the joint British, French, and Israeli invasion of Egypt. Under pressure from the United Nations and the United States, all three countries withdrew from Egyptian territory by 1957. In 1961, he helped to form the Non-Aligned Movement along with five other heads of state: Yugoslavia's Josip Broz Tito, Indonesia's Sukarno, Ghana's Kwame Nkrumah, and India's Jawaharlal Nehru. The member states refused formal alliances with either side during the Cold War. Though Nasser was primarily a Pan-Arabist, he was deeply involved with political affairs in Sub-Saharan Africa. Nasser's rejection of European occupation offered an important example to African leaders seeking independence. In the following excerpt from his book, The Philosophy of the Revolution, *Nasser emphasizes Egypt's independence from European influence, as well as Egypt's dual identity as both an Arab and an African nation.*

We live in a society that has not yet crystallized. It is still boiling over and restless. It has not yet calmed or settled down, so as to continue its gradual evolution parallel with other nations which preceded it along the road.

I believe, without paying any compliment to people's emotions, that our nation has realized a miracle. Any nation, exposed to the same conditions as our country, could be easily lost. It could be swept away by the torrents that fell upon it. But it stood firm in the violent earthquake.

23. Gamal Abdel Nasser, *The Philosophy of the Revolution* (Buffalo, NY: Smith, Keynes & Marshall, 1959).

It is true we nearly lost our equilibrium in some circumstances; but generally we did not fall to the ground. As I consider one normal Egyptian family out of thousands that live in the capital, I find the following: the father, for example, is a turbaned "fellah" from the heart of the country; the mother a lady descended from Turkish stock; the sons of the family are at school adopting the English system; the daughters the French. All this lies between the Thirteenth century and the outward appearances of the Twentieth.

As I see this I feel within me I can comprehend the bewilderment and the confusion that assail us. Then I say to myself, "This society will crystallize; its component parts will hold together; it will form a homogenous entity; but this necessitates that we should strain our nerves during the period of transition."

Such are, then, the roots from which sprang our conditions of today. Such are the sources from which our crisis flows. If I add to these social origins the circumstances for which we expelled Farouk and for which we wish to liberate our country from every foreign soldier; if we add all these together, we shall discover the wide sphere in which we labour and which is exposed from every side, to the winds, to the violent storm that raged in its corners, to flashing lightning and roaring thunder.

. . . .

Many people come to me and exclaim, "You have angered everybody." To which explanation I always reply, "It is not people's anger that influences the situation. The question should be: Was what aroused their anger for the good of the country or for the interest of whom?" I realize we have upset big land-owners; but was it possible not to upset them and yet behold some of us owning thousands of acres, while others do not own the plot of land wherein they are buried after death?

I realize we have aroused the wrath of old politicians; but was it possible not to do so and yet behold our country a victim to their passions, their corruption and their struggle for the spoils of office?

I realize we have angered many government officials; but without this was it possible to spend more than half the budget on officials' salaries and yet allot, as we have done, forty million pounds for productive projects? What would have happened if we had opened the coffers of the treasury of the state, as they had done, and distributed their contents among officials and let come what may thereafter. The year that ensued would have found the Government unable to pay the salaries of officials.

How easy it would have been to satisfy all those malcontents! But what is the price that our country would pay out of its hopes and its future for that satisfaction?

. . . .

We can consider ourselves, therefore, powerful, though not in the loudness of our voices whether we cry, wail, or appeal for help, but powerful when we sit calm and count in figures our capacity for work, powerful in our thorough understanding of the strength of this bond which links us and which makes our territory one.

Such is the first circle in which we must resolve and attempt to move in as much as we possibly can. It is the Arab circle.

If we direct our attention after that to the second circle, the circle of the continent of Africa, I would say, without exaggeration, that we cannot in any way, stand aside, even if we wish to, away from the sanguinary and dreadful struggle now raging in the heart of Africa between five million whites and two hundred million Africans.

We cannot do so for one principal and clear reason, namely that we are in Africa. The people of Africa will continue to look up to us, who guard the northern gate of the continent and who are its connecting link with the world outside. We cannot, under any condition, relinquish our responsibility in helping, in every way possible, in diffusing the light and civilization into the farthest parts of that virgin jungle.

There is another important reason. The Nile is the artery of life of our country. It draws its supply of water from the heart of the continent.

There remains the Sudan, our beloved brother, whose boundaries extend deeply into Africa and which is a neighbour to all the sensitive spots in the centre of the continent.

It is a certain fact that Africa at present is the scene of an exciting ebullition. White man, who represents several European countries, is trying again to repartition the continent. We cannot stand aside in face of what is taking place in Africa on the assumption that it does not concern or affect us.

The third circle now remains; the circle that goes beyond continents and oceans and to which I referred, as the circle of our brethren in faith who turn with us, whatever part of the world they are in, towards the same Kibla in Mecca, and whose pious lips whisper reverently the same prayer.

18

Wind of Change, 1960[24]

Harold Macmillan

As an ever greater number of British colonies became independent, the conservative British prime minister Harold Macmillan (1894–1986) toured British dependencies in Africa to initiate and promote the cause of decolonization, viewing the costs as outweighing the benefits. He delivered his famous 1960 "Wind of Change" speech to the Parliament of South Africa. In South Africa, the white settler population of Dutch and British descent pushed for independence without majority rule. In this speech, Macmillan asserts the unavoidability of the fact that black African nationalism would become a powerful political force. Further, he argues that it is necessary to accept this change lest Africans choose to ally themselves with the Soviet bloc. In effect, the speech marked the end of British support for white rule in South Africa.

The same year of Macmillan's tour, white elites led by Hendrik Verwoerd (1901–1966), the first prime minister of the Republic of South Africa, issued a referendum on the country's independence. For Verwoerd's response to Macmillan see Document 19.

It is, as I have said, a special privilege for me to be here in 1960 when you are celebrating what I might call the golden wedding of the Union. At such a time it is natural and right that you should pause to take stock of your position, to look back at what you have achieved, to look forward to what lies ahead. In the fifty years of their nationhood the people of South Africa have built a strong economy founded upon a healthy agriculture and thriving and resilient industries.

---

24. Harold Macmillan, "Wind of Change," speech to the Cape Town Parliament on February 3, 1960, transcribed from an original recording on YouTube, 42:13, posted by "Roman Styran," March 25, 2016, https://www.youtube.com/watch?v=c07MiYfpOMw (accessed September 17, 2016).

. . . .

No one could fail to be impressed with the immense material progress, which has been achieved. That all this has been accomplished in so short a time is a striking testimony to the skill, energy and initiative of your people. We in Britain are proud of the contribution we have made to this remarkable achievement. Much of it has been financed by British capital . . . but that is not all. We have developed trade between us to our common advantage and our economics are now largely interdependent. You export to us raw materials and food and, of course, gold. And, we in return, send you consumer goods or capital equipment. We take a third of all your exports. And, we supply a third of all your imports. This broad, traditional pattern of investment and trade has been maintained in spite of the changes brought by the development of our two economies and it gives me great encouragement to reflect that the economies of both our countries, while expanding rapidly, have yet remained interdependent and capable of sustaining one another. . . .

. . . .

Today, your readiness to provide technical assistance to the less well-developed parts of Africa is an immense help to the countries that receive it. It is also a source of strength to your friends in the Commonwealth and elsewhere in the western world. You are collaborating in the work of the Commission for Technical Cooperation in Africa south of the Sahara and now in the United Nations Economic Commission for Africa. Your Minister for External Affairs intends to visit Ghana later this year. All this proves your determination as the most advanced industrial country of the continent to play your part in the new Africa of today.

Sir, as I've travelled around the Union I have found everywhere, as I expected, a deep preoccupation with what is happening in the rest of the African continent. I understand and sympathize with your interests in these events and your anxiety about them.

Ever since the break up of the Roman empire one of the constant facts of political life in Europe has been the emergence of independent nations. They have come into existence over the centuries in different forms, different kinds of government, but all have been inspired by a deep, keen feeling of nationalism, which has grown as the nations have grown.

In the twentieth century, and especially since the end of the War, the processes which gave birth to the nation-states of Europe have been repeated all over the world. We have seen the awakening of national consciousness in peoples who have for centuries lived in dependence upon some other power. Fifteen years ago, this movement spread through Asia. Many countries there, of different races and civilisations, pressed their claim to an independent national life.

Today the same thing is happening in Africa, and the most striking of all the impressions I have formed since I left London a month ago is of the strength of this African national consciousness. In different places it takes different forms, but it is happening everywhere.

The wind of change is blowing through this continent, and whether we like it or not, this growth of national consciousness is a political fact. And, we must all accept it as a fact, and our national policies must take account of it.

Good you understand this better than anyone. You are sprung from Europe, the home of nationalism, here in Africa you have yourselves created a free nation. A new nation. Indeed in the history of our times yours will be recorded as the first of the African nationalists. And, this tide of national consciousness, which is now rising in Africa is a fact, for which both you and we, and the other nations of the western world, are ultimately responsible.

For its causes are to be found in the achievements of western civilisation, in the pushing forward of the frontiers of knowledge, in the applying of science to the service of human needs, in the expanding of food production, in the speeding and multiplying of the means of communication, and perhaps above all and more than anything else in the spread of education.

As I have said, this growth of national consciousness in Africa is a political fact, and we must accept it as such. That means, I would judge, that we've got to come to terms with it. I sincerely believe that if we cannot do so we may imperil the precarious balance between the East and West on which the peace of the world depends.

The world today is divided into three main groups. First, what we call the Western Powers. You in South Africa and we in Britain belong to this group, together with our friends and allies in other parts of the Commonwealth, in the United States of America, and in Europe. We call it the Free World. And, then there are the Communists—Russia, her satellites in Europe, and China, whose population will rise by the end of the next ten years to the staggering total of 800 million people. And then, thirdly, there are those parts of the world whose people are at present uncommitted either to Communism or to the western ideas. And, in this context we think first of Asia and then of Africa. As I see it the great issue in this second half of the twentieth century is whether the uncommitted peoples of Asia and Africa will swing to the East or to the West. Will they be drawn into the Communist camp? Or will the great experiments in self-government that are now being made in Asia and Africa, especially within the Commonwealth, prove so successful, and by their example so compelling, that the balance will come down in favour of freedom and order and justice? The struggle is joined, and it is a struggle for the minds of men. What is now on trial is much more than our military strength or our diplomatic and administrative skill. It is our way of life.

The uncommitted nations want to see before they choose. What can we show them to help them choose right? Each of the independent members of the Commonwealth must answer that question for itself. It is a basic principle of our modern Commonwealth that we respect each other's sovereignty in matters of internal policy. At the same time, we must recognize that, in this shrinking world in which we live today, the internal policies of one nation may have effects outside it. So, we may sometimes be tempted to say mind your own business. But in these days, I would expand the old saying so that it runs: mind your own business of course, but mind how it affects my business, too.

If I may be very frank I would venture to say now this: what governments and parliaments in the United Kingdom have done since the last war in according independence to India, Pakistan, Ceylon, Malaya, and Ghana, and what they will do for Nigeria and other countries now nearing independence. All this, although we must take and do take full and sole responsibility for it—we do, in the belief, that it is the only way to establish the future of the Commonwealth and of the free world on sound foundations.

All this, of course, is of deep concern to you. For nothing we do in this small world can be done in a corner, and remain hidden. What we do today in West, Central, and East Africa becomes known to everyone in South Africa whatever his language, colour, or traditions. And, let me sir assure you and all those here assembled and all who may be listening, in all friendliness, that we are well aware of this, that we have acted and will act with full knowledge of the responsibility we have to you and to all our friends.

Nevertheless, I am sure you will agree that in our own areas of responsibility we must each do what we think right. What we British think right derives from a long experience both of failure and success in the management of these affairs. We try to learn and apply the lessons of both. Our judgment of right and wrong and of justice is rooted in the same soil as yours, in Christianity, and the rule of law as the basis of a free society. This experience of our own explains why it has been our aim, in the countries for which we have borne responsibility, not only to raise the material standards of life, but to create a society which respects the rights of individuals, a society in which men are given the opportunity to grow to their full stature. That must, in our view, include the opportunity of an increasing share in political power and responsibility. A society, finally, in which individual merit and individual merit alone is the criterion for man's advancement, whether political or economic.

Finally, in countries inhabited by several different races, it has been our end to find means by which the community can become more of a community and fellowship fostered between its different parts. This problem is by no means confined to Africa nor is it always a problem of a European minority. . . . The attitude of the United Kingdom government towards this problem was clearly expressed by the foreign secretary, Mr. Selwyn Lloyd, speaking at the United Nations General Assembly on the seventeenth of September 1959. These were his words: "In those territories where different races or tribes live side by side, the task is to ensure that all the people may enjoy security and freedom and the chance to contribute as individuals to the progress and well-being of these countries. We," that is the British, "reject the idea of any inherent superiority of one race over another. Our policy, therefore, is non-racial. . . ."

I thought you would wish me to state plainly and with candor the policy which we in Britain stand. It may well be that in trying to do our duty as we see it, we shall sometimes make difficulties for you. If this proves to be so, we much regret it.

19

Response to Harold Macmillan's "Wind of Change" Speech, 1960[25]

Hendrik Verwoerd

For information on this document, see the introduction to Document 18.

The tendency in Africa for nations to become independent, and at the same time to do justice to all, does not only mean being just to the black man of Africa, but also to be just to the white man of Africa.

We call ourselves Europeans, but actually we represent the white men of Africa. They are the people not only in the Union but through major portions of Africa who brought civilisation here, who made the present developments of black nationalism possible. By bringing them education, by showing them this way of life, by bringing in industrial development, by bringing in the ideals which western civilisation has developed itself.

When the white man came to Africa, perhaps to trade, in some cases, perhaps to bring the gospel; has remained to stay. And particularly we in this southern most portion of Africa, have such a stake here that this is our only motherland, we have no where else to go. We set up a country bare, and the Bantu came in this country and settled certain portions for themselves, and it is in line with the thinking of Africa, to grant those fullest rights which we also with you admit all people should have and believe providing those rights for those people in the fullest degree in that part of southern Africa which their forefathers found for themselves and settled in. But similarly, we believe in balance, we believe in allowing exactly those same full opportunities to remain within the grasp of the white man who has made all this possible.

The white man, therefore, has not only an undoubted stake in and right to the land which he developed into a modern industrial state from the empty valleys and isolated mountains, but, according to all principles of morality, it was his, is his, and must remain his.

25. Hendrik Verwoerd, "Response to Harold Macmillan's 'Wind of Change' Speech," given to the South African Parliament on February 3, 1960: http://africanhistory.about.com/od/eraindependence/p/wind_of_change3.htm (accessed September 17, 2016).

20

Speech at the Proclamation of the Congo's Independence, 1960[26]

Patrice Lumumba

Patrice Lumumba (1925–1961) was the first prime minister of Congo, formerly Belgian Congo. In 1958 Lumumba helped to form the Mouvement National Congolais (MNC), a Congolese nationalist party that advocated independence from Belgium. Lumumba was arrested in 1959 on charges of inciting a riot in Stanleyville. He was released after the MNC won a majority in local elections. The Congo became independent on June 30, 1960. Lumumba became the country's first prime minister, with Joseph Kasa-Vubu, of the opposition Alliance des Bakongo, as president.

Immediately after taking office, Lumumba was beset by a number of internal conflicts. Members of the military initiated a violent uprising after Lumumba chose not to increase their salaries. Tensions within the Congo heightened on July 11, 1960 after the province of Katanga declared independence. On July 14, the United Nations Security Council voted to send troops to Congo to quell the military uprising, but the troops were forbidden by the United Nations to intervene in the Katanga conflict. As a result, Lumumba sought financial and military support from the Soviet Union. On September 14, with support from the United States, Colonel Joseph Mobutu staged a coup and placed Lumumba under house arrest. On January 17, 1961, Lumumba was killed by a firing squad.

The following is Lumumba's speech on the occasion of Congolese independence. He discusses the history of Belgium's abuses, but also offers a bold vision for the newly independent Congo's future.

26.   Patrice Lumumba, "Speech at the Proclamation of the Congo's Independence" (June 30, 1960) from *Lumumba Speaks: The Speeches and Writings of Patrice Lumumba, 1958–1961*, translated by Jean Van Lierde. Translation © 1972 by Little, Brown and Company, Inc. Used by permission of Little, Brown and Company.

June 30, 1960

Congolese men and women:

As combatants for independence who today are victorious, I salute you in the name of the Congolese Government.

I ask all my friends, all of you who have fought unceasingly at our side, to make this thirtieth of June, an illustrious date that will be indelibly engraved upon your hearts, a date whose meaning you will teach your children with pride, so that they in turn will tell their children and their children's children the glorious story of our struggle for freedom.

For though this independence of the Congo is today being proclaimed in a spirit of accord with Belgium, a friendly country with which we are dealing as one equal with another, no Congolese worthy of the name can ever forget that we fought to win it [*applause*], a fight waged each and every day, a passionate and idealistic fight, a fight in which there was not one effort, not one provision, not one suffering, not one drop of blood that we ever spared ourselves. We are proud of this struggle amid tears, fire, and blood, down to our very heart of hearts, for it was a noble and just struggle, an indispensible struggle if we were to put an end to the humiliating slavery that had been forced upon us.

The wounds that are the evidence of the fate we endured for eighty years under a colonialist regime are still too fresh and painful for us to be able to erase them from our memory. Backbreaking work has been exacted from us, in return for wages that did not allow us to satisfy our hunger, or to decently clothe or house ourselves, or to raise our children as creatures very dear to us.

We have been the victims of ironic taunts, of insults, of blows that we were forced to endure morning, noon, and night because we were blacks. Who can forget that a black was addressed in the familiar form, not because he was a friend, certainly, but because the polite form of address was to be used only for whites?

We have had our lands despoiled under the terms of what was supposedly the law of the land but was only a recognition of the right of the strongest.

We have known that the law was quite different for whites and blacks; it was most accommodating for the former, and cruel and inhuman for the latter.

We have known the atrocious sufferings of those banished to remote regions because of their political opinions or religious beliefs; exiles in their own country, their fate was truly worse than death.

We have known that there were magnificent mansions for whites in the cities and ramshackle straw hovels for blacks; that a black was never allowed into the so-called European movie theaters or restaurants or stores; that a black traveled in the hold of boats below the feet of the white in his deluxe cabin.

Who can forget, finally, the burst of rifle fire in which so many of our brothers perished, the cells into which the authorities threw those who no longer were willing to submit to a rule where justice meant oppression and exploitation? [*Applause.*]

We have grievously suffered all this, my brothers.

But we who have been chosen to govern our beloved country by the vote of your elected representatives, we whose bodies and souls have suffered from colonialist oppression, loudly proclaim: all this is over and done with now.

The Republic of the Congo has been proclaimed and our country is now in the hands of its own children.

We are going to begin another struggle together, my bothers, my sisters, a sublime struggle that will bring our country peace, prosperity, and grandeur.

We are going to institute social justice together and ensure everyone just remuneration for his labor. [*Applause.*]

We are going to show the world what the black man can do when he works in freedom, and we are going to make the Congo the focal point for the development of all of Africa.

We are going to see to it that the soil of our country really benefits its children. We are going to review all the old laws and make new ones that will be just and noble.

We are going to put an end to the suppression of free thought and see to it that all citizens enjoy to the fullest all the fundamental freedoms laid down in the Declaration of the Rights of Man. [*Applause.*]

We are going to do away with any and every sort of discrimination and give each one the rightful place that his human dignity, his labor, and his devotion to country will have earned him.

We are going to bring peace to the country, not the peace of rifles and bayonets, but the peace that comes from men's hearts and their good will. [*Applause.*]

And in order to achieve all this, dear compatriots, rest assured that we will be able to count not only on our tremendous strength and our immense riches, but also on the assistance of many foreign countries, whose collaboration we will always accept if it is sincere and does not seek to force any policy or any sort whatsoever on us. [*Applause.*]

In this regard, Belgium has finally realized what direction history was moving in and has not attempted to oppose our independence. She is ready to grant us her aid and her friendship, and a treaty to this effect has just been signed between our two equal and independent countries. We for our part, though we shall continue to be vigilant, will respect all commitments freely made.

Thus the new Congo, our beloved republic that my government is going to create, will be a rich, free, and prosperous country, with regard to both its domestic relations and its foreign relations. But in order for us to reach this goal without delay, I ask all of you, Congolese legislators and citizens alike, to aid me with all the strength at your command.

I ask all of you to forget trivial quarrels that are draining our strength and threaten to earn us the contempt of those in other countries.

I ask the parliamentary minority to aid my government by constructive opposition and to stay strictly within legal and democratic paths.

I ask all of you not to shrink from making any sacrifice necessary to ensure the success of our great undertaking.

I ask you, finally, to respect unconditionally the life and property of your fellow citizens and foreigners who have settled in our country. If the behavior of these foreigners leaves something to be desired, our justice will be swift and they will be expelled from the territory of the republic; if, on the other hand, they conduct themselves properly, they must be left in peace, for they too will be working for the prosperity of our country.

The independence of the Congo represents a decisive step toward the liberation of the entire African continent. [*Applause.*]

Your Majesty, Your Excellencies, Ladies and Gentlemen, my dear compatriots, my black brothers, my brothers in the struggle, that is what I wanted to say to you in the name of the government on this magnificent day of our complete and sovereign independence. [*Applause.*]

Our strong, national, popular government will be the salvation of this country.

I invite all Congolese citizens, men, women, and children to set to work to create a prosperous national economy that will be the crowning proof of our economic independence.

Honor to those who fought for national freedom!

Long live independence and African unity!

Long live the independent and sovereign Congo! [*Prolonged applause.*]

21

Declaration on Granting Independence to Colonial Countries and Peoples, 1960[27]

The United Nations General Assembly

On December 14, 1960, the United Nations General Assembly addressed the issue of the collapsing imperial system in Africa and elsewhere. Resolution 1514, which declared the independence of all colonial countries and peoples, was adopted with the approval of eighty-nine countries. While no country opposed the Resolution, nine abstained from the vote. Conspicuously, the majority of abstaining countries possessed colonial interests in Africa, including Belgium, France, Portugal, South Africa, and the United Kingdom. The United States also abstained.

General Assembly Resolution 1514 (XV), December 14, 1960

The General Assembly,

Mindful of the determination proclaimed by the peoples of the world in the Charter of the United Nations to reaffirm faith in fundamental human rights, in the dignity and worth of the human person, in the equal rights of men and women and of nations large and small and to promote social progress and better standards of life in larger freedom,

Conscious of the need for the creation of conditions of stability and well-being and peaceful and friendly relations based on respect for the principles of equal rights and self-determination of all peoples, and of universal respect for, and observance of, human rights and fundamental freedoms for all without distinction as to race, sex, language or religion,

27. The United Nations, excerpt from "Declaration on Granting Independence to Colonial Countries and Peoples" from United Nations General Assembly, *Official Records, Fifteenth Session*, Supplement No. 16 (1960). Reprinted with the permission of the United Nations Secretariat Publications Board.

Recognizing the passionate yearning for freedom in all dependent peoples and the decisive role of such peoples in the attainment of their independence,

Aware of the increasing conflicts resulting from the denial of or impediments in the way of freedom of such peoples, which constitute a serious threat to world peace,

Considering the important role of the United Nations in assisting the movement for independence in Trust and Non-Self-Governing Territories,

Recognizing that the peoples of the world ardently desire the end of colonialism in all its manifestations,

Convinced that the continued existence of colonialism prevents the development of international economic co-operation, impedes the social, cultural and economic development of dependent peoples and militates against the United Nations ideal of universal peace,

Affirming that peoples may, for their own ends, freely dispose of their natural wealth and resources without prejudice to any obligations arising out of international economic co-operation, based upon the principle of mutual benefit, and international law,

Believing that the process of liberation is irresistible and irreversible and that, in order to avoid serious crises, an end must be put to colonialism and all practices of segregation and discrimination associated therewith,

Welcoming the emergence in recent years of a large number of dependent territories into freedom and independence, and recognizing the increasingly powerful trends towards freedom in such territories which have not yet attained independence,

Convinced that all peoples have an inalienable right to complete freedom, the exercise of their sovereignty and the integrity of their national territory,

Solemnly proclaims the necessity of bringing to a speedy and unconditional end colonialism in all its forms and manifestations;

And to this end Declares that:

1. The subjection of peoples to alien subjugation, domination and exploitation constitutes a denial of fundamental human rights, is contrary to the Charter of the United Nations and is an impediment to the promotion of world peace and co-operation.

2. All peoples have the right to self-determination; by virtue of that right they freely determine their political status and freely pursue their economic, social and cultural development.

3. Inadequacy of political, economic, social or educational preparedness should never serve as a pretext for delaying independence.

4. All armed action or repressive measures of all kinds directed against dependent peoples shall cease in order to enable them to exercise peacefully and freely their right to complete independence, and the integrity of their national territory shall be respected.

5. Immediate steps shall be taken, in Trust and Non-Self-Governing Territories or all other territories which have not yet attained independence, to transfer all powers to the peoples of those territories, without any conditions or reservations, in accordance with their freely expressed will and desire, without any distinction as to race, creed or colour, in order to enable them to enjoy complete independence and freedom.

6. Any attempt aimed at the partial or total disruption of the national unity and the territorial integrity of a country is incompatible with the purposes and principles of the Charter of the United Nations.

7. All States shall observe faithfully and strictly the provisions of the Charter of the United Nations, the Universal Declaration of Human Rights and the present Declaration on the basis of equality, non-interference in the internal affairs of all States, and respect for the sovereign rights of all peoples and their territorial integrity.

22

The Challenge of Nationalism, 1962[28]

K. A. Busia

Kofi Abrefa (K. A.) Busia (1913–1978) was a sociologist and prime minister of the Second Republic of Ghana. Busia was born to the royal family of Wenchi (a part of the Ashanti Confederacy). In 1947, he received his D.Phil. in Social Anthropology from Oxford. In 1952, he formed the Ghana Congress Party with former members of Kwame Nkrumah's Convention People's Party (CPP). In 1957, Nkrumah banned all parties that represented specific ethnic, religious, or racial groups. The former members of those parties joined with the Ghana Congress Party to form the United Party, which became the main opposition party to the CPP. As Nkrumah's government strengthened, Busia fled Ghana in 1959 and taught sociology at the University of Leiden, the University of Mexico, and Oxford. He returned to Ghana after Nkrumah was overthrown in 1966. He participated in the formation of the second republic and became its prime minister in 1969. In the following excerpt from his book, The Challenge of Africa, *Busia discusses the dangers of authoritarianism in Africa. He argues that part of the susceptibility of the new African states to authoritarian leaders rests in the legacy of the authoritarian rule of colonialism. He rejects the notion that democratic institutions are somehow incompatible with the new African states.*

African nationalism throws many challenges, some to countries outside Africa, especially the colonial powers, and some to the leaders and peoples of Africa. Some of these challenges have been apparent throughout the problems we have discussed.

The fact that African nationalism is, in the first place, a demand for racial equality is its most conspicuous attribute. Africans demand acceptance as equals in the human family.

28. K. A. Busia, excerpt from "The Challenge of Nationalism" from *The Challenge of Africa.* Copyright © 1962 by K. A. Busia. Reprinted by permission.

This has political dimensions, because colonialism in Africa has been marked by the domination of Africans by Europeans. So the demand for equality finds expression in the demand for the emancipation of all Africa from colonial rule. That is a challenge which African nationalism throws to the European powers that have colonies in Africa.

The demand for emancipation from colonial rule is a demand for national independence; that does not by itself give personal freedom to the individual citizen. The challenge to provide the kind of government that guarantees individual freedom is one thrown to the rulers of the independent states of Africa by their own compatriots. The challenge is also thrown by those outside Africa who, observing the trends in independent African states, contend that democracy is not suited to Africa and that the peoples of Africa themselves prefer authoritarian rule.

That challenge cannot be lightly brushed aside. There are trends that give cause for the contention. One who surveys the independent states of Africa can make an impressive list of these trends: in some states, no opposition parties, or only emasculated ones; a marked growth of monolithic one-party rule; countries in which ruling parties are swallowing up the trade unions, youth organizations, farmers' councils, women's federations, civil servants and other associations—and where one must hold a party card before one can expect to be employed; trends toward one-man rule, and even a personality cult; government or party control of the media of communication, particularly of the press and radio; arbitrary arrests and imprisonment of political opponents without trial; attacks on the independence of the judiciary, or interference with the impartial administration of the law.

There are factors that favor such trends, particularly in newly independent states, just emerged from colonialism. At independence, as already stated, the machinery of government that the new African governments take over is authoritarian; colonial rule engenders subservience to authority, and this can and has been exploited. Often there is no effective public opinion, or no vehicle for its expression; for the institutions—the voluntary societies, trade unions, professional associations, and so on—that, in democratic countries, protect various rights and interests or serve as vehicles for the effective expression of public opinion are either nonexistent, or where they exist are government-sponsored or can be quickly brought under control. Where there are elections to the legislature or councils, it is easy to rig them, for the majority of the citizens are illiterate.

In some states, ethnic or regional or local interests rallied people together to demand what they conceived to be their rights or to resist encroachments on such rights. But such resistances can easily be discredited as reactionary tribalism, whose suppression is a creditable act of nation building.

There is the need for rapid economic development. The task set is to raise living standards to the extent resources and available skills make possible. We have, in this connection, discussed the case presented by those who advocate development in accordance with Marxist-Leninist theory. In practice, it teaches, even demands, the establishment of one-party rule, with pressures to bring trade unions and all other organizations into the ruling party as the best way to achieve economic development. Marxist-Leninism directs development through a monolithic party. It has had its appeal and impact on trends in some of the new states in Africa.

Would-be investors from Western democracies, as we have pointed out, demand strong governments, and thus encourage the development of authoritarian rule.

Even in the old democracies of Europe and America, political scientists have observed trends toward one-man rule as a characteristic development of the present century—the emergence of the heroic leader. The fact is that the increasing role of government in economic affairs, or in establishing the welfare state, or in dealing with international crises in a world whose parts have become increasingly interdependent, tends to strengthen the power of government in a way that constitutes a threat to democracy, even where there are established traditions and institutions to restrain authoritarian tendencies.

In Africa, where parliamentary institutions are new, and where there is such a massive preponderance of conditions favoring authoritarian rule, the battle for personal liberty and democracy is a hard one, with the odds heavily against the few who are fighting it. It has better chances of success where the leaders in power set themselves to establish true democracy and to respect civil liberties. It is a severe moral test calling for wisdom and tolerance. It is well-known that people in power tend to be corrupted by it; at least they do everything they can to remain in power. So it should be recognized that the circumstances under which the battle for personal freedom and democracy has to be fought in Africa are difficult; nevertheless, they do not offer any evidence for the conclusion that democracy is unworkable in Africa, or that the civil liberties stressed as essential in democratic countries are not applicable to Africans.

Independence is coming to Africa at a time and under circumstances that make it easy for governments to be authoritarian and even totalitarian, if they choose to go that way. But none of the prevailing circumstances that are favorable to the establishment of authoritarian rule are unalterable. Personal freedom constitutes a challenge to African nationalism.

The principles of democracy—freedom of speech, including the right to criticize and to propagandize against the government; freedom of assembly and association, including the freedom to organize opposition parties and to propose alternative governments; freedom of the people to choose their government at general elections, and to change them peacefully; freedom of religion; freedom from arbitrary arrest and imprisonment without trial; the rule of law; guarantees for human rights and civil liberties—all these principles of parliamentary government are universal. They can be adopted and applied by any nation that chooses to do so. They can be institutionalized in any culture.

The choice has to be made by the African states. There are leaders of African states who have accepted these principles and are determined to adhere to them. It is a challenge to African leaders to justify their claim for freedom and to give evidence of their maturity by making their states citadels of freedom, national and individual. African nationalism demands of others, in the challenge it throws for emancipation of Africa from colonial rule, justice, respect for human rights and human dignity, wisdom, tact, patience, and integrity. The establishment of democracy in Africa, the guarantee and extension of human rights and personal freedom to the citizens of Africa, justifiably call for the display of the same standards of conduct from Africans. It is a challenge that cannot be evaded; but it must be admitted that those who are trying to meet it are in the minority.

PART THREE: FIGHTING FOR INDEPENDENCE

Introduction

Resistance to imperialism in Africa took many forms. Not only was the nature of resistance itself contested, dividing some actors between non-violent and violent strategies of opposition, its aims differed widely as well. In some instances, acts of resistance followed long-term strategies, with the express purpose of destabilizing the colonial regime. In others, resistance manifested in the sudden and spontaneous rejection of colonial policies and followed no predetermined course. Both contributed to the weakening of colonial regimes and the development of postcolonial nationalism, and are therefore inseparable from the broader story of African independence in the 1950s and 1960s. Further, the place of resistance in the 1950s and 1960s is central to the story of those parts of Africa that did not achieve independence as the rest of Africa underwent decolonization, and where colonialism and white minority rule persisted into the 1970s, 1980s, and 1990s.

The process of decolonization and the later achievement of independence also faced challenges and invited new targets of resistance, including Africans themselves. Leaders who were seen as indifferent to their constituencies or whole segments of the population, and others accused of collaborating with colonial regimes, encountered opposition. This part, therefore, examines the many forms of and rationales for resistance. It is concerned with the words and explanations of individuals who engaged in acts of resistance—whether motivated by grander philosophical visions of freedom and independence, or the challenges of everyday survival. Official statements issued by members of political or guerilla groups and testimonials from individuals who participated in resistance efforts reflect the diverse forms of opposition to colonialism.

While this part covers an array of acts of rebellions and instances of resistance, it also introduces readers to documents pertaining to some of the most oppressive events and features of the European colonial system. It helps to tell the story of the origins of the Algerian War

(1954–1962), which first pitted Algerians against the Pieds-Noirs (Algerians of European descent) and later drew in the French military. Perceived as a pivotal turning point in the global history of imperialism, this protracted war shaped a generation of anti-colonial intellectuals and militants, and transformed the global understanding of the nature of imperialism. Similarly, the British government's response to the Mau Mau Revolt in Kenya exposes readers to the violence inherent to colonialism even as a colonial power claims to be in the process of withdrawing its control. While purportedly preparing to gradually transition Kenya to independence, colonial authorities imprisoned, tortured, and murdered thousands of Kenyan peasant rebels, known as Mau Mau, for attacks on British colonists.

Lusophone (Portuguese-speaking) colonies did not become independent during the period on which this volume focuses. Through the 1960s and into the 1970s, in places like Angola and Mozambique, African guerilla fighters battled against Portuguese colonial forces. Independence only came after the dictatorship of Marcelo Caetano was overthrown in the Carnation Revolution of 1974. In 1975, the Portuguese withdrew from Africa, leading to the independence of Portugal's African colonies. Likewise, where white minority governments prevailed after independence, resistance to exclusionary racist regimes continued into the 1980s and 1990s, when the governments in Rhodesia and South Africa crumbled and systems of apartheid ended. Still, there were active resistance movements in these colonies and states throughout the period that the rest of the colonies became independent states. Therefore, this part includes readings that pertain to the struggles of the 1950s and 1960s in these parts of Africa despite the fact that actual independence would only be realized in subsequent decades.

23

The Mau Mau Oath, 1952[29]

Karari Njama

In 1952, the British colonial government in Kenya declared a state of emergency in response to an anti-colonial uprising among the Kikuyu ethnic group. The British Army together with the British-dominated Kenya Regiment brutally attempted to suppress the so-called "Mau Mau Rebellion," which formally ended in 1960 with the transfer to African majority rule in Kenya. Recent research into this silenced episode in Kenya's late colonial history has uncovered tremendous human rights violations by British authorities against pro–Mau Mau individuals and fomented debate about the event's role in ending British empire in Kenya. The following passage from American anthropologist Donald Bennett's interviews with Karari Njama (published in 1968 as Mau Mau from Within*) describes the initiation into the pro–Mau Mau Gikuyu and Mumbi society. When Njama, a literate schoolteacher and participant in the rebellion, took the oath in September 1952, the movement had broadened in scope, pledging greater anti-colonial militancy and the boycott of European products like beer and cigarettes. Njama's recollections of the ceremony attest to the importance of traditional Kikuyu symbols within the anti-colonial movement.*

By the light of a hurricane lamp, I could see the furious guards who stood armed with *pangas* and *simis*. Right in front of us stood an arch of banana and maize stalks and sugar cane stems tied by a forest creeping and climbing plant. We were harassed to take out our coats, money, watches, shoes and any other European metal we had in our possession. Then the oath administrator, Githinji Mwarari—who had painted his fat face with white chalk—put a band of raw goat's skin on

29.   Karari Njama, excerpt from "Reflections on the Mau Mau Oath" from Donald L. Bennett and Karari Njama, *Mau Mau from Within*. Copyright © 1966 by Donald L. Bennett and Karari Njama. Reprinted with the permission of the Monthly Review Foundation.

the right hand wrist of each one of the seven persons who were to be initiated. We were then surrounded [bound together] by goats' small intestines on our shoulders and feet. Another person then sprayed us with some beer from his mouth as a blessing at the same time throwing a mixture of the finger millet with other cereals on us. Then Githinji pricked our right hand middle finger with a needle until it bled. He then brought the chest of a billy goat and its heart still attached to the kings and smeared them with our blood. He then took a Kikuyu gourd containing blood and with it made a cross on our foreheads and on all important joints saying, 'May this blood mark the faithful and brave members of the Gikuyu and Mumbi Unity; may this same blood warn you that if you betray our secrets or violate the oath, our members will come and cut you into pieces at the joints marked by this blood'.

We were then asked to lick each others blood from our middle fingers and vowed after the administrator: 'If I reveal this secret of Gikuyu and Mumbi to a person not a member, may this blood kill me. If I violate any of the rules of the oath may this blood kill me. If I lie, may this blood kill me'.

We were then ordered to hold each others right hand and in that position, making a line, passed through the arch seven times. Each time the oath administrator cut off a piece of the goat's small intestine, breaking it into pieces, while all the rest in the hut repeated a curse on us: '*Tathu! Ugotuika uguo ungiaria maheni! Muma uroria muria ma!*' ('Slash! May you be cut like this! Let the oath kill he who lies!').

We were then made to stand facing Mt. Kenya, encircled by intestines, and given two dampened soil balls and ordered to hold the left hand soil ball against our navels. We then swore: 'I, (Karari Njama), swear before God and before all the people present here that. . . .

(I) I shall never reveal this secret of the KCA oath—which is of Gikuyu and Mumbi and which demands land and freedom—to any person who is not a member of our society. If I ever reveal it, may this oath kill me! ([Repeated after each vow while] biting the chest meat of a billy goat held together with the heart and lungs.)

(2) I shall always help any member of our society who is in difficulty or need of help.

(3) If I am ever called, during the day or night, to do any work for this society, I shall obey.

(4) I shall on no account ever disobey the leaders of this society.

(5) If I am ever given firearms or ammunition to hide, I shall do so.

(6) I shall always give money or goods to this society whenever called upon to do so.

(7) I shall never sell land to a European or an Asian.

(8) I shall not permit intermarriage between Africans and the white community.

(9) I will never go with a prostitute.

(10) I shall never cause a girl to become pregnant and leave her unmarried.

(11) I will never marry and then seek a divorce.

(12) I shall never allow any daughter to remain uncircumcised.

(13) I shall never drink European manufactured beer or cigarettes.

(14) I shall never spy on or otherwise sell my people to the Government.

(15) I shall never help the missionaries in their Christian faith ruin our traditional and cultural customs.

(16) I will never accept the Beecher Report.

(17) I shall never steal any property belonging to a member of our society.

(18) I shall obey any strike call, whenever notified.

(19) I will never retreat or abandon any of our mentioned demands but will daily increase more and stronger demands until we achieve our goals.

(20) I shall pay 62/50s. and a ram as assessed by this society as soon as I am able.

(21) I shall always follow the leadership of Jomo Kenyatta and Mbiyu Koinange'.

We repeated the oath while pricking the eye of a goat with a kei-apple thorn seven times and then ended the vows by pricking seven times some seven sodom apples. To end the ceremony, blood mixed with some good smelling oil was used to make a cross on our foreheads indicating our reception as members of Gikuyu and Mumbi [while] warning us: 'Forward ever and backward never!' We were then allowed to take our belongings, put on our coats and shoes and were welcomed to stay. We paid 2/50s. each for registration. During the course of our initiation, one person refused to take the oath and was mercilessly beaten. Two guards were crying [out] seeking permission from their chief leader to kill the man. The man learnt that death had approached him and he quickly changed his mind and took the oath.

24

The Road to Freedom Is Via the Cross, 1952[30]

Albert Luthuli

*Albert Luthuli (1898–1967) was a South African politician and for-
mer president of the African National Congress (ANC, 1952–1967).
He was awarded the Nobel Peace Prize in 1960. His political career
in South Africa began when he was elected as tribal chieftain of the
Groutville Mission Reserve. During his tenure as tribal chief, the governing white minority United Party adopted stricter apartheid policies, revoking the rights of non-white Africans to vote in the Cape and
restricting black African land-holding rights to a number of reserves.
In 1944, Luthuli joined the ANC and organized nonviolent cam-
paigns of passive resistance in protest of the government's policies. In
1952, he helped to initiate the Defiance Campaign, a nonviolent
protest insisting on non-cooperation with the government's apartheid
laws. The government subsequently insisted that Luthuli's actions
with the ANC were in conflict with his position as tribal chief and
requested that he renounce his membership as a member of the ANC
or his chieftainship. Refusing to resign from the ANC, Luthuli issued
this public statement explaining his resignation as tribal chief and his
continued support for nonviolent passive resistance against apartheid.*

*A Public Statement made by Albert Luthuli immediately after he was dis-
missed from his position as Chief by the Government in November 1952. It
was issued jointly by the African National Congress and the Natal Indian
Congress.*

I have been dismissed from the Chieftainship of the Abase-Makolweni
Tribe in the Groutville Mission Reserve. I presume that this has been
done by the Governor-General in his capacity as Supreme Chief of the
"Native" people of the Union of South Africa save those of the Cape
Province. I was democratically elected to this position in 1935 by

30. Albert Luthuli, excerpt from "The Road to Freedom Is Via the Cross" from *Let
My People Go*. Copyright © 1962. Reprinted with permission.

the people of Groutville Mission Reserve and was duly approved and appointed by the Governor-General.

PATH OF MODERATION

Previous to being a chief I was a school teacher for about seventeen years. In these past thirty years or so I have striven with tremendous zeal and patience to work for the progress and welfare of my people and for their harmonious relations with other sections of our multi-racial society in the Union of South Africa. In this effort I always pursued what liberal-minded people rightly regarded as the path of moderation. Over this great length of time I have, year after year, gladly spent hours of my time with such organisations as the Church and its various agencies such as the Christian Council of South Africa, the Joint Council of Europeans and Africans and the now defunct Native Representative Council.

In so far as gaining citizenship rights and opportunities for the unfettered development of the African people, who will deny that thirty years of life may have been spent knocking in vain, patiently, moderately and modestly at a closed and barred door?

What have been the fruits of my many years of moderation? Has there been any reciprocal tolerance or moderation from the Government, be it Nationalist or United Party? No! On the contrary, the pasty thirty years have seen the greatest number of Laws restricting our rights and progress until to-day we have reached a stage where we have almost no rights at all: no adequate land for our occupation, our only asset, cattle, dwindling, no security of homes, no decent and remunerative employment, more restrictions to freedom of movement through passes, curfew regulations, influx control measures; in short we have witnessed in these years an intensification of our subjection to ensure and protect white supremacy.

A NEW SPIRIT

It is with this background and with a full sense of responsibility that, under the auspices of the African National Congress (Natal), I have joined my people in the new spirit that moves them to-day, the spirit that revolts openly and boldly against injustice and expresses itself in a determined and non-violent manner. Because of my association with the African National Congress in this new spirit which has found an effective and legitimate way of expression in the non-violent Passive Resistance Campaign, I was given a two-week limit ultimatum by the Secretary for Native Affairs calling upon me to choose between the African National Congress and the chieftainship of the Groutville Mission Reserve. He alleged that my association with Congress in its non-violent Passive Resistance Campaign was an act of disloyalty to the State. I did not, and do not, agree with this view. Viewing non-violent Passive Resistance as a non-revolutionary and, therefore, a most legitimate and humane political pressure technique for a people denied all effective forms of constitutional striving, I saw no real conflict in my dual leadership of any people: leader of this tribe as chief and political leader in Congress.

SERVANT OF PEOPLE

I saw no cause to resign from either. This stand of mine which resulted in my being sacked from the chieftainship might seem foolish and disappointing to some liberal and moderate Europeans and non-Europeans with whom I have worked these many years and with whom I still hope to work. This is no parting of the ways but "a launching farther into the deep." I invite them to join us in our unequivocal pronouncement of all legitimate African aspirations and in our firm stand against injustice and oppression.

I do not wish to challenge my dismissal, but I would like to suggest that in the interest of the institution of chieftainship in these modern times of democracy, the Government should define more precisely and make more widely known the status, functions and privileges of chiefs.

My view has been, and still is, that a chief is primarily a servant of his people. He is the voice of his people. He is the voice of his people in local affairs. Unlike a Native Commissioner, he is part and parcel of the Tribe, and not a local agent of the Government. Within the bounds of loyalty it is conceivable that he may vote and press the claims of his people even if they should be unpalatable to the Government of the day. He may use all legitimate modern techniques to get these demands satisfied. It is conceivable how chiefs could effectively serve the wider and common interest of their own tribe without co-operating with other leaders of the people, both the natural leaders (chiefs) and leaders elected democratically by the people themselves.

MUST FIGHT FEARLESSLY

It was to allow for these wider associations intended to promote the common national interests of the people as against purely local interests that the Government in making rules governing chiefs did not debar them from joining political associations so long as those associations had not been declared "by the Minister to be subversive of or prejudicial to constituted Government." The African National Congress, its non-violent Passive Resistance Campaign, may be of nuisance value to the Government but it is not subversive since it does not seek to overthrow the form and machinery of the State but only urges for the inclusion of all sections of the community in a partnership in the Government of the country on the basis of equality.

Laws and conditions that tend to debase human personality—a God-given force—be they brought about by the State or other individuals, must be relentlessly opposed in the spirit of defiance shown by St. Peter when he said to the rulers of his day: "Shall we obey God or man?" No one can deny that in so far as non-Whites are concerned in the Union of South Africa, laws and conditions that debase human personality abound. Any chief worthy of his position must fight fearlessly against such debasing conditions and laws. If the Government should resort to dismissing such chiefs, it may find itself dismissing many chiefs or causing people to dismiss from their hearts chiefs who are indifferent to the needs of the people through fear of dismissal by the Government. Surely the Government cannot place chiefs in such an uncomfortable and invidious position.

EVEN DEATH

As for myself, with a full sense of responsibility and a clear conviction, I decided to remain in the struggle for extending democratic rights and responsibilities to all sections of the South African community. I have embraced the non-violent Passive Resistance technique in fighting for freedom because I am convinced it is the only non-revolutionary, legitimate and humane way that could be used by people denied, as we are, effective constitutional means to further aspirations.

The wisdom or foolishness of this decision I place in the hands of the Almighty.

What the future has in store for me I do not know. It might be ridicule, imprisonment, concentration camp, flogging, banishment and even death. I only pray to the Almighty to strengthen my resolve so that none of these grim possibilities may deter me from striving, for the sake of the good name of our beloved country, the Union of South Africa, to make it a true democracy and a true union in form and spirit of all the communities in the land.

My only painful concern at times is that of the welfare of my family but I try even in this regard, in a spirit of trust and surrender to God's will as I see it, to say: "God will provide."

It is inevitable that in working for Freedom some individuals and some families must take the lead and suffer: The Road to Freedom is via the CROSS.

MAYIBUYE!

AFRIKA! AFRIKA! AFRIKA![31]

31. See footnote 12.

25

Proclamation of the FLN, 1954[32]

The Algerian National Liberation Front

*On November 1, 1954, the newly-formed Algerian National Libera-
tion Front (FLN), which had split from the more moderate nationalist Mouvement pour le triomphe des libertés démocratiques (MTLD),
officially announced its plan to engage in armed action to win independence from French rule. On the same day, the FLN launched
thirty independent attacks against colonial police and French military
targets on All-Saint's Day. The series of attacks are known as Toussaint Rouge (Red All-Saint's Day). The formation of the FLN and the
Toussaint Rouge attacks effectively marked the beginning of the war to
end French rule in Algeria. Over the course of 1955, the violence in
Algeria would escalate into a full-scale conflict. The war would lead
to the collapse of the Fourth French Republic in 1958 and Algerian
independence in 1962. The following proclamation states the FLN's
reasons for forming and the group's aims.*

Appeal to the Algerian People

TO THE ALGERIAN PEOPLE,
TO THE SUPPORTERS OF THE NATIONAL CAUSE,
To those of you who are called upon to judge us (Algerians in general, militants in particular), by distributing this proclamation our aim
is to clarify for you the profound reasons that have pushed us to act
by explaining our program, the meaning of our action, the soundness
of our views. The goal of all of these remains national independence
in North Africa. Our wish is also to help you avoid the misinforma-
tion coming from imperialism and its administrative agents and other
corrupt sources.

---

32. Translated by Timothy Scott Johnson. Printed with the permission of Timothy
Scott Johnson.

First and foremost, we believe that, after decades of struggle, the national movement has achieved its formative phase. In effect, the goal of a revolutionary movement being to create all of the conditions for a liberatory action, we believe the people have domestically rallied to the call for independence and action; and externally, the climate [of Cold War] détente is favorable to settle minor problems, such as ours, especially with the support of our Arab-Muslim brothers. The events in Morocco and Tunisia are significant in this regard and profoundly affect the process of the struggle for North African liberation. Note that in this domain we have for a very long time been the first to unite in action. Unfortunately this has never been achieved in these three countries.

Today, both Morocco and Tunisia are charging resolutely down this path, and we, relegated to the rearguard, suffer the fate of being left behind. This is why our national movement—held back by years of inaction and lazy habit, poorly led, deprived of the indispensable support of popular opinion, overtaken by events—is progressively falling apart, much to the satisfaction of the colonialism that believed it can claim the greatest victory in its struggle against the Algerian vanguard.

THE MOMENT IS CRITICAL!

In the face of this potentially irreparable situation, a group of responsible and conscious militants, uniting around them the majority of the reasonable and determined nationalist elements, have judged that the moment has come to take the nationalist movement beyond the current impasse caused by infighting, to join forces with their Moroccan and Tunisian brothers in the true revolutionary struggle.

To this effect, we wish to declare ourselves independent of those two factions claiming power. Placing the national interest beyond all petty and erroneous considerations of personality and prestige, conforming to revolutionary principles, our action is specifically directed against colonialism, the lone and blind enemy that has always refused to confer the least amount of freedom through peaceful struggle.

We believe these are all sufficient reasons for our movement of renewal to introduce itself as the NATIONAL LIBERATION FRONT, thus freeing ourselves from all possible half measures and offering all Algerian patriots of every background, all parties and purely Algerian movements, the chance to unite in the struggle for liberation, without any other consideration.

In order to be precise, below are the main points of our political program:

GOAL: National independence through:

1. The restoration of the sovereign, democratic, and social Algerian state under the framework of Islamic principles.

2. The respect for all fundamental freedoms without discrimination based on race or religion.

DOMESTIC OBJECTIVES:

1. A political cleansing by placing the national revolutionary movement on its true path and through the eradication of all vestiges of corruption and reformism, the cause of our current regression.

2. The gathering and organization of all sound energies of the Algerian people in order to liquidate the colonial system.

FOREIGN OBJECTIVES:

1. The internationalization of the Algerian problem.

2. The realization of North African unity under the natural Arab-Muslim framework.

3. In the framework of the United Nations Charter, an affirmation of our good will toward all nations that would support our liberatory action.

MEANS OF STRUGGLE:

Adhering to the revolutionary principles and taking account of domestic and foreign situations, the struggle will continue by all means necessary until our goal is achieved.

To achieve these ends, the FLN will simultaneously have two essential tasks: domestic action involving both political and military action; and, with the support of all of our natural allies, a foreign action intent on making the Algerian problem a problem for the whole world.

This is an overwhelming task that requires the mobilization of all of the nation's energies and resources. It is true the struggle will be long, but the outcome is certain.

Lastly, in order to avoid false interpretations and red herrings, to demonstrate our desire for peace, limit the loss of human life and bloodshed, we put forward an honorable platform for negotiating with the French authorities if they are motivated by good faith and at the same time recognize the right of all those peoples they subjugate to dispose of their own affairs.

1. The recognition of Algerian nationality through an official declaration voiding edicts, decrees, and laws making Algeria a French territory through the denial of the history, geography, language, religion, and customs of the Algerian people.

2. The opening of negotiations with the authorized representatives of the Algerian people on the basis of the recognition of the unified and invisible Algerian sovereignty.

3. The creation of a climate of confidence through the liberation of all political prisoners, the lifting of all emergency measures and the cessation of all hostilities against our combatant forces.

IN RETURN:

1. French cultural and economic interests, honestly acquired, will be respected, along with French persons and families.

2. All French persons desiring to remain in Algeria will have the choice between their French nationality (and will be thus considered foreigners regarding the laws in effect) or to opt for Algerian nationality and, in this case, will be considered Algerians in their rights and duties.

3. The ties between France and Algeria will be defined and will be the object of an agreement between the two powers on the basis of the equality and respect of each.

Algerians! We invite you to consider this charter. Your duty is to join us to save our country and restore its freedom. The FLN is your vanguard. Its victory is your own.

As for us, resolved to continue the struggle, sure of your anti-imperialist sentiments, we give the best of ourselves to the fatherland.

1st November 1954
The National Secretariat

26
The Women's Charter, 1954[33]

The Federation of South African Women

The Federation of South African Women (FSAW) was formed in 1954 by women members of the African National Congress (ANC) Alliance. There were 164 delegates, representing 230,000 black South African women, who attended the founding conference. The FSAW was the central organization for women in the anti-apartheid struggle. In addition to supporting activism against apartheid, the FSAW focused attention on the particular struggles of women and opposed both the sexism women faced under apartheid as well as the sexism women faced within the anti-apartheid movement. The passage of the Natives Abolition of Passes and Co-ordination of Documents Act No 67 of 1952 led to the revision of South Africa's Pass Laws so as not only to apply to black male workers, but to all black South Africans over sixteen years of age. On August 9, 1956, the FSAW organized a march of over 20,000 women against the Pass Laws for Women. The Pass Laws required that non-white South Africans carry a passbook while in white-dominated areas. The Women's Charter adopted at the FSAW's founding conference lays out women's demands in preparation for the meeting of the Congress of the People held in Kliptown on June 26, 1955.

Preamble: We, the women of South Africa, wives and mothers, working women and housewives, African, Indians, European and Coloured, hereby declare our aim of striving for the removal of all laws, regulations, conventions and customs that discriminate against us as women, and that deprive us in any way of our inherent right to the advantages, responsibilities and opportunities that society offers to any one section of the population.

33. The Federation of South African Women, "The Women's Charter" (1954): http://www.sahistory.org.za/topic/womens-charter (accessed October 5, 2016).

A Single Society: We women do not form a society separate from the men. There is only one society, and it is made up of both women and men. As women we share the problems and anxieties of our men, and join hands with them to remove social evils and obstacles to progress.

Test of Civilisation: The level of civilisation which any society has reached can be measured by the degree of freedom that its members enjoy. The status of women is a test of civilisation. Measured by that standard, South Africa must be considered low in the scale of civilised nations.

Women's Lot: We women share with our menfolk the cares and anxieties imposed by poverty and its evils. As wives and mothers, it falls upon us to make small wages stretch a long way. It is we who feel the cries of our children when they are hungry and sick. It is our lot to keep and care for the homes that are too small, broken and dirty to be kept clean. We know the burden of looking after children and land when our husbands are away in the mines, on the farms, and in the towns earning our daily bread.

We know what it is to keep family life going in pondokkies and shanties, or in overcrowded one-room apartments. We know the bitterness of children taken to lawless ways, of daughters becoming unmarried mothers whilst still at school, of boys and girls growing up without education, training or jobs at a living wage.

Poor and Rich: These are evils that need not exist. They exist because the society in which we live is divided into poor and rich, into non-European and European. They exist because there are privileges for the few, discrimination and harsh treatment for the many. We women have stood and will stand shoulder to shoulder with our menfolk in a common struggle against poverty, race and class discrimination, and the evils of the colour bar.

National Liberation: As members of the National Liberatory movements and Trade Unions, in and through our various organisations, we march forward with our men in the struggle for liberation and the defence of the working people. We pledge ourselves to keep high the banner of equality, fraternity and liberty. As women there rests upon us also the burden of removing from our society all the social differences developed in past times between men and women, which have the effect of keeping our sex in a position of inferiority and subordination.

Equality for Women: We resolve to struggle for the removal of laws and customs that deny African women the right to own, inherit or alienate property. We resolve to work for a change in the laws of marriage such as are found amongst our African, Malay and Indian people, which have the effect of placing wives in the position of legal subjection to husbands, and giving husbands the power to dispose of wives' property and earnings, and dictate to them in all matters affecting them and their children.

We recognise that the women are treated as minors by these marriage and property laws because of ancient and revered traditions and customs which had their origin in the antiquity of the people and no doubt served purposes of great value in bygone times.

There was a time in the African society when every woman reaching marriageable stage was assured of a husband, home, land and security.

Then husbands and wives with their children belonged to families and clans that supplied most of their own material needs and were largely self-sufficient. Men and women were partners in a compact and closely integrated family unit.

Women Who Labour: Those conditions have gone. The tribal and kinship society to which they belonged has been destroyed as a result of the loss of tribal land, migration of men away from the tribal home, the growth of towns and industries, and the rise of a great body of wage-earners on the farms and in the urban areas, who depend wholly or mainly on wages for a livelihood.

Thousands of African women, like Indians, Coloured and European women, are employed today in factories, homes, offices, shops, on farms, in professions as nurses, teachers and the like. As unmarried women, widows or divorcees they have to fend for themselves, often without the assistance of a male relative. Many of them are responsible not only for their own livelihood but also that of their children.

Large numbers of women today are in fact the sole breadwinners and heads of their families.

Forever Minors: Nevertheless, the laws and practices derived from an earlier and different state of society are still applied to them. They are responsible for their own person and their children. Yet the law seeks to enforce upon them the status of a minor.

Not only are African, Coloured and Indian women denied political rights, but they are also in many parts of the Union denied the same status as men in such matters as the right to enter into contracts, to own and dispose of property, and to exercise guardianship over their children.

Obstacle to Progress: The law has lagged behind the development of society; it no longer corresponds to the actual social and economic position of women. The law has become an obstacle to progress of the women, and therefore a brake on the whole of society.

This intolerable condition would not be allowed to continue were it not for the refusal of a large section of our menfolk to concede to us women the rights and privileges which they demand for themselves.

We shall teach the men that they cannot hope to liberate themselves from the evils of discrimination and prejudice as long as they fail to extend to women complete and unqualified equality in law and in practice.

Need for Education: We also recognise that large numbers of our womenfolk continue to be bound by traditional practices and conventions, and fail to realise that these have become obsolete and a brake on progress. It is our duty and privilege to enlist all women in our struggle for emancipation and to bring to them all realisation of the intimate relationship that exists between their status of inferiority as women and the inferior status to which their people are subjected by discriminatory laws and colour prejudices.

It is our intention to carry out a nation-wide programme of education that will bring home to the men and women of all national groups the realisation that freedom cannot be won for any one section or for the people as a whole as long as we women are kept in bondage.

An Appeal: We women appeal to all progressive organisations, to members of the great National Liberatory movements, to the trade unions and working class organisations, to the churches, educational and welfare organisations, to all progressive men and women who have the interests of the people at heart, to join with us in this great and noble endeavour.

Our Aims

We declare the following aims:

This organisation is formed for the purpose of uniting women in common action for the removal of all political, legal, economic and social disabilities. We shall strive for women to obtain:

- The right to vote and to be elected to all State bodies, without restriction or discrimination.

- The right to full opportunities for employment with equal pay and possibilities of promotion in all spheres of work.
- Equal rights with men in relation to property, marriage and children, and for the removal of all laws and customs that deny women such equal rights.
- For the development of every child through free compulsory education for all; for the protection of mother and child through maternity homes, welfare clinics, crèches, and nursery schools, in countryside and towns; through proper homes for all, and through the provision of water, light, transport, sanitation, and other amenities of modern civilisation.
- For the removal of all laws that restrict free movement, that prevent or hinder the right of free association and activity in democratic organisations, and the right to participate in the work of these organisations.
- To build and strengthen women's sections in the National Liberatory movements, the organisation of women in trade unions, and through the peoples' varied organization.
- To cooperate with all other organisations that have similar aims in South Africa as well as throughout the world.
- To strive for permanent peace throughout the world.

27

The Freedom Charter, 1955[34]

The South African Congress of the People

Since the late 1940s, the Nationalist Party governments of South Africa—then formally a British dominion—enforced a system of racial segregation and white minority rule in South Africa. In response, a number of South African groups joined in protest against apartheid. These included the African National Congress (ANC), the major political organization agitating for equal rights of black Africans; the South African Indian Congress, who fought for the end of discrimination against South Africa's Indian population; and the South Africa Congress of Democrats, a radical white anti-apartheid organization. Together, they formed the South African Congress Alliance. Hoping to foster support for the Defiance Campaign—a national action of non-cooperation—against apartheid laws initiated in 1952 and promote non-cooperation with the laws, these groups organized a national "Congress of the People" in Kliptown on June 26, 1955 to develop a political program for the country. Penned by delegates from these three groups, the Freedom Charter reflects the broadened political vision of these unified organizations to end apartheid, support a non-racial South Africa, and extend social welfare—including labor and land rights—throughout South Africa's population.

We, the People of South Africa, declare for all our country and the world to know:

that South Africa belongs to all who live in it, black and white, and that no government can justly claim authority unless it is based on the will of all the people;

that our people have been robbed of their birthright to land, liberty and peace by a form of government founded on injustice and inequality;

34. The South African Congress of the People, "The Freedom Charter" (1955): http://www.anc.org.za/ancdocs/history/charter.html (accessed September 15, 2016).

that our country will never be prosperous or free until all our people live in brotherhood, enjoying equal rights and opportunities;

that only a democratic state, based on the will of all the people, can secure to all their birthright without distinction of colour, race, sex or belief;

And therefore, we the people of South Africa, black and white together— equals, countrymen and brothers—adopt this Freedom Charter. And we pledge ourselves to strive together, sparing neither strength nor courage, until the democratic changes set out here have been won.

THE PEOPLE SHALL GOVERN!

Every man and woman shall have the right to vote for and to stand as a candidate for all bodies which make laws;

All people shall be entitled to take part in the administration of the country;

The rights of the people shall be the same, regardless of race, colour or sex;

All bodies of minority rule, advisory boards, councils and authorities shall be replaced by democratic organs of self-government.

ALL NATIONAL GROUPS SHALL HAVE EQUAL RIGHTS!

There shall be equal status in the bodies of state, in the courts and in the schools for all national groups and races;

All people shall have equal right to use their own languages, and to develop their own folk culture and customs;

All national groups shall be protected by law against insults to their race and national pride;

The preaching and practice of national, race or colour discrimination and contempt shall be a punishable crime;

All apartheid laws and practices shall be set aside.

THE PEOPLE SHALL SHARE IN THE COUNTRY'S WEALTH!

The national wealth of our country, the heritage of all South Africans, shall be restored to the people;

The mineral wealth beneath the soil, the Banks and monopoly industry shall be transferred to the ownership of the people as a whole;

All other industry and trade shall be controlled to assist the well-being of the people;

All people shall have equal rights to trade where they choose, to manufacture and to enter all trades, crafts and professions.

THE LAND SHALL BE SHARED AMONG THOSE WHO WORK IT!

Restriction of land ownership on a racial basis shall be ended and all the land redivided amongst those who work it, to banish famine and land hunger;

The State shall help the peasants with implements, seed, tractors and dams to save the soil and assist the tillers;

Freedom of movement shall be guaranteed to all who work on the land;

All shall have the right to occupy land wherever they choose;

People shall not be robbed of their cattle, and forced labour and farm prisons shall be abolished.

ALL SHALL BE EQUAL BEFORE THE LAW!

No one shall be imprisoned, deported or restricted without a fair trial;

No one shall be condemned by the order of any Government official;

The courts shall be representative of all the people;

Imprisonment shall be only for serious crimes against the people, and shall aim at re-education, not vengeance;

The police force and army shall be open to all on an equal basis and shall be the helpers and protectors of the people;

All laws which discriminate on grounds of race, colour or belief shall be repealed.

ALL SHALL ENJOY EQUAL HUMAN RIGHTS!

The law shall guarantee to all their right to speak, to organize, to meet together, to publish, to preach, to worship and to educate their children;

The privacy of the house from police raids shall be protected by law;

All shall be free to travel without restriction from countryside to town, from province to province, and from South Africa to abroad.

Pass Laws, permits, and all other laws restricting these freedoms shall be abolished.

THERE SHALL BE WORK AND SECURITY!

All who work shall be free to form trade unions, to elect their officers and to make wage agreements with their employers;

The State shall recognize the right and duty of all to work, and to draw full unemployment benefits;

Men and women of all races shall receive equal pay for equal work;

There shall be a forty-hour working week, a national minimum wage, paid annual leave, and sick leave for all workers, and maternity leave on full pay for all working mothers;

Miners, domestic workers, farm workers, and civil servants shall have the same rights as all others who work;

Child labour, compound labour, the tot system and contract labour shall be abolished.

THE DOORS OF LEARNING AND OF CULTURE SHALL BE OPENED!

The government shall discover, develop and encourage national talent for the enhancement of our cultural life:

All the cultural treasures of mankind shall be open to all, by free exchange of books, ideas and contacts with other lands;

The aim of education shall be to teach the youth to love their people and their culture, to honour human brotherhood, liberty and peace;

Education shall be free, compulsory, universal and equal for all children;

Higher education and technical training shall be opened to all by means of state allowances and scholarships awarded on the basis of merit;

Adult illiteracy shall be ended by a mass state education plan;

Teachers shall have all the rights of other citizens;

The colour bar in cultural life, in sport, and in education shall be abolished.

THERE SHALL BE HOUSES, SECURITY AND COMFORT!

All people shall have the right to live where they choose, to be decently housed, and to bring up their families in comfort and security;

Unused housing space to be made available to the people;

Rent and prices shall be lowered, food plentiful and no one shall go hungry;

A preventive health scheme shall be run by the state;

Free medical care and hospitalisation shall be provided for all, with special care for mothers and young children;

Slums shall be demolished, and new suburbs built where all have transport, roads, lighting, playing fields, crèches and social centres;

The aged, the orphans, the disabled and the sick shall be cared for by the state;

Rest, leisure and recreation shall be the right of all;

Fenced locations and ghettoes shall be abolished, and laws which break up families shall be repealed.

THERE SHALL BE PEACE AND FRIENDSHIP!

South Africa shall be a fully independent state, which respects the rights and sovereignty of nations;

South Africa shall strive to maintain world peace and the settlement of all international disputes by negotiation—not war;

Peace and friendship amongst all our people shall be secured by upholding the equal rights, opportunities and status of all;

The people of the protectorates—Basutoland, Bechuanaland and Swaziland—shall be free to decide for themselves their own future;

The rights of all the peoples of Africa to independence and self-government shall be recognized, and shall be the basis of close cooperation.

Let all who love their people and their country now say, as we say here:

'THESE FREEDOMS WE WILL FIGHT FOR, SIDE BY SIDE, THROUGHOUT OUR LIVES, UNTIL WE HAVE WON OUR LIBERTY.'

28

Major Program of the Movimento Popular de Libertação de Angola (MPLA), 1956[35]

The People's Movement for the Liberation of Angola

The People's Movement for the Liberation of Angola (MPLA) was formed on December 10, 1956 through a merger of the Angolan Communist Party (PCA) and the Party of the United Struggle for Africans in Angola (PLUA), in an effort to achieve Angolan independence from Portugal. Though originally allied with Communist parties, with the growing membership of other politically aligned groups, the MPLA adopted a Social Democratic political ideology and became a member of the Socialist International. In 1961, the MPLA joined with the African Party for the Independence of Guinea and Cape Verde (PAIGC) in combating Portuguese colonialism. The war for independence from Portugal lasted until 1974. The war came to an end when the Portuguese military staged a coup in Portugal during the Carnation Revolution. The military government divided control of Angola to the three leading political groups: the MPLA, the National Union for the Total Independence of Angola (UNITA), and the National Front for the Liberation of Angola (FNLA). A civil war ensued between the three groups and their supporters until 2002. The following document states the ten primary aims of the MPLA at the outset of the armed conflict with Portugal.

In this hour the concrete and immediate enemies of the Angolan people are the Portuguese colonists and their agents, who will use all measures—violence, assassination, Machiavellism and subterfuge, military force, political and economic power, and cultural obscurantism—to

---

35. The People's Movement for the Liberation of Angola, "Major Program of the Movimento Popular de Libertação de Angola" from Thomas Masaji Okuma, *Angola in Ferment: The Background and Prospects of Angolan Nationalism.* Copyright © 1962 by Thomas Okuma. Reprinted with the permission of Beacon Press, Boston.

maintain their sovereignty in Angola and to continue to oppress and exploit the Angolan people.

MPLA stands for the following program:

1. Immediate and Complete Independence: Liquidation in Angola by all available means of Portuguese colonial rule and all traces of colonialism and imperialism.

   To fight in Common with all the forces of Angolan patriots in a mass popular movement, in order that the Angolan people have the power to install in Angola a republican and democratic regime on the basis of total independence.

   To abolish all the privileges which the colonial regime has conceded to the Portuguese nationals and to foreigners.

   The sovereignty of the Angolan state must belong entirely and uniquely to the Angolan people without distinctions based on ethnic groups, class, age, political and religious beliefs.

   The Angolan nation will have the sacred and inviolable right of self-determination whether in political, economic, diplomatic, military, and cultural planning or in any other sphere.

   Revision of the Angolan position in all treaties, agreements and alliances which Portugal contracted without the free consent of the Angolan people.

   A popular voluntary union with the purpose of liquidating whatever tendency of imperialistic aggression and all the acts and works which prejudice the independence, sovereignty, unity and territorial integrity of Angola.

   The establishment of peace in Angola, based on a program of social justice, and the recognition by other nations of the independence, sovereignty, unity and territorial integrity of Angola.

2. National Unity: To guarantee equality to all the ethnic groups in Angola and to reinforce their unity and to help bring about friendship among them.

   Absolute prohibition of all tendencies to divide the Angolan nation.

   To create conditions in Angola so that the thousands of Angolans who were forced to leave the country because of cruel treatment by the colonial regime would return to Angola.

Regions in which national minorities live in dense numbers and posses individual characters ought to become autonomous.

Each nationality or tribe will have the right to use and develop its own language—written and spoken—and to conserve or recreate its cultural heritage.

In the interest of the Angolan nation, economic and social solidarity must be instigated and developed as well as normal relations—in economic, social and cultural planning—between the autonomous regions and all the nationalities or tribes in Angola.

Freedom of movement for all Angolan citizens which does not encroach upon national boundaries.

3. African Unity: Complete solidarity with all African peoples who are fighting for complete independence and against colonialism and imperialism, and in particular with the peoples and political movements which are fighting against Portuguese colonialism.

To work for the unity of all peoples of the continent of Africa on the basis of respect for liberty, dignity and the right to develop their own political, economic and social systems.

Unity of all African countries based on popular will and expressed through democratic and peaceful means.

Opposition of any move to annex or to pressure one country over another.

In the process of uniting one or more African nations, it resists political, economic, social conquests upon the culture of the working class and the boundaries of each country.

4. Democratic Regime: Republican, democratic and secular government for Angola.

To guarantee freedom of speech, conscience, belief, press, assembly, associations, housing, correspondence, etc., for all the Angolan people.

All Angolan citizens—without distinction of nationality or tribe, of sex, social classification, cultural background, profession, wealth, religious belief or philosophical convictions—will have the right to vote at the age of eighteen years and the right to be elected after twenty-one years of age.

Elections will be based on universal suffrage, equal, direct and secret.

The Assembly of the Angolan nation will be the supreme legislative body of the State.

Members of the Assembly will formulate the first political constitution of the republic of Angola.

All members of the Assembly will have parliamentary immunity.

The Assembly will designate a coalition government which can effect a union among the various nationalities or tribes, social classes; and among the various political parties; and that the government will really express the will of the nation in favor of liberty and progress; and against political, economic, territorial or cultural alienation to the advantage of foreigners.

The government of the republic of Angola will be the supreme body and will exercise the executive power of the State. It will receive its power from the Assembly and will be responsible to that body.

Each autonomous region will have the right to adopt methods particularly suited to its conditions, but not contradictory to the general welfare of Angola.

Africanization of all administrative machinery of the country.

Guarantees of protection in accord with the Universal Declaration of Human Rights to all strangers who respect the laws in existence.

5. Economic Reconstruction and Plan of Production: Economic development through planning stages. Transformation of Angola into a country which is modern, prosperous, vigorous and economically and industrially independent.

Agricultural development, with long range planning, principally the abandoning of a one-crop system; increase in productivity and mechanization of agriculture.

Founding and progressive development of commercial and industrial enterprises, of consumers, wholesale, and producer's cooperatives. Progressive building of heavy and light industries; the latter for the production of consumer goods.

Exploration of the state of potential energy in the country.

Restoration and development of traditional African industries.

Abolition of economic privileges bestowed by the colonial regime upon Portuguese nationals and foreign commercial houses.

Development of communication and transport facilities.

Protection of industry and private enterprise.

Encouragement of industry and of private commerce which are useful to the State and life of the people.

Foreign economic enterprises must conform with the new laws of Angola. Protection of foreign economic activities which are useful to the progress and reinforcement of real independence of the Angolan people.

Development and vigorous activity of economic relations between cities and villages, with the idea of progressively improving rural conditions and the level of life of rural populations.

Effective implementation of a policy which considers, at the same time, the interests of employees and employers.

Establishment of a National Bank and currency. Avoidance of inflation and creation of a stable currency.

Control by the State of the best interest of all of foreign trade of Angola. Revision of the unfair agreement of Angola with Portugal. Combat the balance deficit of the commerce of Angola. A balancing of the books—of receipts and expenditures.

Abolition of the fiscal system introduced by Portuguese colonialists and creation of a new fiscal system; just, rational and simple.

Price control and prohibition of speculations.

6. Agrarian Reform: To introduce agrarian reform that will eliminate the existing injustices in relation to rural ownership; to liquidate private monopoly of special rural production which is contrary to the denationalization of the Angolan soil; to fulfill the principle: the land is for those who till the soil.

Nationalization of land belonging to the enemy of the nationalist movement after immediate and complete independence of Angola; of traitors and proven enemies of the independent and democratic Angolan state.

Definition of the limits of private rural property, having in mind the rural situation of each locality. After revision of title on lands, the purchasing by the State, for a just price, lands which are owned beyond the limits established by law.

Distribution of land to those who do not have it and to those who have insufficient acreage. The beneficiaries of land legally distributed will not have to pay to the expropriators and to the State.

Protection of the right of conquest by farmers in the popular battle for an independent Angola.

7. Just Social Politics and of Progress: The State ought to protect the rights of workers and farmers, and of all social strata who have actively defended the independence of Angola; autonomy and unity of the Angolan people and territorial integrity of the country.

Immediate abolition of the regime of forced labor.

Respect for the independence of syndicates and legal organizations of workers.

An eight-hour day and progressive application of new laws for the protection of workers. The State will fix a minimum wage scale and will guard the rigorous application of the principle, "equal salary for equal work," without discrimination of sex, age and ethnic origin of workers.

Protection of churches, places and objects of worship of legal religious institutions.

In all planning—political, economic, social and cultural— women will have the same rights as men. Women and men are equal before the law.

State assistance to maternity patients and to infants.

Application of social assistance to all Angolan citizens deprived of means and victims of disease, or in situations of forced unemployment, or of old age or infirmity.

Solution for unemployment. Work security for artisans, workers, functionaries and for youths who complete their studies.

Assistance to all citizens who are disabled because of active participation in combat for the independence of Angola. Assistance to families whose members died for the liberation of the Angolan nation.

8. Development of Instruction, Culture and Education: Prohibition of colonial and imperialistic culture and education. Reform of instruction in actual practice. Development of instruction, culture and education in the service of liberty and of peaceful progress of the Angolan people.

   To combat vigorously and rapidly illiteracy throughout the country. Public instruction will become the obligation of the State and will be under its direction.

   To progressively establish compulsory and free primary education. To develop secondary technical-professional schools and to establish higher education.

   Establishment of cultural relations with foreign countries. Formation and perfection of technical units necessary to the building up of the nation. To give impetus to the study of the sciences, technology, letters and arts.

   To institute in rural areas efficient and adequate medical and sanitary aid for rural populations. Equal development on a national scale of medical and sanitary assistance.

   Elimination of prostitution and alcoholism.

   Stimulation and support of progressive youth activities. To support and protect, throughout the country, physical culture.

9. National Defense: Establishment of an army for national defense, with sufficient power, intimately linked with the people and commanded wholly by Angolan citizens.

   To arm, equip and unqualifiedly train an army. To install and unify new military and political instruction for the army. To establish democratic relations between officers and enlisted men. To consolidate discipline. Within the army to develop and create a national conscience, and to combat all regional tendencies.

   Prohibition of foreign military bases on the national territory.

10. Independent and Peaceful Foreign Relations: To establish and maintain diplomatic relations with all the countries of the world on the basis of the following principles: mutual respect of national sovereignty and territorial integrity; nonaggression;

noninterference in internal matters; equal and reciprocal advantages; peaceful coexistence.

Respect for the Charter of the United Nations.

Nonalignment to whatever military bloc.

Special relations with our good neighbors and collaboration with the surrounding nations of Angola.

Protection of Angolan residents in foreign countries.

29

White Supremacy and African Nationalism, 1959[36]

Ndabaningi Sithole

A Methodist minister born in Southern Rhodesia (present-day Zimbabwe), Ndabaningi Sithole (1920–2000) became one of the most important critics of racism in Africa with the publication of his book African Nationalism *(1959). In 1963, Sithole founded the Zimbabwe African National Union (ZANU) party along with Robert Mugabe. Although Rhodesia achieved independence from Britain in 1965, the white minority government of Ian Smith banned the party and its activities. Owing to the state repression of ZANU, between 1964 and 1974 Sithole was imprisoned for his political activities. During this decade of incarceration, a civil war, the so-called Rhodesian Bush War, erupted between the Smith government, the military wing of ZANU, and the military wing of ZANU's rival party, the Zimbabwe African People's Union. The war came to an end after the Lancaster House Agreement, which ended white minority rule and permitted the creation of a multi-racial democracy in the newly renamed state of Zimbabwe Rhodesia. In 1980, the same year that Britain and the United Nations formally recognized Zimbabwe's independence, Sithole's former ally Robert Mugabe defeated him in the presidential elections. Mugabe's government persecuted Sithole, who sought asylum in the United States from 1983 to 1992. After his return to Zimbabwe, in 1997, Sithole was tried and convicted on dubious charges of plotting Mugabe's assassination. Sithole died while in exile in Philadelphia, Pennsylvania.*

In this excerpt from African Nationalism, *Sithole argues that white supremacy rests on the notion of the superiority of white people over people of color. This conception of racial superiority serves to legitimate the domination of Africans. In opposition to racial discrimination, Sithole champions African nationalism, claiming it is the expression of African's rejection of domination.*

36. Ndabaningi Sithole, "White Supremacy and African Nationalism" from *African Nationalism.* Copyright © 1959. Reprinted with permission.

The overall European policy in Africa may be summed up in two words—white supremacy, and this is what the African means when he says, 'White people, from Cape to Cairo, are the same'. That is, they have a mania to rule Africa. This European policy is a great challenge to Africa, and since it is the nature of human existence to respond to challenge, the African peoples, despite their great geographical, linguistical, and ethnical differences, have been united by this challenge to which they are now responding positively and persistently. The law of 'the greater the challenge, the greater the stimulus' is in full operation on the continent of Africa. So long as the challenge remains, it would seem that the African peoples will continue, by every conceivable effort, to devise ways and means of overthrowing white domination without necessarily driving the white man out of Africa. The chances are that the white man, because he is too proud and too greedy to share life on an equal basis with the African, may leave Africa if equality of races becomes an accomplished fact.

If European policy had adopted, right from the beginning, an inclusive rather than an exclusive policy, it seems reasonable to surmise that African nationalism, as it is today, would have been almost unknown. This is pure speculation and we do not pretend to know what would have happened if an inclusive policy had been followed; so that here we shall speak in terms of possibilities rather than of actualities.

On examination, the basic ingredients that go to make up the present African nationalism may be enumerated as the African's desire to participate fully in the central government of the country; his desire for economic justice that recognizes fully the principle of 'equal pay for equal work' regardless of the colour of the skin; his desire to have full political rights in his own country; his dislike of being treated as a stranger in the land of his birth; his dislike of being treated as means for the white man's end; and his dislike of the laws of the country that prescribe for him a permanent position of inferiority as a human being. It is this exclusive policy of white supremacy that has created a deep dissatisfaction among the African peoples. It is this exclusive policy that has brought to the fore the African's consciousness of kind. It seems reasonable to say that the present African nationalism is, paradoxically, the child of white supremacy, the product of an exclusive policy.

The question arises: since this exclusive policy has been largely responsible for the emergence of African nationalism, what European policy would have done a better job? We suggest seriously that an inclusive policy would have done it. By definition an inclusive policy takes in all those who come under its purview, and this is its chief merit since it does not ignore the needs of one section of the population in favour of the other. An exclusive policy, by its very nature, implies a disregard of one section of the people in favour of the other, and this is the real fatal weakness of white supremacy. A government that is orientated towards white supremacy fails miserably to serve the basic interests of a multiracial society. Those whose interests are deliberately ignored become dissatisfied and seek a government that has a truly inclusive view of the affairs of the country.

But even if we accept that an inclusive European policy would have done a much better job than the present exclusive European policy, the very fact that the policy is described as European implies that it is external and foreign, and is exclusive in its actual essence, since Africa is multiracial. An inclusive policy forged in Africa on the anvil of true equal footing of all those races living in Africa, would be, in the main, acceptable to all.

To conclude our survey, we may now say that white supremacy is a stubborn rejection of the African by the white man, and that African nationalism is a reaction to that rejection. The African does not so much resent rejection in foreign countries, but he loathes it in the land of his birth. He wants to feel accepted by his fellow-men as man, and white supremacy is standing in his way, and he is determined to brush it aside. African nationalism is a struggle against white supremacy, and this struggle will continue to go on until white supremacy in Africa has given way to sound common sense—namely, that people, regardless of their colour or race, do not like to be treated as unwanted strangers in the land of their birth. The victory of African nationalism will therefore be the triumph of human personality and dignity.

30

The Struggle for Independence in Mozambique, 1963[37]

Eduardo Mondlane

Eduardo Mondlane (1920–1969) was the son of a tribal chieftain in Portuguese East Africa (modern-day Mozambique). He was educated in Portugal and the United States, receiving his Ph.D. in Anthropology from Northwestern University in 1953. Initially working as a research officer for the United Nations, Mondlane left to pursue an academic career in 1957 as an assistant professor of anthropology at Syracuse University. As a growing number of African states gained independence, Mondlane became increasingly frustrated with the Portuguese refusal to grant its colonies independence. In 1962, Mondlane left the United States for Tanzania, where he helped form and supervise the Mozambican Liberation Front (FRELIMO). From FRELIMO's offices in Dar es Salaam, Mondlane, serving as the group's president, helped secure financial support and training for guerrilla fighters resisting Portuguese rule. He was killed when a bomb, presumably sent by Portuguese intelligence, was set off at the FRELIMO headquarters.

In the following excerpt from a talk given at the Fourth International Conference of the American Society for African Culture at Howard University in 1963, Mondlane discusses the history of Portuguese rule in Mozambique and explains the emergence of FRELIMO, including his personal involvement with the group and attempts to secure international support for Mozambique's independence movement.

Soon after the formation of the Front, a congress was planned for that same year to formulate the main lines of the policy of the new organization

---

37. Eduardo C. Mondlane, "The Struggle for Independence in Mozambique," in *Southern Africa in Transition*, edited by John A. Davis and James K. Baker, published for The American Society for African Culture (New York: Frederick A. Praeger, 1966).

and to elect a group of officers to carry out its work. The congress was to meet in Dar es Salaam and bring together representatives of the various political groups of Mozambique exiled in East Africa and of as many groups within Mozambique as could send delegates.

The congress convened at the end of September and was attended by eighty delegates and more than five hundred observers from Dar es Salaam, Tanga, Lindi, Morogoro, Songea—cities in Tanganyika where there were more than 100,000 Mozambican workers, including thousands of refugees who had recently arrived from Mozambique. There were also observers from Zanzibar, where more than 30,000 Mozambicans work in the shipping industry and on clover farms and plantations. From Mombasa came several people representing a Mozambican community of more than 20,000 dock workers; a few people came from the Rhodesias and Nyasaland. In sum, the first congress of our party was a representative one.

The FRELIMO Congress examined carefully the current situation in Mozambique and recommended a program for the Central Committee to carry out during the year. During the discussions, the following points were noted: 1) that the people of Mozambique were still under the subjection of Portuguese colonialism, characterized by political, economic, social, and cultural oppression; 2) that the Portuguese government in Mozambique suppressed the basic freedoms to which modern man is entitled; 3) that the Portuguese government failed to recognize the primacy of the interests of Mozambicans, and that it opposed the right of the people to determine their own destinies, continuing to insist upon labeling Mozambique as an "overseas province"; and 4) that Portugal, instead of seeking a peaceful solution to the conflict between her people and the people of Mozambique, continued to use fascist methods of repression, reinforcing the military and police apparatus by the dispatch of military contingents, massacring innocent people, and imprisoning and torturing people suspected of nationalistic tendencies. (I might add that the latest statistics indicate that there are approximately 30,000 Portuguese soldiers, well equipped with NATO arms, in Mozambique.)

The Congress noted that the reforms that Portugal had recently promulgated were within the framework of the same colonialist spirit that has always typified Portuguese action and were, therefore, unacceptable. It stated that the people of Mozambique were forced to seek effective methods of self-defense and called up all Mozambican patriots to unite under FRELIMO's banner to fight for the independence of their country. It also called attention to the existence of an alliance among the racist powers of Portugal, South Africa, and the so-called Central African Federation, aided by a multifarious system of economic interests financed in London and New York, and urged all freedom-loving peoples of the world to condemn and act in such a way as to frustrate the inhuman activities of these forces.

The Congress of FRELIMO declared its determination to promote the efficient organization of the struggle of the Mozambican people for national liberation and adopted the following program for the Central Committee: 1) to develop and consolidate the organizational structure of FRELIMO; 2) to develop unity among Mozambicans; 3) to utilize the energies and capabilities of each member of FRELIMO to the fullest; 4) to promote and accelerate the training of cadres; 5) to use every effort to achieve freedom in Mozambique; 6) to develop literacy programs for Mozambican people, creating schools whenever possible; 7) to encourage and support the formation and consolidation of trade unions and students' and women's organizations; 8) to encourage cooperation with nationalist organizations of Angola, Guinea, and Cape Verde; 9) to promote the social and cultural development of Mozambican women; 10) to procure all means of self-defense and prepare the people for every eventuality; 11) to appeal for financial support from organizations that sympathize with the cause of the people of Mozambique; 12) to establish permanent centers of information and propaganda in all parts of the world; and 13) to seek diplomatic, moral, and material help for the cause of freedom in Mozambique, especially from the already independent states of Africa, and from all peace and freedom-loving countries of the world.

It would be unwise for me to indicate what we are doing to implement those resolutions which had to do with direct action within Mozambique. There are, however, two direct areas of recommended action—diplomatic action and education—that can be outlined publicly. Since the formation of FRELIMO, diplomatic contacts have been intensified in all parts of the world. We have made certain that our point of view is well understood by those committees of the United Nations which are directly responsible for gathering information on Portuguese colonies. As soon as the meetings of the Congress ended, I flew back to New York to petition the Fourth Committee of the General Assembly (which was discussing Mozambique) to consider our territory. We also intensified our contacts with international conferences in Africa, Asia, and the Americas. At the annual conference of PAFMECSA,[38] which met in Leopoldville, Vice-President Simango of FRELIMO presented a petition on our behalf. We sent a team of five members of the Central Committee to the Moshi conference of the Afro-Asian Solidarity Council to present our case. In the United States, I attended the first American Negro Leadership Conference on Africa, where I presented a background paper on conditions in Mozambique. Our university students in Europe and North America are united in an organization called União Nacional dos Estudantes de Moçambique, which cooperates with FRELIMO in informing people outside of Africa of our case against Portuguese colonialism. We hope that through this knowledge the representatives of the peace-loving peoples of the world will be able to take the proper steps to convince Portugal of the stupidity of her position.

In response to the instructions of the Congress to regard the education of the Mozambican people as a priority matter, the Central Committee has begun a crash program on three levels: university, secondary school, and mass literacy. We have requested scholarships from most of the independent countries of the world for Mozambicans who have had enough education to attend schools above the secondary level. We have also appealed to the United Nations to help us in this respect. As a result, we have received scholarship offers from many countries in Eastern Europe, North and South America, Western Europe, and Asia, and have sent students to the United States, where facilities for both training and transportation have been liberally given by governmental and private bodies; to France, where training, especially in medicine, is being given to several Mozambicans; and to Italy, where Mozambicans are studying law and economics. We have also sent some students to the Soviet Union. Because we have more scholarships offered to us than we can use, we are making plans to develop a crash secondary-school program in Mozambique to prepare students for university entrance. We have already asked private groups in the United States and elsewhere for funds to coordinate the efforts of those educational organizations which are now trying to help us with training facilities. In addition, we would like to prepare literacy programs to reach the millions of our people who are not able to read and write, for we believe that without a literate populace our efforts for a stable, progressive, and peaceful Mozambique

38.   Pan-African Freedom Movement of East, Central, and South Africa.

cannot succeed. We appeal, therefore, to all those who believe in the effectiveness of these programs to give us whatever help they can afford.

Our struggle against Portuguese colonialism is a formidable one. We will do everything we can to hasten the demise of colonialism in Mozambique, even if it means giving up our own lives. For some time we believed that the people of the world were committed to morality and the rule of law, but as we went forth to present our case to the United Nations, to governments within each country, and to the press of the world, we began to realize that interests other than morality and the merits of our case to be more important. For example, we know that the United States and her NATO allies are the paramount sources of military and economic power for Portugal. When we presented the facts at our disposal to the people of the United States, they seemed to fall on deaf ears. Even the press lacked interest in reporting on our plight. Instead, the American people are being fed propaganda through high-powered public-relations firms receiving money from Portugal and through various Anglo-American interests. But the people of Mozambique will appeal to all those who believe in freedom for their help in this struggle against Portuguese colonialism. Our people will not rest until they have gained their independence.

31

I Am Prepared to Die, 1964[39]

Nelson Mandela

Nelson Mandela (1918–2013) was a South African anti-apartheid leader and former president of South Africa (1994–1999). He was a member of the Xhosa ethnic group. Mandela trained as a lawyer at the University of Witwatersrand, where in 1944 he became involved with the African National Congress (ANC). Mandela founded the African National Congress Youth League (ANCYL) that year, initially following the ANC's ideals of peaceful non-compliance and protest. However, in 1960, the South African government banned the ANC. State violence and apartheid policies escalated. The implementation of Pass Laws, designed to segregate and restrict the movement of South Africa's non-white population, and the Sharpeville Massacre, when police fired upon 5,000–7,000 anti–Pass Laws protestors and killed 69, disenchanted many members of the ANC with its traditionally nonviolent stance. In response, Mandela co-founded a military organization of the ANC known as the Umkhonto we Sizwe (MK), or "Spear of the Nation." The founding of Umkhonto led to a deep rift within the ANC between advocates of nonviolence and defenders of violent action. It pitted younger ANC members against established leaders like Albert Luthuli (see Document 24).

In 1961, Mandela defied the Pass Laws by traveling throughout Africa to garner support, where he addressed political leaders and received guerilla warfare training. Upon his return to South Africa, Mandela was arrested in 1962 and sentenced to five years imprisonment. Shortly thereafter police arrested the majority of Umkhonto leadership and between 1963 and 1964 tried Umkhonto's leaders with 221 counts of sabotage for attempting to overthrow the apartheid system, known as the Rivonia Trial. Mandela delivered the speech

39. Nelson Mandela, excerpt from "I Am Prepared to Die" (Statement from the dock at the opening of the defence case in the Rivonia Trial Pretoria Supreme Court, 20 April 1964), from *In His Own Words* by Nelson Mandela. Copyright © 2003 by the Nelson Mandela Foundation. Used by permission of Little, Brown and Company.

*excerpted here at the opening of his defense case on April 20, 1964.
In it he defends Umkhonto's means of violent anti-apartheid protest,
arguing that the national government denied the ANC avenues for
peaceful protest. Mandela also discusses the tremendous disparity in
social standing between whites and non-whites in South Africa. Mandela spent 27 years in prison, much of it in the prison at Robben
Island, before he was released—and the ANC legalized—in 1990.
Mandela was awarded the Nobel Peace Prize in 1993.*

I have already mentioned that I was one of the persons who helped to
form Umkhonto. I, and the others who started the organization, did
so for two reasons. Firstly, we believed that as a result of Government
policy, violence by the African people had become inevitable, and that
unless responsible leadership was given to canalize and control the feelings of our people, there would be outbreaks of terrorism which would
produce an intensity of bitterness and hostility between the various races
of this country which is not produced even by war. Secondly, we felt that
without violence there would be no way open to the African people to
succeed in their struggle against the principle of white supremacy. All
lawful modes of expressing opposition to this principle had been closed
by legislation, and we were placed in a position in which we had either
to accept a permanent state of inferiority, or to defy the Government.
We chose to defy the law. We first broke the law in a way which avoided
any recourse to violence; when this form was legislated against, and then
the Government resorted to a show of force to crush opposition to its
policies, only then did we decide to answer violence with violence.

But the violence which we chose to adopt was not terrorism. We
who formed Umkhonto were all members of the African National Congress, and had behind us the ANC tradition of non-violence and negotiation as a means of solving political disputes. We believe that South
Africa belongs to all the people who live in it, and not to one group, be
it black or white. We did not want an interracial war, and tried to avoid
it to the last minute.

In 1960 there was the shooting at Sharpeville, which resulted in
the proclamation of a state of emergency and the declaration of the
ANC as an unlawful organization. My colleagues and I, after careful
consideration, decided that we would not obey this decree. The African
people were not part of the Government and did not make the laws by

which they were governed. We believed in the words of the Universal Declaration of Human Rights, that 'the will of the people shall be the basis of authority of the Government', and for us to accept the banning was equivalent to accepting the silencing of the Africans for all time. The ANC refused to dissolve, but instead went underground. We believed it was our duty to preserve this organization which had been built up with almost fifty years of unremitting toil. I have no doubt that no self-respecting White political organization would disband itself if declared illegal by a government in which it had no say.

In 1960 the Government held a referendum which led to the establishment of the Republic. Africans, who constituted approximately 70 per cent of the population of South Africa, were not entitled to vote, and were not even consulted about the proposed constitutional change. All of us were apprehensive of our future under the proposed White Republic, and a resolution was taken to hold an All-In African Conference to call for a National Convention, and to organize mass demonstrations on the eve of the unwanted Republic, if the Government failed to call the Convention. The conference was attended by Africans of various political persuasions. I was the Secretary of the conference and undertook to be responsible for organizing the national stay-at-home which was subsequently called to coincide with the declaration of the Republic. As all strikes by Africans are illegal, the person organizing such a strike must avoid arrest. I was chosen to be this person, and consequently I had to leave my home and family and my practice and go into hiding to avoid arrest.

The stay-at-home, in accordance with ANC policy, was to be a peaceful demonstration. Careful instructions were given to organizers and members to avoid any recourse to violence. The Government's answer was to introduce new and harsher laws, to mobilize its armed forces, and to send Saracens, armed vehicles, and soldiers into the townships in a massive show of force designed to intimidate the people. This was an indication that the Government had decided to rule by force alone, and this decision was a milestone on the road to Umkhonto.

Some of this may appear irrelevant to this trial. In fact, I believe none of it is irrelevant because it will, I hope, enable the Court to appreciate the attitude eventually adopted by the various persons and bodies concerned in the National Liberation Movement. When I went to jail in 1962, the dominant idea was that loss of life should be avoided. I now know that this was still so in 1963.

I must return to June 1961. What were we, the leaders of our people, to do? Were we to give in to the show of force and the implied threat against future action, or were we to fight it and, if so, how?

We had no doubt that we had to continue the fight. Anything else would have been abject surrender. Our problem was not whether to fight, but was how to continue the fight. We of the ANC had always stood for a non-racial democracy, and we shrank from any action which might drive the races further apart than they already were. But the hard facts were that fifty years of non-violence had brought the African people nothing but more and more repressive legislation, and fewer and fewer rights. It may not be easy for this Court to understand, but it is a fact that for a long time the people had been talking of violence—of the day when they would fight the White man and win back their country—and we, the leaders of the ANC, had nevertheless always prevailed upon them to avoid violence and to pursue peaceful methods. When some of us discussed this in May and June of 1961, it could not be denied that our policy to achieve a non-racial State by non-violence had achieved nothing, and that our followers were beginning to lose confidence in this policy and were developing disturbing ideas of terrorism.

It must not be forgotten that by this time violence had, in fact, become a feature of the South African political scene. There had been violence in 1957 when the women of Zeerust were ordered to carry passes; there was violence in 1958 with the enforcement of cattle culling in Sekhukhuniland; there was violence in 1959 when the people of Cato Manor protested against pass raids; there was violence in 1960 when the Government attempted to impose Bantu Authorities in Pondoland. Thirty-nine Africans died in these disturbances. In 1961 there had been riots in Warmbaths, and all this time the Transkei had been a seething mass of unrest. Each disturbance pointed clearly to the inevitable growth among Africans of the belief that violence was the only way out—it showed that a Government which uses force to maintain its rule teaches the oppressed to use force to oppose it. Already small groups had arisen in the urban areas and were spontaneously making plans for violent forms of political struggle. There now arose a danger that these groups would adopt terrorism against Africans, as well as Whites, if not properly directed. Particularly disturbing was the type of violence engendered in places such as Zeerust, Sekhukhuniland, and Pondoland amongst Africans. It was increasingly taking the form, not of struggle against the Government—though this is what prompted it—but of civil strife amongst themselves, conducted in such a way that it could not hope to achieve anything other than a loss of life and bitterness.

At the beginning of June 1961, after a long and anxious assessment of the South African situation, I, and some colleagues, came to the conclusion that as violence in this country was inevitable, it would be unrealistic and wrong for African leaders to continue preaching peace and non-violence at a time when the Government met our peaceful demands with force.

This conclusion was not easily arrived at. It was only when all else had failed, when all channels of peaceful protest had been barred to us, that the decision was made to embark on violent forms of political struggle, and to form Umkhonto we Sizwe. We did so not because we desired such a course, but solely because the Government had left us with no other choice.

Our fight is against real, and not imaginary, hardships or, to use the language of the State Prosecutor, 'so-called hardships'. Basically, we fight against two features which are the hallmarks of African life in South Africa and which are entrenched by legislation which we seek to have repealed. These features are poverty and lack of human dignity, and we do not need communists or so-called 'agitators' to teach us about these things.

South Africa is the richest country in Africa, and could be one of the richest countries in the world. But it is a land of extremes and remarkable contrasts. The whites enjoy what may well be the highest standard of living in the world, whilst Africans live in poverty and misery. Forty per cent of the Africans live in hopelessly overcrowded and, in some cases, drought-stricken Reserves, where soil erosion and the overworking of the soil makes it impossible for them to live properly off the land. Thirty per cent are labourers, labour tenants, and squatters on white farms and work and live under conditions similar to those of the serfs of the Middle Ages. The other 30 per cent live in towns where they have developed economic and social habits which bring them closer in many respects to white standards. Yet most Africans, even in this group, are impoverished by low incomes and high cost of living.

. . . .

Poverty goes hand in hand with malnutrition and disease. The incidence of malnutrition and deficiency diseases is very high amongst Africans.

Tuberculosis, pellagra, kwashiorkor, gastro-enteritis, and scurvy bring death and destruction of health. The incidence of infant mortality is one of the highest in the world. According to the Medical Officer of Health for Pretoria, tuberculosis kills 40 people a day (almost all Africans), and in 1961 there were 58,491 new cases reported. These diseases not only destroy the vital organs of the body, but they result in retarded mental conditions and lack of initiative, and reduce powers of concentration. The secondary results of such conditions affect the whole community and the standard of work performed by African labourers.

The complaint of Africans, however, is not only that they are poor and the whites are rich, but that the laws which are made by the whites are designed to preserve this situation. There are two ways to break out of poverty. The first is by formal education, and the second is by the worker acquiring a greater skill at his work and thus higher wages. As far as Africans are concerned, both these avenues of advancement are deliberately curtailed by legislation.

The present Government has always sought to hamper Africans in their search for education. One of their early acts, after coming into power, was to stop subsidies for African school feeding. Many African children who attended schools depended on this supplement to their diet. This was a cruel act.

There is compulsory education for all white children at virtually no cost to their parents, be they rich or poor. Similar facilities are not provided for the African children, though there are some who receive such assistance. African children, however, generally have to pay more for their schooling than whites. According to figures quoted by the South African Institute of Race Relations in its 1963 journal, approximately 40 per cent of African children in the age group between seven to fourteen do not attend school. For those who do attend school, the standards are vastly different from those afforded to white children. In 1960–1961 the per capita Government spending on African students at State-aided schools was estimated at R12.46. In the same years, the per capita spending on white children in the Cape Province (which are the only figures available to me) was R144.57. Although there are no figures available to me, it can be stated, without doubt, that the white children on whom R144.57 per head was being spent all came from wealthier homes than African children on whom R12.46 per head was being spent.

The quality of education is also different. According to the Bantu Educational Journal, only 5,660 African children in the whole of South Africa passed their Junior Certificate in 1962, and in that year only 362 passed matric. This is presumably consistent with the policy of Bantu education about which the present Prime Minister said, during the debate on the Bantu Education Bill in 1953:

"When I have control of Native education I will reform it so that Natives will be taught from childhood to realize that equality with Europeans is not for them. . . . People who believe in equality are not desirable teachers for Natives. When my Department controls Native education it will know for what class of higher education a Native is fitted, and whether he will have a chance in life to use his knowledge."

The other main obstacle to the economic advancement of the African is the industrial colour-bar under which all the better jobs of industry are reserved for Whites only. Moreover, Africans who do obtain employment in the unskilled and semi-skilled occupations which are open to them are not allowed to form trade unions which have recognition under the Industrial Conciliation Act. This means that strikes of African workers are illegal, and that they are denied the right of collective bargaining which is permitted to the better-paid White workers. The discrimination in the policy of successive South African Governments towards African workers is demonstrated by the so-called 'civilized labour policy' under which sheltered, unskilled Government jobs are found for those white workers who cannot make the grade in industry, at wages which far exceed the earnings of the average African employee in industry.

The Government often answers its critics by saying that Africans in South Africa are economically better off than the inhabitants of the other countries in Africa. I do not know whether this statement is true and doubt whether any comparison can be made without having regard to the cost-of-living index in such countries. But even if it is true, as far as the African people are concerned it is irrelevant. Our complaint is not that we are poor by comparison with people in other countries, but that we are poor by comparison with the white people in our own country, and that we are prevented by legislation from altering this imbalance.

The lack of human dignity experienced by Africans is the direct result of the policy of white supremacy. White supremacy implies black inferiority. Legislation designed to preserve white supremacy entrenches this notion. Menial tasks in South Africa are invariably performed by

Africans. When anything has to be carried or cleaned the white man will look around for an African to do it for him, whether the African is employed by him or not. Because of this sort of attitude, whites tend to regard Africans as a separate breed. They do not look upon them as people with families of their own; they do not realize that they have emotions—that they fall in love like white people do; that they want to be with their wives and children like white people want to be with theirs; that they want to earn enough money to support their families properly, to feed and clothe them and send them to school. And what 'house-boy' or 'garden-boy' or labourer can ever hope to do this?

Pass Laws, which to the Africans are among the most hated bits of legislation in South Africa, render any African liable to police surveillance at any time. I doubt whether there is a single African male in South Africa who has not at some stage had a brush with the police over his pass. Hundreds and thousands of Africans are thrown into jail each year under Pass Laws. Even worse than this is the fact that Pass Laws keep husband and wife apart and lead to the breakdown of family life.

Poverty and the breakdown of family life have secondary effects. Children wander about the streets of the townships because they have no schools to go to, or no money to enable them to go to school, or no parents at home to see that they go to school, because both parents (if there be two) have to work to keep the family alive. This leads to a breakdown in moral standards, to an alarming rise in illegitimacy, and to growing violence which erupts not only politically, but everywhere. Life in the townships is dangerous. There is not a day that goes by without somebody being stabbed or assaulted. And violence is carried out of the townships in the white living areas. People are afraid to walk alone in the streets after dark. Housebreakings and robberies are increasing, despite the fact that the death sentence can now be imposed for such offences. Death sentences cannot cure the festering sore.

Africans want to be paid a living wage. Africans want to perform work which they are capable of doing, and not work which the Government declares them to be capable of. Africans want to be allowed to live where they obtain work, and not be endorsed out of an area because they were not born there. Africans want to be allowed to own land in places where they work, and not to be obliged to live in rented houses which they can never call their own. Africans want to be part of the general population, and not confined to living in their own ghettoes. African men want to have their wives and children to live with them where they work, and not be forced into an unnatural existence in men's hostels. African women want to be with their menfolk and not be left permanently widowed in the Reserves. Africans want to be allowed out after eleven o'clock at night and not to be confined to their rooms like little children. Africans want to be allowed to travel in their own country and to seek work where they want to and not where the Labour Bureau tells them to. Africans want a just share in the whole of South Africa; they want security and a stake in society.

Above all, we want equal political rights, because without them our disabilities will be permanent. I know this sounds revolutionary to the whites in this country, because the majority of voters will be Africans. This makes the white man fear democracy.

But this fear cannot be allowed to stand in the way of the only solution which will guarantee racial harmony and freedom for all. It is not true that the enfranchisement of all will result in racial domination. Political division, based on colour, is entirely artificial and, when it disappears, so will the domination of one colour group by another. The ANC has spent half a century fighting against racialism. When it triumphs it will not change that policy.

This then is what the ANC is fighting. Their struggle is a truly national one. It is a struggle of the African people, inspired by their own suffering and their own experience. It is a struggle for the right to live.

During my lifetime I have dedicated myself to this struggle of the African people. I have fought against white domination, and I have fought against black domination. I have cherished the ideal of a democratic and free society in which all persons live together in harmony and with equal opportunities. It is an ideal which I hope to live for and to achieve. But if needs be, it is an ideal for which I am prepared to die.

32

Announcement of Unilateral Declaration of Independence, 1965[40]

Ian Smith

As more former European colonies throughout the world gained independence, the white settler population of the British colony of Southern Rhodesia (modern-day Zimbabwe) feared that independence would bring about the end of white minority rule. In comparison to other British colonies in Africa, Southern Rhodesia, since 1923 a self-governing colony, had a relatively large white settler community. On November 11, 1965, Southern Rhodesia's prime minister, Ian Smith (1919–2007), declared the country's unilateral independence. Until 1979, the white minority controlled the state and the government of Rhodesia, renamed following the declaration of independence in 1965. Initially, Smith sought international recognition of the state as an autonomous realm within the British Commonwealth. However, it was not until 1979 that both Britain and the wider international community formally recognized the Rhodesian state. Until this point, the country's rule was contested in a violent civil war fought between Smith's white minority government, the ZANU, and the ZAPU (for more information see Document 29 and the introduction on Ndabaningi Sithole). In 1978, Smith agreed to allow for the creation of a bi-racial democracy and, in 1979, the Republic of Zimbabwe was founded with Robert Mugabe as its first president. Smith, who remained active in the Zimbabwean parliament, became one of Mugabe's most vocal critics.

Together, this and the next selection, Document 33, pertain to the Unilateral Declaration of Independence of Rhodesia. Here, Smith frames the Declaration as a rejection of Britain's withdrawal from Africa

40. Ian Smith, "Announcement of Unilateral Declaration of Independence" (November 11, 1965), Modern History Sourcebook: Rhodesia: Unilateral Declaration of Independence Documents, 1965, from the *East Africa and Rhodesia Newspaper*, November 18, 1965, pp. 204–5: http://www.fordham.edu/halsall/mod/1965Rhodesia-UDI.html#Ian%20Smith (accessed October 5, 2016).

and as a defense against the radicalizing political climate on the continent. See Document 33 for British Prime Minister Harold Wilson's (1916–1995) condemnation of the Declaration. The Smith Declaration and the debate that it incited reveals the contested notions of African independence. In this case, claims of independence were invoked not by an indigenous African population. Rather, a white settler community, many of whom had resided permanently in Southern Rhodesia since the late nineteenth century, sought to abolish colonial ties.

Now I would like to say a few words to you. Today, now that the final stalemate in negotiations has become evident, the end of the road has been reached.

It has become abundantly clear that it is the policy of the British Government to play us along with no real intention of arriving at a solution which we could possibly accept. Indeed, in the latest verbal and confidential message delivered to me last night we find that on the main principle which is in dispute the two Governments have moved further apart.

I promised the people of this country that I would continue to negotiate to the bitter end and that I would leave no stone unturned in my endeavours to secure an honourable and mutually accepted settlement.

It now falls to me to tell you that negotiations have come to an end. No one could deny that we have striven with might and main and at times bent over backwards to bridge the gap which divides us from the British Government.

. . . Let no one believe that this action today marks a radical departure from the principles by which we have lived, or be under any misconception that now the Constitution will be torn up and that the protection of the rights of all peoples which are enshrined in that Constitution will be abrogated and disregarded.

Neither let it be thought that this event marks a diminution in the opportunities which our African people have to advance and prosper in Rhodesia. Far from this being the case, it is our intention, in consultation with the chiefs, to bring them into the Government and administration as the acknowledged leaders of the African people on a basis acceptable to them.

It is our firm intention to abide by the Constitution. Indeed, we have never asked for anything other than independence on the basis of the present Constitution, and only such amendments are included as are necessary to adapt it to that of an independent country.

With regard to the position of Members of Parliament, judges, civil servants, and members of the armed forces, as well as the police, provision has been made for all of them to carry on their duties, and all are deemed to have complied with the requirements of the New Constitution. They will continue to carry on their normal work. All present laws shall continue to operate and the courts will enforce them in the normal manner.

We are doing no more than assuming the right which various British Ministers have in the past indicated were ours. And in fact this Constitution was the one which would carry us to independence.

Let no one be persuaded that this action marks a change in our attitude towards our neighbours in Africa, to whom we have ceaselessly extended the hand of friendship and to whom we have nothing but goodwill and the best of intentions.

We have never sought, nor will we ever seek, to interfere or in any way attempt to influence their policy and their internal affairs. All we ask in return is their goodwill in permitting us to look after what are, after all, our own private and domestic matters. . . .

There can be no solution to our racial problems while African nationalists believe that, provided they stirred up sufficient trouble, they will be able to blackmail the British Government into bringing about a miracle on their behalf by handing the country over to irresponsible rule.

There will be no happiness in this country, while the absurd situation continues to exist where people such as ourselves, who have ruled ourselves with an impressive record for over 40 years, are denied what is freely granted to other countries, who have ruled themselves in some cases for no longer than a year.

There can never be long-term prosperity, which is so necessary for the nurturing of our endeavours to improve the standard of living and increase the happiness and better the lot of all our people, whilst the present uncertainty exists.

No businessman could ever seriously contemplate massive long-term investment in a country in which chaos and confusion will always be future possibilities.

Whatever the short-term economic disadvantages may be, in the long term steady economic progress could never be achieved unless we are masters in our own house. . . .

That some economic retributions will be visited upon us there is no doubt. Those who seek to damage us do not have any great concern for the principles to which they endlessly pay lip service; for if they really believed in these principles, which they ceaselessly proclaim, then they could not possibly deny the many disasters which have been brought about by the premature withdrawal of European influence from countries in Africa and Asia who were nowhere near ready for it.

There is no doubt that the talk of threats and sanctions is no more than appeasement to the United Nations, the Afro-Asian bloc, and certain members of the Commonwealth; and undoubtedly some action will be taken.

But I cannot conceive of a rational world uniting in an endeavour to destroy the economy of this country, knowing, as they undoubtedly do, that in many cases the hardest hit will be the very people on whose behalf they would like to believe they are invoking these sanctions. We for our part will never do anything in the nature of taking revenge on any neighbouring African State for what other countries may do to us. . . .

We may be a small country, but we are a determined people who have been called upon to play a role of world-wide significance.

We Rhodesians have rejected the doctrinaire philosophy of appeasement and surrender. The decision which we have taken today is a refusal by Rhodesians to sell their birthright. And, even if we were to surrender, does anyone believe that Rhodesia would be the last target of the Communists in the Afro-Asian block?

We have struck a blow for the preservation of justice, civilization, and Christianity; and in the spirit of this belief we have this day assumed our sovereign independence. God bless you all.

33

The Position of the British Government on the Unilateral Declaration of Independence by Rhodesia, 1965[41]

Prime Minister Harold Wilson

On November 11, 1965, British Prime Minister Harold Wilson (1916–1995) gave the following speech in British Parliament, articulating the position of the British government on the Unilateral Declaration of Independence by Rhodesia (see Document 32). Wilson condemns the Declaration, arguing that it is an illegal act that should not be formally recognized by the British government. Wilson responded to the Declaration by attempting to economically isolate the new state and the United Nations Security Council imposed sanctions on Rhodesia until 1979 (see the introduction to Document 32 for more information).

I repeat that the British Government condemn the purported declaration of Independence by the former Government of Rhodesia as an illegal act and one which is ineffective in law. It is an act of rebellion against the Crown and against the Constitution as by law established, and actions taken to give effect to it will be treasonable. The Governor, in pursuance of the authority vested in him by Her Majesty The Queen, has today informed the Prime Minister and other Ministers of the Rhodesian Government that they cease to hold office. They are now private persons and can exercise no legal authority in Rhodesia.

The British Government wish to make it clear that it is the duty of all British subjects in Rhodesia, including all citizens of Rhodesia, to remain loyal to The Queen and to the law of the land, and to recognise

41. Harold Wilson, excerpt from "Position of the British Government on the Unilateral Declaration of Independence by Rhodesia" (speech in Parliament, November 11, 1965). As found in Hansard, *Parliamentary Debates, House of Commons*, Official Report, 5th Series, Vol. 720 (H.M.S.O., 1966), columns 349–56. Used by permission.

the continuing authority and responsibility for Rhodesia of the Government of the United Kingdom.

The British Government are in close touch with all other Commonwealth Governments about the consequences of this illegal act and about the measures we should take. The British Government will, of course, have no dealings with the rebel régime. The British High Commissioner is being withdrawn and the Southern Rhodesian High Commissioner in London has been asked to leave. Export of arms, including spares, have, of course, been stopped. All British aid will cease. Rhodesia has been removed from the sterling area. Special exchange control restrictions will be applied. Exports of United Kingdom capital to Rhodesia will not be allowed. Rhodesia will no longer be allowed access to the London capital market.

Our Export Credits Guarantee Department will give no further cover for exports to Rhodesia. The Ottawa Agreement of 1932 which governs our trading relations with Rhodesia is suspended. Rhodesia will be suspended forthwith from the Commonwealth Preference Area and her goods will no longer receive preferential treatment on entering the United Kingdom. There will be a ban on further purchases of tobacco from Southern Rhodesia. We propose to suspend the Commonwealth Sugar Agreement in its relation to Rhodesia and to ban further purchases of Rhodesian sugar. We shall not recognise passports issued or renewed by the illegal Southern Rhodesian regime. . . .

It is the duty of everyone owing allegiance to the Crown in Rhodesia or elsewhere to refrain from all acts which would assist the illegal régime to continue in their rebellion against the Crown. Members of the armed forces and the police in Southern Rhodesia should refrain from taking up arms in support of the illegal régime, and from doing anything which will help them to pursue their unlawful courses. Public servants in Rhodesia should not do any work for the illegal régime which would tend to further the success of the rebellion. It is the duty of all private citizens owing allegiance to the Crown, wherever they may be, in Rhodesia or outside, to refrain from acts which will give support to the illegal regime. . . .

But I cannot end this statement about a problem with which my right hon. Friend the Secretary of State and other colleagues and myself have been so intimately concerned for so long without expressing the deep sense of tragedy which each of us feels—personal tragedy, but not only personal tragedy'. It is a tragedy affecting a great people, including many thousands who have made their homes there and who are plunged into a maelstrom not of their own making, and of millions more who are denied the inalienable human right of self-expression and self-determination.

Heaven knows what crimes will be committed against the concept of the rule of law and of human freedom for which this House has always stood: this progressive unfolding of the regulations which have been signed under the state of emergency—and there are more to come—are an ominous warning.

The illegal regime which now claims power and authority in Rhodesia marked its usurpation of authority—with a proclamation which borrowed for the purposes of small and frightened men the words of one of the historic documents of human freedom, even to the point of appropriating the historic reference to "a respect for the opinions of mankind."

34

The Weapon of Theory, 1966[42]

Amilcar Cabral

Amilcar Cabral (1924–1973) was a prominent nationalist and political leader, born in Portuguese Guinea (modern-day Guinea-Bissau). As a student in Lisbon, Cabral became active in the independence movements of African nations under Portuguese domination. In 1956, he founded the African Party for the Independence of Guinea and Cape Verde (PAIGC) and helped found the People's Movement for the Liberation of Angola (MPLA) (for more on the MPLA see Document 28). From 1963 until his assassination in 1973, Cabral led the PAIGC's guerrilla operations against the Portuguese army. "The Weapon of Theory" was a speech Cabral delivered to the First Solidarity Conference of the Peoples of Africa, Asia, and Latin America on January 6, 1966, in Havana, Cuba. The following excerpt from the speech reflects the influence of Marxism on Cabral's thought. Cabral explains that national liberation promises to free the productive forces of the nation from imperialist exploitation. He also argues that national liberation necessitates the use of violence to combat the violence of the imperialist system.

We are not going to use this platform to vilify imperialism. There is an African proverb very common in our country—where fire is still an important tool and a treacherous friend—this shows the state of underdevelopment in which colonialism is going to leave—this proverb goes: "When your hut is burning, it is no use beating the tom-tom." In a Tricontinental dimension, this means that we are not going to succeed in eliminating imperialism by shouting or by slinging insults, spoken or written. For us, the worst or best we can say about imperialism, whatever its form, is to take up arms and struggle. That is what we are doing

42. Amilcar Cabral, "The Weapon of Theory" (address delivered to the first Tricontinental Conference of the Peoples of Asia, Africa and Latin America, Havana, January, 1966), from *Unity and Struggle: Speeches and Writings of Amilcar Cabral*. Reprinted with the permission of Monthly Review Foundation.

and will go on doing until foreign domination has been totally elimi-
nated from our African countries.

. . . .

Our agenda includes topics whose importance and acuteness are beyond
doubt and in which one concern is predominant: *The Struggle*. We note,
however, that one type of struggle we regard as fundamental is not
explicitly mentioned in this agenda, although we are sure that it was
present in the minds of those who drew it up. We are referring to *the
struggle against our own weaknesses*. We admit that other cases may differ
from ours. Our experience in the broad framework of the daily struggle
we wage has shown us that, whatever difficulties the enemy may create, the aforenamed is the most difficult struggle for the present and
the future of our peoples. This struggle is the expression of the internal
contradictions in the economic, social and cultural (therefore historical)
reality of each of our countries. We are convinced that any national or
social revolution which not founded on adequate knowledge of this reality runs grave risks of poor results or of being doomed to failure.

Absence of Ideology

When the African people say, in their plain language, that "no matter how hot the water from your well, it will not cook your rice," they
express with singular simplicity a basic principle, not only of physics but
also of political science. We know in fact that the unfolding behaviour
(development) of a phenomenon-in-motion, whatever its external con-
ditioning, depends mainly on its internal characteristics. We also know
that on the political level—however fine and attractive the reality of others may be—we can only truly transform our own reality, on the basis of
detailed knowledge of it and our own efforts and sacrifices.

It is worth recalling in this Tricontinental gathering, so rich in
experiences and examples, that however great the similarity between our
cases and however identical our enemies, unfortunately and fortunately,
national liberation and social revolution are not exportable commodities. They are (and increasingly so every day) a local, national, product—
more or less influenced by (favourable or unfavourable) external factors
but essentially determined and conditioned by the historical reality of
each people. Victory is only achieved by the adequate resolution of the

various internal contradictions characterizing this reality. The success of the Cuban Revolution, taking place only ninety miles from the biggest imperialist and anti-socialist power of all time, seems to us, in the form and content of its evolution, to be a practical and conclusive illustration of the validity of this principle.

We must however recognize that we ourselves and the other liberation movements in general (we are referring here above all to the African experience) have not been able to pay sufficient attention to this significant question of our common struggle.

The ideological deficiency, not to say the total lack of ideology, on the part of the national liberation movements—which is basically explained by ignorance of the historical reality which these movements aspire to transform—constitutes one of the greatest weaknesses, if not the greatest weakness, of our struggle against imperialism. We nevertheless believe that a sufficient number of varied experiences have already been accumulated to enable us to define a general line of thought and action in order to eliminate this deficiency. A full discussion of this matter could therefore be useful, and would enable this Conference to make a valuable contribution towards improving the present and future action of the national liberation movements. This would be a practical way of helping these movements, and, in our opinion, no less important than political support or assistance with money, weapons and other material.

It is with the intention of contributing, although modestly, to this discussion, that we present here our view on *presuppositions and objectives of national liberation in relation to the social structure.* This view is shaped by our own experience of struggle and of a critical appreciation of the experiences of others. To those who see in this view as being theoretical, we would recall that every practice gives birth to a theory. If it is true that a revolution can fail, even though it be based on perfectly conceived theories, nobody has yet made successfully practised Revolution without a revolutionary theory.

. . . .

Imperialism

The political report drawn up by the International Preparatory Committee of this Conference, for which reaffirm our complete support, placed imperialism, clearly and by succinct analysis, in its economic context and historical position. We will not repeat here what has already been said before this assembly. We shall merely say that imperialism may be defined as the worldwide expression of the profit motive and the ever-increasing accumulation of *surplus values* by monopoly financial capital, in two regions of the world: first in Europe and, later, in North America. And if we wish to place the fact of imperialism within the general direction of the evolution of the epoch-making factor that has changed the face of the world—capital and the process of accumulation—we might say that imperialism is piracy transplanted from the seas to dry land, piracy reorganised, consolidated and adapted to the aim of plundering the natural and human resources of our peoples. But if we can calmly analyse the phenomenon of imperialism, we shall not shock anybody if we have to admit that imperialism, which everything goes to show is really the last stage in the evolution of capitalism was a historical necessity, a consequence of the development of productive forces and the transformations of the mode production, in the general context of mankind, considered as a dynamic whole. This is a necessity like those today of the national liberation of peoples, the destruction of capitalism and the advent of socialism.

. . . .

On the question of the effects of imperialist domination on the social structure and the historical process of our peoples, we should first of all examine the general forms of imperialist domination. There are at least two forms:

1. Direct domination—by means of a political power made up of agents foreign to the dominated people (armed forces, police, administrative agents and settlers)—which is conventionally called *classical colonialism* or *colonialism*.

2. Indirect domination—by means of a political power made up mainly or completely of native agents—which is conventionally called *neo-colonialism*.

In the first case, the social structure of the dominated people, at whatever stage they are, can suffer the following experiences:

a. Total destruction, generally accompanied by immediate or gradual elimination of the aboriginal population and consequent replacement by an exotic population.

b. Partial destruction, generally accompanied by more or less intensive settlement by an exotic population.

c. Ostensible preservation, brought about by confining the aboriginal society to areas or special reserves generally offering no means of living and accompanied by massive implantation of an exotic population.

The two latter cases, which are those we must consider in the context of the problematic of national liberation, are widely present in Africa. One can say that in either case the main effect by the impact of imperialism on the historical process of the dominated people is paralysis, stagnation (even in some cases, regression) in that process. However, this paralysis is not complete. In one sector or another of the socio-economic whole in question, noticeable transformations may occur, caused by the continuing action of some internal (local) factors, or as a result of the action of new factors introduced by the colonial domination, such as the introduction of money and the development of urban conglomerations. Among these transformations, we should particularly note, in certain cases, the gradual loss of prestige of the native ruling classes or strata, the forced or voluntary exodus of part of the peasant population to the urban centres, with the consequent development of new social strata: salaried workers, employees of the State and in commerce and the liberal professions, and an unstable stratum of workless. In the countryside, there grows up with very varied intensity, and always with ties to the urban milieu, a stratum made up of petty farm-owners. In the case of neocolonialism, whether the majority of the colonized population is aboriginal or of exotic origin, imperialist action in the form of creating a local bourgeoisie or pseudo-bourgeoisie, in fee to the ruling class of the dominating country.

The transformations in the social structure are not so marked in the lower strata, above all in the countryside, where the structure largely retains the characteristics of the colonial phase, but the creation of a native pseudo-bourgeoisie, which generally develops out of a petty bourgeoisie of bureaucrats and intermediaries in the trading system (compradores), accentuates the differentiation between the social strata. By strengthening the economic activity of the native elements, this opens up new perspectives in the social dynamic, notably by the gradual development of an urbanized working class and the introduction of private agricultural property, which slowly gives rise to the appearance of an agricultural proletariat. These more or less noticeable transformations of the social structure, determined by a significant rise in the level of productive forces, have a direct influence on the historical process of the socio-economic whole in question. While in classical colonialism this process is paralysed, neocolonialist domination, by allowing the social dynamic to be awakened—conflicts of interest between the native social strata or class struggle—creates the illusion that the historical process is returning to its normal evolution. This illusion is reinforced by the existence of a political power (national State), composed of native elements. It is only an illusion, since in reality the subjection of the native "ruling" class to ruling class of the dominating country limits or holds back the full development of the national productive forces. But in the specific conditions of the present-day world economy, this subjection is an inevitability, and thus the native pseudo-bourgeoisie, however strongly nationalist, cannot fulfill the historical function that would fall to this class: it cannot *freely* guide the development of productive forces, in short it cannot be a *national bourgeoisie*. For, as we have seen, the productive forces are the motive force of history, and total freedom of the process of their development is an indispensible condition for their full functioning.

We see, therefore, that both in colonialism and in neocolonialism the essential characteristic of imperialist domination remains the same—denial of the historical process of the dominated people, by means of violent usurpation of the freedom of the process of development of the national productive forces. This observation, which identifies the essence of the two apparent forms of imperialist domination, seems to us to be of primordial importance for the thought and action of national liberation movements.

On the basis of the foregoing, we can state that national liberation is the phenomenon in which a socio-economic whole rejects the denial of its historical process. In other words, the national liberation of a people is the regaining of the historical personality of that people, it is their return to history through the destruction of the imperialist domination to which they were subjection.

Now we have seen that the principal and permanent characteristic of imperialist domination, whatever its form, is the usurpation by violence of the freedom of the process of development of the dominated socio-economic whole. We have also seen that this freedom, and it alone, can guarantee the normal course of the historical process of a people. We can therefore conclude that national liberation exists when, and only when, the national productive forces have been completely freed from all and any kind of domination.

. . . .

The Role of Violence

The facts make it unnecessary for us to waste words proving that the essential instrument of imperialist domination is violence. If we accept the principle that *the national liberation struggle is a revolution*, and that it is not over at the moment when the flag is hoisted and the national anthem is played, we shall find that there is and there can be no national liberation without the use of liberating violence, on the part of the national forces, in answer to the criminal violence of the agents of imperialism. Nobody can doubt that imperialist domination, whatever its local characteristics, implies a state of permanent violence against the nationalist forces. There is no people in the world which, after being subjected to the imperialist yoke (colonialist or neocolonialist), has gained independence (nominal or effective) without victims. The important thing is to decide what forms of violence have to be used by the national liberation forces, in order not only to answer the violence of imperialism but also to ensure, through the struggle, the final victory of their cause, that is true national independence.

The past and recent experience of various peoples; the present situation of national liberation struggle in the world (especially the cases of Vietnam, Congo, and Zimbabwe); as well as the very situation of permanent violence, or at least contradictions and upheavals, in certain countries which have gained independence by the so-called peaceful way show us not only that compromises with imperialism are counter-productive, but also that the normal road of national liberation, imposed on peoples by imperialist repression, is *armed struggle*.

35

Freedom for Namibia, 1968[43]

Andimba Toivo ya Toivo

In 1920 the League of Nations placed the former German colony of Namibia under South African rule. The country became subject to the apartheid system instated in South Africa in 1948 with the election of the National Party (NP) to government. In 1957, the Ovambo-land People's Congress (OPC) was founded to campaign for Namibia's independence and the end of white minority rule. The OPC, renamed the South West African People's Organization (SWAPO) in 1960, engaged in a guerrilla war against the South African government from 1966 to 1989. The war endured despite the fact that the United Nations recognized SWAPO as the legitimate representative of Namibia in 1972. After seventy years of South African rule, Namibia at last achieved independence in 1990.

One of the founders of the OPC, Andimba Toivo ya Toivo (born in 1924) was a leader of the Namibian independence movement and prominent statesman. For his involvement with OPC and later SWAPO, Toivo was imprisoned on Robben Island in South Africa along with others suspected of undermining the NP and the white minority government of South Africa. Toivo's speech at his 1968 trial for his advocacy of Namibian independence is excerpted here. In it, Toivo cites the independence of other former colonies as a precedent for Namibia's independence from South Africa. He explains that the Namibian people had always viewed South Africa's rule of Namibia as illegitimate.

A Court can only do justice in political cases if it understands the position of those that it has in front of it. The State has not only wanted to convict us, but also to justify the policy of the South African government. We will not even try to present the other side of the picture,

43. Andimba Toivo ya Toivo, "Freedom for Namibia," in *The Africa Reader: Independent Africa*, edited by Wilfred Cartey and Martin Kilson (New York: Vintage Books, 1970).

because we know that a Court that has not suffered in the same way as we have, cannot understand us. This is perhaps why it is said that one should be tried by one's equals. We have felt from the very time of our arrest that we were not being tried by our equals but by our masters, and that those who have brought us to trial very often do not even do us the courtesy of calling us by our surnames. Had we been tried by our equals, it would not have been necessary to have any discussion about our grievances. They would have been known to those set to judge us.

It suits the government of South Africa to say that it is ruling South West Africa with the consent of its people. This is not true. Our organization, S.W.A.P.O., is the largest political organization in South West Africa. We consider ourselves a political party. We know that whites do not think of blacks as politicians—only as agitators. Many of our people, through no fault of their own, have had no education at all. This does not mean that they do not know what they want. A man does not have to be formally educated to know that he wants to live with his family where he wants to live, and not where an official chooses to tell him to live; to move about freely and not require a pass; to earn a decent wage; to be free to work for the person of his choice for as long as he wants; and finally, to be ruled by the people that he wants to be ruled by, and not those who rule him because they have more guns than he has.

Our grievances are called "so-called" grievances. We do not believe South Africa is in South West Africa in order to provide facilities and work for non-whites. It is there for its own selfish reasons. For the first forty years it did practically nothing to fulfill its "sacred trust." It only concerned itself with the welfare of the whites.

Since 1962, because of the pressure from inside by the non-whites and especially my organization, and because of the limelight placed on our country by the world, South Africa has been trying to do a bit more. It rushed the Bantustan Report so that it would at least have something to say at the World Court.

Only one who is not white and has suffered the way we have can say whether our grievances are real or "so-called."

Those of us who have some education, together with our uneducated brethren, have always struggled to get freedom. The idea of our freedom is not liked by South Africa. It has tried in this Court to prove through the mouths of a couple of its paid chiefs and a paid official that S.W.A.P.O. does not represent the people of South West Africa. If the government of South Africa were sure that S.W.A.P.O. did not represent

the innermost feelings of the people in South West Africa, it would not
have taken the trouble to make it impossible for S.W.A.P.O. to advocate
its peaceful Policy.

South African officials want to believe that S.W.A.P.O is an irresponsible organization and that it is an organization that resorts to the
level of telling people not to get vaccinated. As much as white South
Africans may want to believe this, this is not S.W.A.P.O. We sometimes
feel that it is what the government would like S.W.A.P.O. to be. It may
be true that some member or even members of S.W.A.P.O. somewhere
refused to do this. The reason for such refusal is that some people in our
part of the world have lost confidence in the governors of our country
and they are not prepared to accept even the good that they are trying
to do.

Your government, my Lord, undertook a very special responsibility
when it was awarded the mandate over us after the First World War. It
assumed a sacred trust to guide us toward independence and to prepare
us to take our place among the nations of the world. South Africa has
abused that trust because of its belief in racial supremacy (that white
people have been chosen by God to rule the world) and apartheid. We
believe that for fifty years South Africa has failed to promote the development of our people. Where are our trained men? The wealth of our
country has been used to train your people for leadership, and the sacred
duty of preparing the indigenous people to take their place among the
nations of the world has been ignored.

I know of no case in the last twenty years of a parent who did not
want his child to go to school if the facilities were available, but even if,
as it was said, a small percentage of parents wanted their children to look
after cattle, I am sure that South Africa was strong enough to impose its
will on this, as it has done in so many other respects. To us it has always
seemed that our rulers wanted to keep us backward for their benefit.

Nineteen hundred sixty-three for us was to be the year of our freedom. From 1960 it looked as if South Africa could not oppose the world
forever. The world is important to us. In the same way as all laughed in
Court when they heard that an old man tried to bring down a helicopter
with a bow and arrow, we laughed when South Africa said that it would
oppose the world. We knew that the world was divided, but as time
went on it at least agreed that South Africa had no right to rule us.

I do not claim that it is easy for men of different races to live at
peace with one another. I myself had no experience of this in my youth,

and at first it surprised me that men of different races could live together in peace. But now I know it to be true and to be something for which we must strive. The South African government creates hostility by separating people and emphasizing their differences. We believe that by living together, people will learn to lose their fear of each other. We also believe that this fear which some of the whites have of Africans is based on their desire to be superior and privileged, and that when whites see themselves as part of South West Africa, sharing with us all its hopes and troubles, then that fear will disappear. Separation is said to be a natural process. But why, then, is it imposed by force and why then is it that whites have the superiority?

Head-men are used to oppress us. This is not the first time that foreigners have tried to rule indirectly—we know that only those who are prepared to do what their masters tell them become head-men. Most of those who had some feeling for their people and who wanted independence have been intimidated into accepting the policy from above. Their guns and sticks are used to make people say they support them.

I have come to know that our people cannot expect progress as a gift from anyone, be it the United Nations or South Africa. Progress is something we shall have to struggle and work for. And I believe that the only way in which we shall be able and fit to secure that progress is to learn from our own experience and mistakes.

Your Lordship emphasized in your judgment the fact that our arms came from communist countries, and also that words commonly used by communists were to be found in our documents. But my Lord, in the documents produced by the State there is another type of language. It appears even more often than the former. Many documents finish up with an appeal to the Almighty to guide us in our struggle for freedom. It is the wish of the South African government that we should be discredited in the Western world. That is why it calls our struggle a communist plot; but this will not be believed by the world. The world knows that we are not interested in ideologies. We feel that the world as a whole has a special responsibility towards us. This is because the land of our fathers was handed over to South Africa by a world body. It is a divided world, but it is a matter of hope for us that it at least agrees about one thing—that we are entitled to freedom and justice.

Other mandated territories have received their freedom. The judgment of the World Court was a bitter disappointment to us. We felt betrayed and we believed that South Africa would never fulfill its trust.

Some felt that we would secure our freedom only by fighting for it. We knew that the power of South Africa is overwhelming, but we also knew that our case is a just one and our situation intolerable—why should we not also receive our freedom?

We are sure that the world's efforts to help us in our plight will continue, whatever South Africans may call us.

That is why we claim independence for South West Africa. We do not expect that independence will end our troubles, but we do believe that our people are entitled—as are all peoples—to rule themselves. It is not really a question of whether South Africa treats us well or badly, but that South West Africa is our country and we wish to be our own masters.

There are some who will say that they are sympathetic with our aims, but that they condemn violence. I would answer that I am not by nature a man of violence and I believe that violence is a sin against God and my fellow men. S.W.A.P.O. itself was a nonviolent organization, but the South African government is not truly interested in whether opposition is violent or nonviolent. It does not wish to hear any opposition to apartheid. Since 1963, S.W.A.P.O. meetings have been banned. It is true that it is the Tribal Authorities who have done so, but they work with the South African government, which has never lifted a finger in favor of political freedom. We have found ourselves voteless in our own country and deprived of the right to meet and state our own political opinions.

Is it surprising that in such times my countrymen have taken up arms? Violence is truly fearsome, but who would not defend his property and himself against a robber? And we believe that South Africa has robbed us of our country.

36

The Ahiara Declaration, 1969[44]

Chukwuemeka Odumegwu Ojukwu

On May 30, 1967, the southeastern region of Nigeria seceded to form the Republic of Biafra, intensifying the ethnic and religious conflicts that had beset Nigeria's government in the seven years since the country's independence from Britain. Biafra seceded after Christian Igbos, the predominant ethnic group of the southeastern region, were massacred in the Hausa- and Fulani-dominated North. The massacres took place in response to the 1966 coup d'état against the Nigerian government. Several Igbo officers had been involved with the coup and blame for the coup was directed at the Igbo population. After peace negotiations with the Nigerian government failed, Colonel Chukwuemeka Odumegwu Ojukwu (1933–2011), military governor of the southeastern region, proclaimed the independence of the Republic of Biafra from Nigeria, inciting a war between supporters of the Biafran state and forces loyal to a unified Nigerian state. The Nigerian-Biafran War ended on January 15, 1970, when Biafran forces agreed to a ceasefire with the Nigerian government, reintegrating the former Republic of Biafra into the Nigerian state.

In the following document, selected from a speech given on June 1, 1969 in the southeastern town of Ahiara on the occasion of the second anniversary of Biafran independence, Ojukwu explains the motivations behind the secession of Biafra. He directs his criticisms against Nigeria and calls on Biafrans to reject a Nigerian national identity. The text illustrates the multifaceted interpretations of African independence. Although independence during the 1960's wave of decolonization frequently concerned the liberation of African nations from European oppression, the meaning of independence and national belonging continued to be contested among Africans within newly independent states.

44.   Chukwuemeka Odumegwu Ojukwu, *Ahiara Declaration: The Principles of the Biafran Revolution*, edited by Obi Harrison Ekwonna (Glenn Dale, MD: Rising Star Publications, 2003).

RE-DISCOVERING INDEPENDENCE

From the moment we assumed the illustrious name of the ancient kingdom of Biafra, we were re-discovering the original independence of a great African people. We accepted by this revolutionary act the glory, as well as the sacrifice of true independence and freedom. We knew that we had challenged the many forces and interests which had conspired to keep Africa and the Black Race in subjection forever. We knew they were going to be ruthless and implacable in defence of their age-old imposition on us and exploitation of our people. But we were prepared and remain prepared to pay any price for our freedom and dignity.

And in this we were not mistaken. Five weeks after we had proclaimed our independence[,] Nigeria, goaded by her foreign masters, declared war on us.

For two years now we have fought a difficult war in defence of our Fatherland. From the beginning we have never been in doubt about our ultimate victory. But, seeing the odds ranged against us, the world did not believe that we had any chance of success whatever the merit of our case. Perhaps our determination and persistence are making the world think again. Biafra today is no longer a lost cause. For us, Biafra's eventual triumph has never been in doubt: Biafra has always been the shining light at the end of our dark tunnel. In the two years of our grim struggle, we have learned important lessons about ourselves, about our society and about the world. In some ways this struggle has been a journey in self-discovery and self-realisation.

Our Revolution is a historic opportunity given to us to establish a just society; to revive the dignity of our people at home and the dignity of the Black-man in the world. We realise that in order to achieve those ends we must remove those weaknesses in our institutions and organisations and those disabilities in foreign relations which have tended to degrade this dignity. This means that we must reject Nigerianism in all its guises.

THE PEOPLE

Fellow countrymen, are we going to say no to Nigerianism and then let a few unpatriotic people among us soil our Revolution with the stain of Nigeria? Are we going to watch the very disease which caused the demise of Nigeria take root in our new Biafra? Are we prepared to embark on another revolution perhaps more bloody to put right the inevitable disaster? I ask you, my countrymen, can we afford another spell of strife when this one is over to correct social inequalities in our Fatherland? I say NO. A thousand times no. The ordinary Biafran says no. When I speak of the ordinary Biafran I speak of the People. The Biafran Revolution is the People's Revolution. Who are the People? you ask. The farmer, the trader, the clerk, the business man, the housewife, the student, the civil servant, the soldier, you and I are the people. Is there anyone here who is not of the people? Is there anyone here afraid of the People—anyone suspicious of the People? Is there anyone despising the People? Such a man has no place in our Revolution. If he is a leader, he has no right to leadership because all power, all sovereignty, belongs to the People. In Biafra the People are supreme; the People are master; the leader is servant. You see, you make a mistake when you greet me with shouts of "Power, Power." I am not power—you are. My name is Emeka. I am your servant, that is all.

SHAKING OFF NIGERIANISM

Fellow countrymen, we pride ourselves on our honesty. Let us admit to ourselves that when we left Nigeria, some of us did not shake off every particle of Nigerianism. We say that Nigerians are corrupt and take bribes, but here in our country we have among us some members of the Police and the Judiciary who are corrupt and who "eat" bribe. We accuse Nigerians of inordinate love of money, ostentatious living and irresponsibility, but here, even while we are engaged in a war of national survival, even while the very life of our nation hangs in the balance, we see some public servants who throw huge parties to entertain their friends; who kill cows to christen their babies. We have members of the Armed Forces who carry on "attack" trade instead of fighting the enemy. We have traders who hoard essential goods and inflate prices thereby increasing the people's hardship. We have "money-mongers" who aspire to build hundreds of plots on land as yet unreclaimed from the enemy; who plan to buy scores of lorries and buses and to become agents for those very foreign businessmen who have brought their country to grief. We have some civil servants who think of themselves as masters rather than servants of the people. We see doctors who stay idle in their villages while their countrymen and women suffer and die. When we see all these things, they remind us that not every Biafran has yet absorbed the spirit of the Revolution. They tell us that we still have among us a member of people whose attitudes and outlooks are Nigerian. It is clear that if our Revolution is to succeed, we must reclaim these wayward Biafrans. We must Biafranize them. We must prepare all our people for the glorious roles which await them in the Revolution. If after we shall have tried to reclaim them and have failed then they must be swept aside. The people's revolution must stride ahead and like a battering ram, clearing all obstacles in its path. Fortunately, a vast majority of Biafrans are prepared for these roles.

When we think of our Revolution, therefore, we think about these things. We think about our ancient heritage, we think about the challenge of today and the promise of the future. We think about the changes which are taking place at this very moment in our personal lives and in our society. We see Biafrans from different parts of the country living together, working together, suffering together and pursuing together a common cause. We see our doctors, scientists, engineers and technologists responding to the demands of the Revolution with brilliant inventions and innovations. We see our Armed Forces with their severely limited resources holding back an aggressor who is massively equipped by the neo-imperialist enemies of African freedom. We see men of learning and mass information spreading with patriotic zeal the true story and significance of the Biafran struggle. We see our farmers determined to win the war against starvation imposed on us by the enemy. We see our ordinary men and women—the people—pursuing, in their different but essential ways, the great task of our national survival. We see every sign that this struggle is purifying and elevating the masses of our people. Every day of the struggle bears witness to actions by our countrymen and women which reveal high ideals of patriotic courage, service and sacrifice; actions which show the will and determination of our people to remain free and independent but also to create a new and better order of society for the benefit of all.

In the last five or six months, I have devised one additional way of learning at first hand how the ordinary men and women of our country see the Revolution. I have established a practice of meeting every Wednesday with a different cross-section of our people to discuss the problems of the Revolution. These meetings have brought home to me the great desire for change among the generality of our people. I have heard a number of criticisms and complaints by people against certain things; I have also noticed groups forming themselves and trying to put right some of the ills of society. All this indicates both that there is a change in progress and a need for more change. Thus, the Biafran Revolution is not dreamt up by an elite; it is the will of the People. The People want it. They are fighting and dying to defend it. Their immediate concern is to defeat the Nigerian aggressor and so safeguard the Biafran Revolution.

PART FOUR: CONSOLIDATING INDEPENDENCE

Introduction

Following independence, Africans living in newly independent nation-states began the process of state-building. Creating functioning states rested not only on transferring governing institutions into African hands, but also on overcoming legacies of economic dependence, social inequality, and uneven development. With the impulse for imperial reform after the Second World War, colonial powers had intensified development strategies and targeted the modernization of both colonial administrations and economies. This redoubled effort was uneven in its implementation and outcome, disrupting traditional ways of life and the organization of family labor. African nationalists thus inherited states that were in some places oriented toward an industrial economy, and in other places agrarian. The inadequacy of and disruption caused by colonial development schemes proved a powerful rallying point for anti-colonial activism. However, following independence, African leaders themselves appropriated the language of development. They continued to invoke it, speaking in terms of the needs of Africans to undertake development for themselves. Once in power, the heads of state tried to implement ambitious development programs at the levels of the economy, politics, and culture.

In some parts of Africa, structures of colonial governance were maintained and reformed, in other places scrapped altogether. Creating sovereign nations with centralized power sometimes meant disempowering local authorities and breaking down regional and tribal allegiances. Groups seeking political autonomy were often compelled to join the new states. Democracy could also be perceived as an obstacle to development. Heads of state, eager to realize their programs or simply wishing to consolidate their power, confronted competing views and agendas, which, at times, led to the suppression of oppositional political formations. Consequently, authoritarian regimes emerged in some states in the years after independence. Still, newly formed African governments had to forge unified states out of historically, politically, and culturally heterogeneous populations. The new African states were often quite fragile. The colonial system, in ways both deliberate and unintentional, had redrawn historic borders and redefined tribal and ethnic identities, breaking apart historically unified groups, and splintering others. New governments attempted to cultivate new national identities to foster loyalty by framing development as a cooperative process. Africans tried to define the new Africa using familiar historical and cultural idioms by claiming the heritage of pre-colonial African cultures and naming their states after pre-colonial polities.

Against the backdrop of the Cold War, African states entered a global conflict in which it was urgent to choose sides. The political ideologies that Africans embraced, and the countries with whom they sought to forge commercial and political ties, mattered crucially for the Cold War powers, who supplied money, advisors, weapons, and, less frequently, soldiers. They also, often, helped to dictate the kinds of development programs that Africans undertook. The modernization schemes developed in concert with their Western or Soviet allies were often ambitious, and relied on tremendous financial investments in an effort to modernize states quickly. Such programs seemed feasible in the economic climate of the 1960s. However, when the economic crisis of the 1970s wracked the global economy, African states were among the hardest hit. These young and fragile states fell into heavy debt and were forced to relinquish the control and supervision of national economies over to international bodies like the World Bank and the International Monetary Fund. The internationalization of development aid in Africa continues to signify the ways in which foreign states and capital impact the political, social, and natural landscapes of the African continent.

This part focuses on the project of state-building and cultural and political development following independence. It considers the different political ideologies that African leaders advocated and their experiments with different systems of government. It also includes documents pertaining to the ways African thinkers aspired to forge alliances and cooperation among their independent states. Finally, it offers accounts of political suppression by African heads of state, providing insights into the seeds of authoritarian rule.

37

I Speak of Freedom, 1961[45]

Kwame Nkrumah

Kwame Nkrumah (1909–1972) was the first president of Ghana and a major proponent of Pan-Africanism. Nkrumah was heavily influenced by the work of the Afro-Caribbean Marxist intellectuals C. L. R. James and George Padmore (see Document 11). Together with Padmore, Nkrumah helped organize the Fifth Pan-African Congress in 1945 (see Document 9). After Nkrumah's return to the Gold Coast (present-day Ghana), he organized the various trade unions into the Convention People's Party (CPP).

Ghana became an autonomous Commonwealth state in 1957 and, three years later, an independent republic with Nkrumah as president. Nkrumah traveled abroad regularly to promote Pan-African cooperation. However, at home, support for Nkrumah had dwindled. His unpopular policies included banning religious and ethnic parties in 1957; the 1958 Trade Union Act, which banned unions from striking; and the Preventive Detention Act, which he used to arrest and imprison his political opponents. In 1964, Nkrumah proposed a constitutional amendment to make the CPP Ghana's only legal party. While on a state visit to North Vietnam and China in 1966, a military coup overthrew the Nkrumah government. Nkrumah never returned to Ghana.

In the following preface to his book I Speak of Freedom, *Nkrumah outlines his Pan-African political philosophy, stressing that the newly independent African nations remain susceptible to recolonization or foreign intervention. Nkrumah suggests that the U.N. might serve as a tool for Western interests. The only way to preserve the gains of independence and extend them into the creation of strong and prosperous states, Nkrumah asserts, is through strengthening Pan-African unity.*

45. Kwame Nkrumah, excerpt from *I Speak of Freedom*. Copyright © 1961 by Kwame Nkrumah. Reprinted with permission of Panaf Books.

The movement for independence in Africa which gained momentum after the Second World War has spread like a prairie fire throughout the length and breadth of Africa. The clear, ringing call for freedom which the eight independent states of Africa sounded in Accra in April 1958, followed by the All-African Peoples' Conference in December of that year, stirred up the demand for independence from Conakry to Mogadishu, from Fort Lamy to Leopoldville. The 'wind of change' has become a raging hurricane, sweeping away the old colonialist Africa. The year 1960 was Africa's year. In that year alone, seventeen African states emerged as proud and independent sovereign nations. Now the ultimate freedom of the whole of Africa can no more be in doubt.

For centuries, Europeans dominated the African continent. The white man arrogated to himself the right to rule and to be obeyed by the non-white; his mission, he claimed, was to 'civilise' Africa. Under this cloak, the Europeans robbed the continent of vast riches and inflicted unimaginable suffering on the African people.

All this makes a sad story, but now we must be prepared to bury the past with its unpleasant memories and look to the future. All we ask of the former colonial powers is their goodwill and co-operation to remedy past mistakes and injustices and to grant independence to the colonies in Africa.

The new African nations from the very nature of things cannot but be economically weak at the early stages of their nationhood as compared with the older and long-established nations of the world. The long dependence on European and American financial and technical enterprise has prevented the growth of local capital and the requisite technical knowledge to develop their resources. They need economic help, but in seeking outside aid they lay themselves open to a grave new danger which not merely threatens but could even destroy their hard-won freedom.

It is unreasonable to suppose that any foreign power, affluent enough to give aid to an African state, would not expect some measure of consideration or favour from the state receiving the aid. History has shown how one colonial empire in liquidation can easily be replaced by another, more insidious, because it is a disguised form of colonialism. The fate of those territories in Europe and North Africa which once formed the Turkish Empire is a warning to Africa today. It would be a tragedy if the initial weakness of the emergent African nations should lead to a new foreign domination of Africa brought about by economic forces.

It may be argued that the existence of the United Nations Organization offers a guarantee for the independence and the territorial integrity of all states, whether big or small. In actual fact, however, the U.N. is just as reliable an instrument for world order and peace as the Great Powers are prepared to allow it to be. The present division of the world into rival blocs, and the dictates of power politics, offer little hope that this international body will ever become an effective instrument for world peace. Recent events in the Congo have not helped to foster confidence in the U.N. in the face of Great Power interests. Patrice Lumumba, democratically elected Prime Minister of the Congo Republic, who himself invited the U.N. to the Congo, was murdered along with two of his ministers because the U.N. failed in its mission to maintain law and order.

It is clear that we must find an African solution to our problems, and that this can only be found in African unity. Divided we are weak; united, Africa could become one of the greatest forces for good in the world.

Although most Africans are poor, our continent is potentially extremely rich. Our mineral resources, which are being exploited with foreign capital only to enrich foreign investors, range from gold and diamonds to uranium and petroleum. Our forests contain some of the finest woods to be grown anywhere. Our cash crops include cocoa, coffee, rubber, tobacco and cotton. As for power, which is an important factor in any economic development, Africa contains over 40% of the potential water power of the world, as compared with about 10% in Europe and 13% in North America. Yet so far, less than 1% has been developed. This is one of the reasons why we have in Africa the paradox of poverty in the midst of plenty, and scarcity in the midst of abundance.

Never before have a people had within their grasp so great an opportunity for developing a continent endowed with so much wealth. Individually, the independent states of Africa, some of them potentially rich, others poor, can do little for their people. Together, by mutual help, they can achieve much. But the economic development of the continent must be planned and pursued as a whole. A loose confederation designed only for economic co-operation would not provide the necessary unity of purpose. Only a strong political union can bring about full and effective development of our natural resources for the benefit of our people.

The political situation in Africa today is heartening and at the same time disturbing. It is heartening to see so many new flags hoisted in place of the old; it is disturbing to see so many countries of varying sizes and at different levels of development, weak and, in some cases, almost helpless. If this terrible state of fragmentation is allowed to continue it may well be disastrous for us all.

There are at present some 28 states in Africa, excluding the Union of South Africa, and those countries not yet free. No less than nine of these states have a population of less than three million. Can we seriously believe that the colonial powers meant these countries to be independent, viable states? The example of South America, which has as much wealth, if not more than North America, and yet remains weak and dependent on outside interests, is one which every African would do well to study.

Critics of African unity often refer to the wide differences in culture, language and ideas in various parts of Africa. This is true, but the essential fact remains that we are all Africans, and have a common interest in the independence of Africa. The difficulties presented by questions of language, culture and different political systems are not insuperable. If the need for political union is agreed by us all, then the will to create it is born; and where there's a will there's a way.

The present leaders of Africa have already shown a remarkable willingness to consult and seek advice among themselves. Africans have, indeed, begun to think continentally. They realise that they have much in common, both in their past history, in their present problems and in their future hopes. To suggest that the time is not yet ripe for considering a political union of Africa is to evade the facts and ignore realities in Africa today.

The greatest contribution that Africa can make to the peace of the world is to avoid all the dangers inherent in disunity, by creating a political union which will also by its success, stand as an example to a divided world. A Union of African states will project more effectively the African personality. It will command respect from a world that has regard only for size and influence. The scant attention paid to African opposition to the French atomic tests in the Sahara, and the ignominious spectacle of the U.N. in the Congo quibbling about constitutional niceties while the Republic was tottering into anarchy, are evidence of the callous disregard of African Independence by the Great Powers.

We have to prove that greatness is not to be measured in stockpiles of atom bombs. I believe strongly and sincerely that with the deep-rooted wisdom and dignity, the innate respect for human lives, the intense humanity that is our heritage, the African race, united under one federal government, will emerge not as just another world bloc to flaunt its wealth and strength, but as a Great Power whose greatness is indestructible because it is built not on fear, envy and suspicion, nor won at the expense of others, but founded on hope, trust, friendship and directed to the good of all mankind.

The emergence of such a mighty stabilising force in this strife-worn world should be regarded not as the shadowy dream of a visionary, but as a practical proposition, which the peoples of Africa can, and should, translate into reality. There is a tide in the affairs of every people when the moment strikes for political action. Such was the moment in the history of the United States of America when the Founding Fathers saw beyond the petty wranglings of the separate states and created a Union. This is our chance. We must act now. Tomorrow may be too late and the opportunity will have passed, and with it the hope of free Africa's survival.

38

Tensions in African Development, 1961[46]

Tom Mboya

Tom Mboya (1930–1969) became a prominent trade unionist in Kenya, then a British colony, after forming the Kenya Local Government Workers' Union. In 1955, Mboya received a scholarship to study at Oxford University from Britain's Trades Union Congress. In 1957, he formed the People's Congress Party. In 1958, he attended the All-African Peoples' Conference in Ghana and was elected the conference chairman. In 1960, the People's Congress Party was one of the parties to merge to form the Kenya African National Union (KANU). Mboya was one of KANU's prominent members, and he was a rival of Jomo Kenyatta. He served in Kenyatta's government as minister for Economic Planning and Development when he was assassinated in 1969. Suspicions that Kenyatta, a member of the Kikuyu ethnic group, had Mboya, a Luo, killed, led to mass demonstrations when Kenyatta attended Mboya's funeral.

In the following 1961 speech at New College, Oxford, Mboya discusses Africa's underdevelopment in the wake of independence. He advocates both democratic participation in government and emphasizes the role played by voluntary democratic bodies such as trade unions. Further, he calls for a restructuring of the civil service, whose members had previously only received training to serve colonial interests. Both his vision for the formation of unions and the restructuring of the civil service reflect Mboya's early experience as both a trade unionist and civil servant.

Africa is one of the underdeveloped continents of the world. Socially, Africa is underdeveloped in the sense that its tribal components have not yet found a proven basis for collective action. It is still possible for tribal differences to provoke inter-country tension, especially because

46. Tom Mboya, "Tensions in African Development," *The Challenge of Nationhood: A Collection of Speeches and Writings by Tom Mboya* (New York: Praeger, 1970).

the boundaries were drawn up artificially without regard to ethnic groupings. On the basis of tribe alone, the bulk of Africa can wrap itself in all sorts of claims and counter-claims, struggles and convulsions. Whether or not tribalism is going to be a cause of widespread tensions in Africa will depend on the honesty and quality of African leadership.

Further, Africa is socially underdeveloped because there is almost no social and cultural traffic between English- and French-speaking Africa. The culture imposed on us sticks like burrs. English-speaking Africans, formerly subjects of Britain, are most familiar with the etiquette, language, economics, and politics of Great Britain. They constantly listen to the B.B.C. and the local English programmes. They might listen to the Voice of America, Russia, or India if their outlook is wide. But most of them are uninformed when it comes to the events, news, and institutions of the Portuguese or ex-French territory next door. Similarly, the French-speaking Africans, formerly French subjects, know more about France—its politics, economics, literature, and philosophy—than they know about the English-speaking countries surrounding their own. This lack of communication is a definite source of tension in this continent. Education, and teaching of both the French and English languages on both sides, concerted efforts to revive the old cultural links, communication at economic and commercial levels are some of the ways in which these barriers can be broken. Again, these undertakings call for very honest leadership. Trade unions can provide the links to start with, but the extent to which they can be used as links in the chain is dependent on whether they all agree to function with some measure of freedom from their own governments.

Economically, Africa is underdeveloped in the sense that mass poverty is universal. This poverty is not entirely due to poor natural resources, and could be lessened by methods already proved successful in other parts of the world. It is reflected in deficiencies like the shortage of schools, social services, hospitals, universities, and technical institutions. It is further reflected in the number of our women who die in childbirth, the universality of malnutrition, the high incidence of various diseases, low wages, and in the contrast between the wealth of Europe and North America on the one hand, and the poverty prevailing in Africa on the other. The continent as a whole is underdeveloped. Poverty is a threat because our people have already learned that they are entitled to a better life. It is difficult to restrain the surging expectations on the part of our people for more education, more health facilities, higher wages, and all the other conditions of a better life.

A very fertile source of tension exists in the realisation that the colonial powers who have hitherto been responsible for the economic development of Africa have either not done their best in developing the continent or have taken so much out of it as to render the Africans poor. It is not mere propaganda to say that, under colonial rule, economic, human and social development in Africa has been unduly subordinated and subjected to the profit motive. Capital from the metropolitan countries sought profits for the benefit of the owners and their countries. African countries have been developed to supply the demands of the metropolitan economies, and in this process deliberate efforts to combat poverty in Africa were forgotten. Arising from the way our economies have been developed are numerous frictions and tensions which most African leaders have already recognised and are doing their best to minimise. It is a fact, that because of the 'colonial' nature of our economies, a unique economic isolation has been forced on various parts of our continent. Our African currencies, now pegged to the currencies of present or ex-metropolitan countries, are exchanged with a great deal of difficulty. Our transport and communication systems have been designed for political rather than economic convenience. Inter-African trade is hampered by exchange difficulties, transport bottle-necks, and unfair tariffs—all instituted by colonial rule.

Africa is still largely dependent on Europe. This fact is, in itself, another source of tension because dependence is not consistent with our national pride and makes a sham of the independence we are supposed to have won. If one studies the direction of African international trade and balance of trade of the various African countries, one cannot avoid arriving at the conclusion that the present arrangements are inequitable. Better arrangements must be made so that the prices of our primary commodities exported from Africa are in line with the ever-increasing import propensity of the African economies. The economies of African countries are adversely affected by fluctuations in world prices of the commodities they export and these fluctuations have political repercussions. The solution for this kind of problem is partly political and partly economic.

There are other sources of friction in the development of Africa. One of them concerns the relationship between our people and industry. Under colonial rule, some economic structures have emerged in our countries which are not suitable and which must either be changed or considerably modified. I think the system of relations between workers and employers in Africa is one of these. Wage-earning in Africa is already a strongly based institution; there are millions of Africans who have no other means of livelihood. Like other workers, these Africans expect that wage-earning will prove human and gratifying. As workers and citizens they expect the same respect accorded to other citizens. They want to feel that they are an integral part of industry, doing something meaningful and valuable for the country; they want security in employment, and above all they want dignity accorded to their labour. They want to be consulted on all matters which affect them.

It is unfortunate that these very natural expectations are far from realisation in practically all parts of Africa. The main explanation for this sad state of affairs is the fact that the employer–employee relationship, as developed in colonial Africa, has lacked mutual respect and goodwill. First of all, it has been poisoned by racialism, because the bulk of the employers of African labour have been, and even at this time still are, governments which, even after independence, still exercise the colonial vice of regimenting and suppressing workers. Also, most private employers are non-Africans whose relations with their employees are capitalistic. They regard African workers in terms of colonial stereotypes such as 'they are lazy', 'their needs are few', and so on, and consequently pay them very low wages and order them about as in the heyday of colonial rule.

It is true that illiteracy, lack of trained trade union officials, and a narrow base of industrial development are still impeding the growth of strong and independent democratic trade unions to protect the interests of the African working classes. But a start towards improvement has already been made, and tension between the African worker and his employer will assume vital significance unless the whole system of industrial relations is given an immediate democratic and African orientation. The same goes for the whole development we now call 'Africanisation'. We support it because we believe that it is a necessary concomitant to political independence. But if it is attempted without raising the whole base of living of the working masses, then a gambit will be open. There will be a lot of friction between the African substitutes for colonial administrators (who will be in a new ivory tower) and the working people (whose lot will not have changed). This situation would be dynamite. Unless the rate of developing skills and of capital formation is accelerated, Africanisation, though good and logical, will be a source of tension. In this, as in other respects, the search for the capital and the know-how for the promotion of quick economic and social development is a very important consideration.

In connexion with this problem of capital and skill shortage, I would like to point out an aspect which I regard as very serious. This is the lack of education. This deficiency is actually the main source of tension in Africa. Because of the lack of trained men and women, even independent African countries have to depend on outside experts to help them run the countries. We then have a situation in which the ministers are Africans but the technicians are Russians, Poles, or Yugoslavs in country A; French, Swedes, and Americans in country B; British, Canadian, and American in country C; American, British, Swiss, Yugoslav, and Russian in country D. This is a bad situation: first, because it helps to perpetuate the political and economic Balkanisation of Africa; second, because it increases the cost of development projects, since the foreign staff employed have to be paid the high salaries they are used to in their own countries; and lastly, because it increases the dangers of neo-colonialism.

Following independence—or even before—all African countries are faced with the problem of what kind of political structure to adopt in order to ensure internal peace, order, and continuity of economic activities. The leaders must establish and maintain order to enable the government to promote economic and social development. The responsibility for virtually all types of development becomes the concern of the government; for the indigenous people are poor and they still lack business and commercial skill. On its part, government finds itself with many projects in hand, but without capital or technical know-how to sustain development. Added to these difficulties is the fact of the autocratic background of colonial rule dressed up in institutions such as the judiciary, civil service, municipalities, police, etc.—all copied from the metropolitan country but put to very little democratic use all along.

Will democracy survive in Africa? To those who think that democracy will survive only if the colonial institutions are preserved, I have this to say: 'You will be disappointed'. To those willing to understand the difficulties we face in fulfilling the aims of African nationalism outlined above, viz., increasing the wealth and power of our countries to enable us to preserve the freedom and dignity of every individual citizen, I would say that the whole aim must be fulfilled simultaneously.

The problem of deciding what constitutes democracy and what institutions are best for its realisation can be a mere academic exercise. What is necessary is that force must be minimised and persuasion substituted for it as a tool of governmental action. A government sometimes needs unusual powers to implement some decisions, and it must be recognised that the use of this kind of power will be much more frequent in the emerging countries, with unproven foreign institutions grafted on, than in the politically and economically stable countries, with numerous conventions or generally accepted codes of political conduct.

There are two other internal factors I consider necessary to democracy: free association of all the people of the country with the control and the functioning of the government at all levels; and the existence of various democratic voluntary bodies, such as free trade unions, cultural and professional associations, and a large body of people with independent thinking and outlook to help influence the activities of those in power. Whether there will be two or more political parties is not a *sine qua non* of democracy. External structures and institutions must be judged by their effects on the people. The challenge we face in Africa will lead to the emergence of new political institutions, and some of the colonial political structures will either be discarded deliberately or will die a natural death. But the good or suitable ones will remain. In bending these institutions to the services of the peoples they have hitherto been by-passing, there will be necessary modifications all over. Even the judiciary will have to be modified. The administration of the civil service will also have to undergo a complete metamorphosis.

I envisage a complete revolution in the structure and functioning of the civil service of a country like Kenya when it is shorn of European domination and the 'colonial mentality'. The vital question here is, what will be the relations between the civil servants and the politicians? This is not a difficult thing. So far, our civil service has served the colonial purposes of preserving order—to enable the colonial governments to collect taxes and to enable colonial capital investments to pay dividends. For the advancement of independent African countries, the purposes of the civil service must range far wider. They will be expected to work for order and security of the person and property of everybody; they will be expected to deal justly with everybody. They will be expected to work under and to carry out much more extensive and egalitarian economic and social policies, unlike those of the colonial regime. Colonial administration hardly trains for this kind of work; there is always tension in the civil service in the transitional period following independence. The civil service must assume its independence of politicians and political parties, for this is the only way to ensure its continuity.

Colonial administrations have a habit of exercising the policy of 'divide and rule', even if this is not in the long-term interests of the country under its jurisdiction. They recruit police from specified tribes, certain grades of labour from others, clerks from elsewhere. This makes the civil service unrepresentative and provides the basis for tribal conflict. Allied to this is the question of the imbalance in the economic and social development in the various regions of colonial Africa. This fact is a source of very serious tension.

I have said a lot about tensions in the development of Africa and about changing relations between African countries and the former or present colonial powers. What of the future relationship? What I have to say on this matter is not new; it has been said again and again by African leaders and others. Our relations with former metropolitan powers must be reviewed, and new relations both economic and political must be based on genuine equality. We all agree that this is the next step. And let this equality be carried to its logical conclusion. If we are equal, only help us where we need help; stop being paternalistic. We need a continuing flow of technical, specialist, financial, and other types of aid. We will take it from you, and from any other nations ready to offer aid with no strings attached. Do not grumble when we take it. We take it because we need it, and we take it because it is given free. Remember, we are also capable of gauging the ulterior motives of all those who offer to help us. This ability is not the monopoly of the rich and developed people alone. We need technical and financial aid, both private and public. Improved relations with former metropolitan countries can be achieved if existing inequitable economic relations are put on new levels of equality; if on both sides every effort is made to heal the scars of colonial association; if our associations with ex-metropolitan countries such as the Commonwealth, Common Market, etc., are shorn of the difficulties involved in the economic and political relations between the African countries. There is a lot we can do to get along together, I think.

Our relations with the two leading world powers, the United States and the Soviet Union, must be brought under the same reckoning. They have vast wealth; they are squandering millions on nuclear armament to 'protect' us, while they fail to protect us from poverty, ill-health, illiteracy, and our other basic enemies. We have made it clear to them that we shall never accept the role they are trying to devise for us, namely, that of pawns in their power game. No, this we shall never accept. Our internal and external policies will consistently be governed by what is best for our people, for our development and our future.

Lastly, we have the concept of African unity and solidarity and the realisation of the 'African personality'. In the effort to break away from the colonial past, with its artificial divisions, its psychological and economic enslavement, its misrepresentation overseas and within Africa, African nationalism faces the challenge of creating trust, confidence, leadership, and effective regional economic and political cooperation. Neo-colonialism, attempts at Balkanisation, and outright Cold War manoeuvres have to be watched, in addition to the challenge of personal ambitions, tribalism, lack of communication, and certain language difficulties, which must be checked in the interest of a given region, and of Pan-Africanism in general.

39

Decision to Co-operate with Uganda, 1961[47]

Kabaka Mutesa II

Buganda is a traditional kingdom that exists within the modern state of Uganda. In 1894, Buganda became a British protectorate. But Kabaka (King) Mwanga II revolted against British rule in 1897 and was defeated, forcing him to escape to German East Africa where he died. The incoming British commissioner of Uganda and the chiefs of Buganda negotiated a new arrangement. The Buganda Agreement of 1900 secured the chiefs support for the British colonial administration, but it also left the Bugandan system of governance largely intact. Buganda remained a self-governing kingdom, and the royal family of the Kabakas continued their line of succession. This arrangement became complicated during the decolonization process. The impending independence of Uganda called into question the future status of Buganda.

The following statement by Kabaka Mutesa II (1924–1969) is part of a larger dialogue occurring in the late 1950s and early 1960s revolving around the question of Bugandan sovereignty. In it, the Kabaka concedes to negotiations with the incoming Ugandan government, but makes references to the rights of the kingdom that had been recognized by British colonial authorities. Uganda became independent in 1962, and four years later President Milton Obote abolished the kingdom of Buganda. After decades of war in Uganda, the kingdom was reestablished in 1993 with autonomy. This document illustrates the ways in which a kingdom that was largely successful in maintaining its independence during the colonial era was compelled to deal with the new realities brought about by African independence and state-building.

---

47. Kabaka Mutesa II, "Decision to Co-operate with Uganda" (Kabaka Mutesa II to the Lukiiko, September 16, 1961), in *The Mind of Buganda: Documents of the Modern History of an African Kingdom*, edited by D. A. Low (Berkeley: University of California Press, 1971).

With the agreement of the members of the Buganda Constitutional Committee, I have sent Dr Lumu and Mr C. M. S. Mukasa to bring to you my personal message [from London] regarding the progress so far made in the discussions about the kingdom's political future.

As you know, I was invited by Her Majesty's Government to come and discuss matters concerning Buganda's political position, especially at this time when the British protection is about to end. It is for the same reason that the Buganda Constitutional Committee was invited to come and complete the negotiations which had been taking place between the Lukiiko's delegates and Her Majesty's Representative at Entebbe.

With regard to the talks that we have had since we arrived in London, it appears that the Colonial Secretary is up to now unable to conclude any of the outstanding matters; but he has agreed to hold talks with the Buganda Committee, as requested in the Lukiiko Resolution of 29th August, 1961. The Colonial Secretary has, however, assured both the Committee and me that these matters will be finalized. We have accepted that assurance. But the Colonial Secretary on his part wants Buganda's representatives to be part of the Conference in which the representatives of the other parts of Uganda will be taking part and to present our proposals as to our future relationship with the rest of Uganda. That Conference opens on 18th September.

The Representatives of Buganda did, however, make it clear that despite the above assurance, they have no mandate to participate in the Conference unless the Lukiiko, of which they are representatives, has agreed. The Colonial Secretary saw this point and I have accordingly sent the aforesaid messengers to you.

Considering the assurances which the Colonial Secretary has given me and the Committee after detailed and careful discussions and also after examining what may happen in the future, it appears that Buganda's participation in that Conference will not prejudice Buganda's position at all. Therefore, it seems to us to be advisable that the Lukiiko should permit its representatives to take their places in the Conference; this will also enable Buganda to present its case regarding its future relationship with the rest of Uganda.

Part of the understanding (with the Colonial Secretary) is also the assurance that we shall not lose whatever was already agreed with the Queen's Representative at Entebbe and that outstanding matters will soon be finalized. Any conclusions will, of course, be brought and laid before the Lukiiko, as is the usual practice.

Having regard to the Colonial Secretary's assurances as stated above, and the advice that we have received from our (legal) Advisers, the Committee and I consider it desirable that my aforesaid messengers bring the Lukiiko's endorsement when they return!

I send you all my greetings; my subjects that are here also send you their regards and assure you that they are firm and will not relent or falter.

40

Regional Government, 1962[48]

Sir Ahmadu Bello

Sir Ahmadu Bello (1910–1966) was the first premier of the Northern Nigeria Region. The son of an heir to the Sokoto Caliphate, Bello made an unsuccessful bid to become the new Sultan in 1938, but was given the honorary title of Sardauna and joined the Sokoto Native Authority Council. After studying in Britain, Bello returned to Northern Nigeria and became the leader of the Northern People's Congress (NPC). Throughout his career, Bello was a strong advocate of the interests of Northern Nigeria's primarily Muslim population. In 1957, Northern Nigeria became independent of British rule and the NPC became the leading party. In 1960, Nigeria became independent and established a federal government. Bello retained his position as premier of Northern Nigeria. Bello was assassinated during the 1966 coup d'état that helped precipitate the Nigerian Civil War (see Document 36 for more about the secession of Biafra).

In the following excerpt from his autobiography, Bello addresses the issues surrounding the formation of Nigeria's new federal government. While he defends the idea of a central government, he also explains the need for local government. He also engages contentious issues, such as the future of the Emirs and chiefs in regional politics, as well as the controversy over the fact that women had been enfranchised in the rest of Nigeria but not in the North.

. . . [W]e discovered that the old British bickerings were not without reason and that, unless you fought hard, the Regions would certainly be left out and the central government would get away with most of the cake.

That is why we are so keen on our Regional self-government. This is the only guarantee that the country will progress evenly all over,

---

48. Sir Ahmadu Bello, "Regional Government" from *My Life*. Copyright © 1962 by Sir Ahmadu Bello. Reprinted with the permission of Cambridge University Press.

for *we* can spend the money we receive, and the money we raise, in the directions best suited to us. To show what I mean, you have only to consider the former backwardness of our educational and medical provision, compared with that of areas near Lagos. As I have suggested elsewhere, if it had not been for the Native Authorities the North would have been left completely standing in these and other important developments.

Eight years have passed from the last crisis and we see clearly now that Nigeria must stand as one and that, as things are, the existing external boundaries cannot readily be changed—nor can those of the Regions. But that does not necessarily bind us to the present *form* of Government at the Centre. Obviously we cannot be left with a vacuum there; for example, someone must look after foreign affairs, foreign trade, and defence, to name the more important: but who? As things are in the present constitution, the North has half the seats in the House of Representatives. My party might manage to capture these, but it is not very likely for the present to get any others: on the other hand, a sudden grouping of the Eastern and Western parties (with a few members from the North opposed to our party) might take power and so endanger the North.

This would, of course, be utterly disastrous. It might set back our programme of development ruinously: it would therefore force us to take measures to meet the need. What such measures would have to be is outside my reckoning at the moment, but God would provide a way. You can therefore see that the political future must rest on an agreeable give and take between the parties.

So long as all respect the common purpose, all will be well.

And so, what about the future of the Emirs? You will have noticed in this book my insistence on the theme that the old Emirates were originally much more democratic than they were when the British left them, and that we have been doing our best since then to put things back; to ensure that the Chiefs are surrounded by a wide body of suitable councillors, mostly chosen by election, whose advice they must take.

We are also determined that they and their Administrations—and this, of course, applies also to the Conciliar Administrations—must accept the technical advice of the Regional Government and must at all times keep us in touch with the important events in their areas; that means especially anything likely to endanger the peace. Their areas must develop in step, each with each.

The immense prestige of their office is thus harnessed to the machine of modern progress and cannot, I am sure, fail to have a notable effect in bringing the country forward. To remove or endanger this prestige in *any way*, or even to remove any of their traditional trappings, would be to set the country back for years, and indeed, were such changes to be drastic, it might well need another Lugard to pull things together again. We must get away from the idea that they are effete, conservative, and diehard obstructionists: nothing could be farther from the truth. I agree that there are one or two very elderly chiefs who probably do not fully appreciate all that is being done for their territories, but even these have progressive councils and their successors will be men educated and brought up to modern ideas.

I have insisted throughout that we are working on the principles of democracy in this Region. I must here stress the word 'principles'. There are many Europeans who are strongly convinced that the only form of democracy which is democratic is that in use in their own country. We observe that these differ from each other: the USA form is utterly different from that found in Great Britain; the Italian is different from the French, and I understand that it differs within itself from decade to decade. But they all have a common denominator, the vote of the common man: what they vote for may vary from place to place, but in each country they have, from time to time, the (often abused) privilege of casting their vote in favour of a certain man or a certain policy.

We have now established the use throughout this country—so primitive in many ways—of the ballot box. In spite of anxious fears expressed in many quarters, its use has been successful (and in our own last election in this Region, overwhelmingly successful) and that will, I am sure, continue to be the case. The people so elected meet in open parliament and not only discuss the matters laid before them by the Government they have themselves chosen, but are at liberty to put forward their own motions and to raise their own questions, without fear or favour. The Government, on its side, is bound to make clear statements of its proposed policy and to be as convincing as is possible in debate. The opposition is at full liberty to say what it likes about these proposals or to produce alternatives.

The real control, however, over the Government, to my mind, comes from the 'tail' of the party. The Government must carry this tail with it or risk defeat. This is not a unique situation and obtains everywhere. In any group of people you are bound to have different opinions on the same subjects. And the more people you have, the more strongly will such differing opinions be held.

. . . .

In the old days, when the British were the 'government', all parties concentrated on demanding self-government to the exclusion of all else, and had no well-defined policy beyond a general desire for 'development'. Attacking the existing government was the main occupations and it was not particularly difficult and did not demand any real thought. Naturally, when the British withdrew gradually, and the power passed, there was no one to attack and, as we had got self-government, there was nothing more to be said about it. So far no burning question has arisen on which we are likely to take sides strongly.

As things are there is no real reason to think that the Oppositions in the Regions are ever likely to be in a position, in the foreseeable future, to form a Government and this can only be irritating to them. So far there is nothing to indicate any likelihood of a 'landslide' in votes in favour of the Opposition parties, except possibly in the West. This produces, I think, a rather careless attitude of mind and a regrettable tendency to be unrealistic. This does not, of course, apply to the Federation where things are delicately balanced.

We already have a good deal of socialism and a degree of state-ownership—railways, telephones, radio and electricity, and so on—and hospitals and schools are mostly free or very cheap. We might come to a showdown on nationalisation of mines (but the coal mines are already national property and always have been) or on the future of Chiefs. We would resist any interference with the tin mines, for it is a specialised trade and would be expensive for us to run; indeed, it is more than doubtful whether we would get as much profit from nationalised mines as we do, with no effort on our part, from royalties and fees of various kinds. But until something of the sort comes along, I don't think that there is much alternative to the present form of the parties. And so the possibilities of a real Opposition on the Westminster model are rather thin; as I have said, I do not think it matters very much.

We are often taken to task about votes for women. The Eastern and Western Regions have given their women the vote, and during the recent Cameroons plebiscite the United Nations insisted on them registering and voting. I agree that no particular harm has been done, though

I must claim that no outstanding good has come of it. I daresay that we shall introduce it in the end here, but—and this is important—it is so contrary to the customs and feelings of the greater part of the men of this Region that I would be very loath to introduce it myself. The education of women must reach a far greater strength, and the numbers of properly educated women must be increased to many times the present, before the vote would be used to full advantage.

It would, of course, greatly strengthen our position as a party—for all the women would vote in the same direction as their menfolk and thus our support would be more than doubled by a stroke of the pen. But the unrest and trouble that would ensue would, I am convinced, be serious and widespread, and I would not like to have to deal with it in the present circumstances. Most of the men, and certainly all the older ones, would be quite incapable of understanding the need for such revolutionary change.

41

Ujamaa: The Basis of African Socialism, 1962[49]

Julius Nyerere

Julius Nyerere (1922–1999) was the first president of Tanzania (formerly Taganyika) and a founding theoretician of African socialist political philosophy, Ujamaa. As a student in Edinburgh, Nyerere was introduced to British socialist thought and began to work on synthesizing it with what he saw as the traditional African political structures of communal living. On his return to Tanganyika, then a British colony, he joined the nationalist movement and formed the Tanganyika African National Union (TANU). TANU became the most influential party under Nyerere's leadership, both campaigning for independence and promoting the idea of Ujamaa. When Tanganyika became independent in 1961, Nyerere was elected the country's first prime minister. In 1964, the Republic of Tanzania was formed with Nyerere as president. During his presidency, Tanzania became one of the poorest African nations and became reliant on foreign loans. He voluntarily left office in 1985. Before exiting office, Nyerere attempted to guide Tanzania along a socialist path of development and governance. Though other African intellectuals and politicians, such as Kwame Nkrumah, embraced socialism, Nyerere's political philosophy differed by focusing on the strengthening of regional rather than Pan-African or continental unity. The following excerpt from his essay of 1962 provides a fuller account of Nyerere's concept of Ujamaa. He emphasizes that a modern African form of socialism can be derived from the historical tradition of communal living and collective cooperation, the foundation of traditional African societies.

In traditional African society everybody was a worker. There was no other way of earning a living for the community. Even the Elder, who appeared to be enjoying himself without doing any work and for

---

49. Julius Nyerere, "Ujamaa: The Basis of African Socialism" from *Essays on Socialism*. Copyright © 1968 by Julius Nyerere. Reprinted with permission.

whom everybody else appeared to be working, had, in fact, worked hard all his younger days. The wealth he now appeared to possess was not his, personally; it was only 'his' as the elder of the group which had produced it. He was a guardian. The wealth itself gave him neither power nor prestige. The respect paid to him by the young was his because he was older than they, and had served his community longer; and the 'poor' Elder enjoyed as much respect in our community as the 'rich' Elder.

When I say that in traditional African society everybody was a worker, I do not use the word 'worker' simply as opposed to 'employer' but also as opposed to 'loiterer' or 'idler.' One of the most socialistic achievements of our society was the sense of security it gave to its members, and the universal hospitality on which they could rely. But it is too often forgotten, nowadays, that the basis of this great socialistic achievement was this: that it was taken for granted that every member of society—barring only the children and the infirm—contributed his fair share of effort towards the production of its wealth. Not only was the capitalist, or the landed exploiter, unknown to traditional African society, but we did not have that other form of modern parasite—the loiterer, or idler, who accepts the hospitality of society as his 'right' but gives nothing in return! Capitalistic exploitation was impossible. Loitering was an unthinkable disgrace.

Those of us who talk about the African way of life, and, quite rightly, take a pride in maintaining the tradition of hospitality which is so great a part of it, might do well to remember the Swahili saying: '*Mgeni siku mbili; siku ya tatu mpe jembe*'—or, in English, 'Treat your guest as a guest for two days; on the third day give him a hoe!' In actual fact, the guest was likely to ask for the hoe even before his host had to give him one—for he knew what was expected of him, and would have been ashamed to remain idle any longer. Thus, working was part and parcel, was indeed the very basis and justification of his socialist achievement of which we are so justly proud.

There is no such thing as socialism without work. A society which fails to give its individuals the means to work, or having given them the means of work, prevents them from getting a fair share of the products of their own sweat and toil, needs putting right. Similarly, an individual who can work—and is provided by society with the means to work— but does not do so, is equally wrong. He has no right to expect anything from society because he contributes nothing to society.

The other use of the word 'worker,' in its specialized sense of 'employee' as opposed to 'employer,' reflects a capitalistic attitude of mind which was introduced into Africa with the coming of colonialism and is totally foreign to our own way of thinking. In the old days the African had never aspired to the possession of personal wealth for the purpose of dominating any of his fellows. He had never had laborers or 'factory hands' to do his work for him. But then came the foreign capitalists. They were wealthy. They were powerful. And the African naturally started wanting to be wealthy too. There is nothing wrong in our wanting to be wealthy; nor is it a bad thing for us to want to acquire the power which wealth brings with it. But it most certainly is wrong if we want the wealth and the power so that we can dominate somebody else. Unfortunately there are some of us who have already learned to covet wealth for that purpose, and who would like to use the methods which the capitalist uses in acquiring it. That is to say, some of us would like to use, or exploit, our brothers for the purpose of building up our own personal power and prestige. This is completely foreign to us, and it is incompatible with the socialist society we want to build here.

Our first step, therefore, must be to re-educate ourselves; to regain our former attitude of mind. In our traditional African society we were individuals within a community. We took care of the community, and the community took care of us. We neither needed nor wished to exploit our fellow men.

And in rejecting the capitalist attitude of mind which colonialism brought into Africa, we must reject also the capitalist methods which go with it. One of these is the individual ownership of land. To us in Africa land was always recognized as belonging to the community. Each individual within our society had a right to the use of land, because otherwise he could not earn his living and one cannot have the right to life without having the right to some means of maintaining it. But the African's right to land was simply the right to use it: he had no other right to it, nor did it occur to him to try and claim one.

The foreigner introduced a completely different concept, the concept of land as a marketable commodity. According to this system, a person could claim a piece of land as his own private property whether he intended to use it or not. I could take a few square miles of land, call them 'mine,' and then go off to the moon. All I had to do to gain a living from 'my' land was to charge a rent to the people who wanted to use it. If this piece of land was in an urban area I had no need to develop it at all; I could leave it to the fools who were prepared to develop all the other pieces of land surrounding 'my' piece, and in doing so automatically to raise the market value of mine. Then I could come down from the moon and demand that these fools pay me through their noses for the high value of 'my' land; a value which they themselves had created for me while I was enjoying myself on the moon! Such a system is not only foreign to us, it is completely wrong. Landlords, in a society which recognizes individual ownership of land, can be, and usually are, in the same class as the loiterers I was talking about: the class of parasites.

We must not allow the growth of parasites here in Tanganyika. The TANU government must go back to the traditional African custom of land holding. That is to say, a member of society will be entitled to a piece of land on condition that he uses it. Unconditional, or 'freehold,' ownership of land (which leads to speculation and parasitism) must be abolished. We must, as I have said, regain our former attitude of mind—our traditional African socialism—and apply it to the new societies we are building today. TANU has pledged itself to make socialism the basis of its policy in every field. The people of Tanganyika have given us their mandate to carry out that policy, by electing a TANU government to lead them. So the government can be relied upon to introduce only legislation which is in harmony with socialist principles.

But, as I said at the beginning, true socialism is an attitude of mind. It is therefore up to the people of Tanganyika—the peasants, the wage-earners, the students, the leaders, all of us—to make sure that this socialist attitude of mind is not lost through the temptations to personal gain (or to the abuse of positions of authority) which may come our way as individuals, or through the temptation to look on the good of the whole community as of secondary importance to the interests of our own particular group.

Just as the Elder, in our former society, was respected for his age and his service to the community, so, in our modern society, this respect for age and service will be preserved. And in the same way as the 'rich' elder's apparent wealth was really only held by him in trust for his people, so, today, the apparent extra wealth which certain positions of leadership may bring to the individuals who fill them, can be theirs only in so far as it is a necessary aid to the carrying out of their duties. It is a 'tool' entrusted to them for the benefit of the people they serve. It is not 'theirs' personally; and they may not use any part of it as a means of accumulating more for their own benefit, nor as an 'insurance' against the day when they no longer hold the same positions. That would be to betray the people who entrusted it to them. If they serve the community while they can, the community must look after them when they are no longer able to do so.

In tribal society, the individuals or the families within a tribe were 'rich' or 'poor' according to whether the whole tribe was rich or poor. If the tribe prospered, all the members of the tribe shared in its prosperity. Tanganyika, today, is a poor country. The standard of living of the masses of our people is shamefully low. But if every man and woman in the country takes up the challenge and works to the limit of his or her ability for the good of the whole society, Tanganyika will prosper; and that prosperity will be shared by all her people.

But it must be shared. The true socialist may not exploit his fellows. So that if the members of any group within our society are going to argue that, because they happen to be contributing more to the national income than some other groups, they must therefore take for themselves a greater share of the profits of their own industry than they actually need; and if they insist on this in spite of the fact that it would mean reducing their group's contribution to the general income and thus slowing down the rate at which the whole community can benefit, then that group is exploiting (or trying to exploit) its fellow human beings. It is displaying a capitalistic attitude of mind.

There are bound to be certain groups which, by virtue of the 'market value' of their particular industry's products, will contribute more to the nation's income than others. But the others may actually be producing goods or services which are of equal, or greater, intrinsic value although they do not happen to command such a high artificial value. For example, the food produced by the peasant farmer is of greater social value than the diamonds mined at Mwadui. But the mine-workers of Mwadui could claim quite correctly, that their labor was yielding greater financial profits to the community than that of the farmers. If, however, they went on to demand that they should therefore be given most of that extra profit for themselves, and that no share of it should be spent on helping the farmers, they would be potential capitalists!

This is exactly where the attitude of mind comes in. It is one of the purposes of Trade Unions to ensure for the workers a fair share of the profits of their labor. But a 'fair' share must be fair in relation to the whole society. If it is greater than the country can afford without having to penalize some other section of society, then it is not a fair share.

Trade Union leaders and their followers, as long as they are true social-ists, will not need to be coerced by the government into keeping their demands within the limits imposed by the needs of society as a whole. Only if there are potential capitalists amongst them will the socialist government have to step in and prevent them from putting their capital-ist ideas into practice!

As with groups, so with individuals. There are certain skills, certain qualifications, which, for good reasons, command a higher rate of salary for their possessors than others. But, here again, the true socialist will demand only that return for his skilled work which he knows to be a fair one in proportion to the wealth or poverty of the whole society to which he belongs. He will not, unless he is a would-be capitalist attempt to blackmail the community by demanding a salary equal to that paid to his counterpart in some far wealthier society.

. . . .

The foundation, and the objective, of African socialism is the extended family. The true African socialist does not look on one class of men as his brethren and another as his natural enemies. He does not form an alli-ance with the "brethren" for the extermination of the 'non-brethren.' He rather regards all men as his brethren—as members of his ever extending family. That is why the first article of TANU's Creed is '*Binadamu wote ni ndugu zangu, na Afrika ni moja*.' If this had been originally put in English, it could have been 'I believe in Human Brotherhood and the Unity of Africa.'

'*Ujamaa*,' then, or 'familyhood,' describes our socialism. It is opposed to capitalism, which seeks to build a happy society on the basis of the exploitation of man by man; and it is equally opposed to doctri-naire socialism which seeks to build its happy society on a philosophy of inevitable conflict between man and man.

We, in Africa, have no more need of being 'converted' to social-ism than we have of being 'taught' democracy. Both are rooted in our own past—in the traditional society which produced us. Modern Afri-can socialism can draw from its traditional heritage the recognition of 'society' as an extension of the basic family unit. But it can no longer confine the idea of the social family within the limits of the tribe, nor, indeed, of the nation. For no true African socialist can look at a line drawn on a map and say, 'The people on this side of that line are my brothers, but those who happen to live on the other side of it can have no claim on me.' Every individual on this continent is his brother.

It was in the struggle to break the grip of colonialism that we learned the need for unity. We came to recognize that the same socialist attitude of mind which, in the tribal days, gave to every individual the security that comes of belonging to a widely extended family, must be preserved within the still wider society of the nation. But we should not stop there. Our recognition of the family to which we all belong must be extended yet further—beyond the tribe, the community, the nation, or even the continent—to embrace the whole society of mankind. This is the only logical conclusion for true socialism.

42

Speech at the Organization of African Unity, Addis Ababa, 1963[50]

Sir Abubakar Tafawa Balewa

Sir Abubakar Tafawa Balewa (1912–1966) came from the largely Muslim northern part of Nigeria. Starting as a teacher, by the 1940s Balewa was active in Northern politics. In 1949, he formed the Northern People's Congress (NPC). In 1957, he became chief minister and his NPC entered into a coalition with Dr. Nnamdi Azikiwe's National Council of Nigeria and the Cameroons (NCNC) party. He acted as the prime minister of the First Nigerian Republic from 1960 until his assassination in 1966 during the coup that precipitated the Nigerian Civil War (also see Documents 36 and 40).

Though a strong advocate of the formation of the Organization of African Unity (OAU), Balewa expressed reservations about the formation of a strong political union. In this excerpt from his speech, he argues for unity based on the cooperation of sovereign states. As a means of encouraging cooperation, collaboration, and African development, Balewa recommends the creation of an African Common Market. What follows is the speech by Balewa on the occasion of the creation of the OAU at Addis Abba, Ethiopia, on May 24, 1963.

It has always been our view in Nigeria that personal contacts and the exchange of ideas are the basis of mutual understanding. I am pleased to say that, from now on, there will be no question of the so-called Monrovia and Casablanca Blocs. We all belong to Africa.

There have been quite a lot of views on what we mean by African unity. Some of us have suggested that African unity should be achieved

50. Sir Abubakar Tafawa Balewa, "Speech at the Organization of African Unity," *Mr. Prime Minister: A Selection of Speeches Made by Alhaji the Right Honourable Sir Abubakar Tafawa Balewa, K.B.E., M.P., Prime Minister of the Federal Republic of Nigeria* (Apapa: Nigerian National Press, Ltd., 1964).

by political fusion of the different states in Africa; some of us feel that African unity could be achieved by taking practical steps in economic, educational, scientific and cultural co-operation, and by trying first to get the Africans to understand themselves before embarking on the more complicated and more difficult arrangement of political union. My country stands for the practical approach to the unity of the African continent. We feel that, if this unity is to last, we must start from the beginning. Nigeria's stand is that if we want this unity in Africa we must first agree to certain essential things: The first is that African States must respect one another. There must be acceptance of equality by all the States. No matter whether they are big or small, they are all sovereign and their sovereignty is sovereignty. The size of a state, its population or its wealth should not be the criterion. It has been pointed out many times that the smaller States in Africa have no right to exist because they are too small. We in Nigeria do not agree with this view. It was unfortunate that the African States have been broken up into different groups by the Colonial powers. In some cases, a single tribe has been broken up into four different States. You might find a section in Guinea, a section in Mali, a section in Sierra Leone and perhaps a section in Liberia. That was not our fault because, for over sixty years, these different units have been existing, and any attempt, on the part of any African country to disregard this fact might bring trouble to this continent. This is the thing we want to avoid and, for this reason, Nigeria recognizes all the existing boundaries in Africa, and recognizes the existence of all the countries in Africa. This I think, Sir, is the basis of the unity which we in Nigeria pray for on our continent.

As I have said, we have to start from the beginning. I have listened to speeches in this conference, and there have been only very few members who spoke on the desirability of having a political union. Almost all the speeches indicate that a more practical approach is much preferred by the majority of the delegation. I am glad to say that the stand we have taken right from the beginning is the stand of nearly almost all the countries in this conference. It appears from the speeches as if we were just sitting idle and doing nothing towards the achievement of this unity. For our part, in Nigeria, we are already co-operating with some of our neighbours. For example, the other day, my friend, the President of Malagasy said he could not contact Lagos by telephone from Cotonou. This is no longer the case. Now he can speak direct. What we are trying to do is to link up with all our neighbours by means of telecommunications and by exchanging more postal facilities; and we are already entering into bilateral agreements with many of our neighbours. We are discussing this matter with the Republic of the Cameroun, discussing our common problems with Tchad, Congo Leopoldville, with Dahomey, and also we have a direct link with Togo. We hope to continue in this work because we feel that, if we are to unite, it is important that our communications system should be excellent and transport facilities should be such that it would enable us to move freely around, to move not only ourselves but to move our goods to different parts of the continent.

Also, we have been trying in Nigeria to join other states in trying to discuss common problems—educational and scientific problems.

We feel that it is very important for the nationals of different African countries to have the opportunity of mixing at all levels, not only at the Heads of States and Governments level, not only at the Foreign Ministers level, but also at all other levels. Let our peoples travel to different countries in Africa; let them get to know themselves and to understand themselves. This, I am sure, will bring great understanding among all the peoples of this continent. So far, our communications system is not what we would like it to be; our transport is bad. This is not our fault. It was the fault of the Colonial Powers because they designed everything for their own purposes. It is up to us now—those of us who shape the destiny of our countries—to do what we can to improve matters.

Many of the speakers have told us that mere resolutions, mere condemnations is not enough; it is time for action. I would call upon the conference that we now start on the real work. It is in our hands to build, to create and to develop a new Africa, which all of us are anxious to do.

Now, Mr. President, the Hon. President of the Sudan, I think, when he spoke, told us that we should be frank. I think it was the President of Malagasy who said that we in Africa do not want to speak the truth. We have a saying in Nigeria, which is that 'Truth is bitter'. Mr. President, I want to be frank; I want to tell the bitter truth. To my mind we cannot achieve this African unity as long as some African countries continue to carry on subversive activities in other African countries.

Sir, many of the members have spoken very strongly on the decolonization of the continent. I want to say that we in Nigeria are prepared to do anything to secure the freedom of the continent of Africa. There has been a suggestion that we should pull our resources together, that we should make arrangements, if necessary, to help the nationalists in different countries in Africa, which are still dependent, to fight their way to independence. We in Nigeria are prepared to do anything towards the liberation of all African countries. I have observed that when we give assistance to another country which is fighting for its independence, some of us are in the habit of imposing obligations on those States. That is wrong. If we give assistance to African people in any dependent territory, we should not ask for any obligation on their part; because that would come almost to the same point that many of the speakers have made that they would only accept foreign aid without any strings attached. I do not believe that any aid, no matter from where it comes, is without strings attached to it. Let us not fall into the same trap. If we assist any dependent territory in Africa, we must see to it that we do not attach conditions to our assistance. This is very, very important if we want to establish the solidarity of the continent of Africa, to make sure that any assistance we give is free.

It is good, Sir, that we have a common pool, but a conference like this cannot discuss the details of such an organization; and it is our view that, immediately after leaving this conference, or before we should appoint a committee—a standing committee—to go into the details of this matter. On the question of colonialism and racial discrimination, I am afraid that we in Nigeria will never compromise.

Now, I come to a very vital matter, which is the development of the continent. The African continent is very rich in resources but, unfortunately these resources are not developed yet. We are born at a very difficult time: we have not the necessary capital, the necessary equipment, or the necessary know-how for the development of our continent. Therefore, we find it absolutely necessary to rely on outsiders for the development of the African territories. I would like to tell the conference that we must take every care to know whom we invite to assist in the development of our resources, because there is a fear, which is also my personal fear, that, if we are not careful, we may have colonialism in a different form. Colonialism can take many different forms. Our countries can be colonized economically, if we are not careful. Just as we have fought political domination, it is also important that we fight against economic domination by other countries.

Let us not forget that we in Africa are part of the world. We have our international obligations as well. Whatever we do, we cannot isolate ourselves from the rest of the world. Therefore, in all that we do, and in all that we say, we should be careful because we belong to one human society. Mr. President, I always tell people that I do not believe in African personality, but in human personality. The African is a human being and, therefore, we have to see to the development of the human personality in Africa. I think any talk of African personality is based on an inferiority complex. I do not regard any human being—red, white, brown, yellow or green—as superior to me. I regard myself as equal to anybody. I am a human being.

Now, some people have suggested, and this is a thing which is already underway, the establishment of an African Development Bank. I hope that, when the Ministers of Finance of different countries of Africa meet in Khartoum, they will be able to produce something which should be of benefit to all of us. Also, a suggestion has been made for the establishment of an African Common Market. This is a very good idea; but I must say that we in Nigeria feel that it is a very complicated matter. We want an African Common Market. But, can we do it by taking the continent as a whole? Or can we do it by certain groupings in Africa? What appears to us to be more practical is that we should have an African Common Market based on certain groupings. We are thinking, Sir, of a North African grouping, which will include the Sudan; a West African grouping which will extend to the River Congo; and an East African grouping, which will include the Central African countries. If we base our examination on these groupings, I think we will arrive at a very successful establishment of an African Common Market, because I think it is good for the trade in Africa. For example, the inter-State trade in Africa is 10%, while 90% is done with countries outside Africa. There is no reason why we should not increase the inter-State trade on this continent. I think, Sir, that if we are able to establish an African Common Market we shall overcome many difficulties and we shall be in a Position to stand on our own in relation to the other parts of the world. My fear of our being colonised will disappear if we are able to establish this African Common Market.

The question of disarmament was raised by several speakers. I think all of us feel strongly about this question. Although some feel that disarmament can never be achieved, still others feel that it is most important that the great Powers will continue to talk about it; because the more they talk about it, the less danger there would be of an open clash. I am glad that they have seen fit to invite some of the African countries to participate in their disarmament talks. The most essential thing which is desirable is to effect disarmament. It is desirable to ban nuclear testing; it is most important that we exercise every possible influence we can upon the great Powers to destroy those bombs which they have already got. If there is a war now, there would be nothing left—everything would go. We are now just starting to develop our country. The mere fact that Africa has been declared a nuclear-free zone will not make Africa free in the event of a world war. If there is war, we in Africa will be directly involved. It is our concern that there should be peace in the world, and that there should be understanding among the great Powers. Some people have suggested that we should organize ourselves into a Defence Bloc. Well, Mr. President and Your Excellencies, all of us have been talking about the bad nature of the armament race. It has been suggested that we should embark on an arms race in Africa. All of us know very well that we are at present incapable of joining in such a race. Our idea is that we should not be talking about an arms race. All we should talk about, Sir, is how to stop it, and I would not suggest that we should join in that race at all.

A suggestion was also made that we should come together as a bloc in the United Nations. Well, that is a very good idea; but I must tell the conference that we in Nigeria hate the idea of blocs, and we do not like it. If we can find some kind of name for it, such as African committee or an African 'something', it will be much better, because the whole idea of blocs is revolting. I think we should try to find better names for these different groupings. I think that we have been working for sometime now in the United Nations where our different representatives meet and discuss matters of common interest. May I suggest to the conference that it is time now that we find a permanent small secretariat or such an African Committee in New York? That does not mean, of course, that we will instruct our delegates to close their eyes to the wider issues of world problems. But, as a Continent which has suffered for so long and also as a people who have suffered for so long, I think we have to do everything to get our proper position in the United Nations Organization. Some of us have suggested that we should seek greater representation in the Security Council and also in all the bodies of the United Nations Organization. Well, this has been our stand all the years we have been independent. I said so in New York; I said it in Monrovia. It is absolutely essential that the African continent must have more appropriate representation in the Security Council and all the bodies of the United Nations, because we have more to gain thereby. That world organization, I have always maintained, is a sure guarantee of the independent sovereignty of our African states.

Mr. President, many of the points have been made. Many members have said that we cannot leave Addis Ababa without a charter. I hope we shall not leave here without some kind of charter. I hope our Foreign Ministers will produce a charter before we leave this city.

43

Founding Charter, 1963[51]

Organization of African Unity

In 1963, as an increasing number of African states moved toward territorial sovereignty, thirty-two representatives of African governments met in Addias Ababa, Ethiopia, and on May 25 of that year formed the Organization of African Unity (OAU). The chief aim of the OAU was to strengthen the unity of African states. Emperor Haile Selassie I of Ethiopia became the Organization's first chairperson. In 2002, the African Union replaced the Organization, as the OAU became seen as increasingly ineffectual in dealing with Africa's internal problems because of its commitment to non-interference in state sovereignty. The Founding Charter lays out the shared commitment of African governments to the cooperation of African states. While promoting mutual support between member states, the Founding Charter ultimately upholds the sovereignty of each participating nation.

We, the Heads of African States and Governments assembled in the City of Addis Ababa, Ethiopia,

Convinced that it is the inalienable right of all people to control their own destiny,

Conscious of the fact that freedom, equality, justice and dignity are essential objectives for the achievement of the legitimate aspirations of the African peoples,

Conscious of our responsibility to harness the natural and human resources of our continent for the total advancement of our peoples in all spheres of human endeavor,

---

51. Organization of African Unity, "Founding Charter" (May 25, 1963). Reprinted with the permission of the African Union.

Inspired by a common determination to promote understanding among our peoples and cooperation among our states in response to the aspirations of our peoples for brother-hood and solidarity, in a larger unity transcending ethnic and national differences,

Convinced that, in order to translate this determination into a dynamic force in the cause of human progress, conditions for peace and security must be established and maintained,

Determined to safeguard and consolidate the hard-won independence as well as the sovereignty and territorial integrity of our states, and to fight against neocolonialism in all its forms,

Dedicated to the general progress of Africa,

Persuaded that the Charter of the United Nations and the Universal Declaration of Human Rights, to the Principles of which we reaffirm our adherence, provide a solid foundation for peaceful and positive cooperation among States,

Desirous that all African States should henceforth unite so that the welfare and well-being of their peoples can be assured,

Resolved to reinforce the links between our states by establishing and strengthening common institutions,

Have agreed to the present Charter.

ESTABLISHMENT

Article I

1. The High Contracting Parties do by the present Charter establish an Organization to be known as the ORGANIZATION OF AFRICAN UNITY.
2. The Organization shall include the Continental African States, Madagascar and other Islands surrounding Africa.

PURPOSES

Article II

1. The Organization shall have the following purposes:
   (a) To promote the unity and solidarity of the African States;

(b) To coordinate and intensify their cooperation and efforts to achieve a better life for the peoples of Africa;

(c) To defend their sovereignty, their territorial integrity and independence;

(d) To eradicate all forms of colonialism from Africa; and

(e) To promote international cooperation, having due regard to the Charter of the United Nations and the Universal Declaration of Human Rights.

2. To these ends, the Member States shall coordinate and harmonize their general policies, especially in the following fields:

(a) Political and diplomatic cooperation;

(b) Economic cooperation, including transport and communications;

(c) Educational and cultural cooperation;

(d) Health, sanitation and nutritional cooperation;

(e) Scientific and technical cooperation; and

(f) Cooperation for defense and security.

PRINCIPLES

Article III

The Member States, in pursuit of the purposes stated in Article II solemnly affirm and declare their adherence to the following principles:

1. The sovereign equality of all Member States.

2. Non-interference in the internal affairs of States.

3. Respect for the sovereignty and territorial integrity of each State and for its inalienable right to independent existence.

4. Peaceful settlement of disputes by negotiation, mediation, conciliation or arbitration.

5. Unreserved condemnation, in all its forms, of political assassination as well as of subversive activities on the part of neighboring States or any other States.

6. Absolute dedication to the total emancipation of the African territories which are still dependent.

7. Affirmation of a policy of non-alignment with regard to all blocs.

MEMBERSHIP

Article IV

Each independent sovereign African State shall be entitled to become a Member of the Organization.

RIGHTS AND DUTIES OF MEMBER STATES

Article V

All Member States shall enjoy equal rights and have equal duties.

Article VI

The Member States pledge themselves to observe scrupulously the principles enumerated in Article III of the present Charter.

INSTITUTIONS

Article VII

The Organization shall accomplish its purposes through the following principal institutions:

1. The Assembly of Heads of State and Government.
2. The Council of Ministers.
3. The General Secretariat.
4. The Commission of Mediation, Conciliation and Arbitration.

THE ASSEMBLY OF HEADS OF STATE AND GOVERNMENT

Article VIII

The Assembly of Heads of State and Government shall be the supreme organ of the Organization. It shall, subject to the provisions of this Charter, discuss matters of common concern to Africa with a view to coordinating and harmonizing the general policy of the Organization. It may in addition review the structure, functions and acts of all the organs and any specialized agencies which may be created in accordance with the present Charter.

Article IX

The Assembly shall be composed of the Heads of State and Government or their duly accredited representatives and it shall meet at least once a year. At the request of any Member State and on approval by a two-thirds majority of the Member States, the Assembly shall meet in extraordinary session.

Article X

1. Each Member State shall have one vote.
2. All resolutions shall be determined by a two-thirds majority of the Members of the Organization.
3. Questions of procedure shall require a simple majority. Whether or not a question is one of procedure shall be determined by a simple majority of all Member States of the Organization.
4. Two-thirds of the total membership of the Organization shall form a quorum at any meeting of the Assembly.

Article XI

The Assembly shall have the power to determine its own rules of procedure.

THE COUNCIL OF MINISTERS

Article XII

1. The Council of Ministers shall consist of Foreign Ministers or other Ministers as are designated by the Governments of Member States.
2. The Council of Ministers shall meet at least twice a year. When requested by any Member State and approved by two-thirds of all Member States, it shall meet in extraordinary session.

Article XIII

1. The Council of Ministers shall be responsible to the Assembly of Heads of State and Government. It shall be entrusted with the responsibility of preparing conferences of the Assembly.

2. It shall take cognizance of any matter referred to it by the Assembly. It shall be entrusted with the implementation of the decision of the Assembly of Heads of State and Government. It shall coordinate inter-African cooperation in accordance with the instructions of the Assembly conformity with Article II (2) of the present Charter.

Article XIV

1. Each Member State shall have one vote.
2. All resolutions shall be determined by a simple majority of the members of the Council of Ministers.
3. Two-thirds of the total membership of the Council of Ministers shall form a quorum for any meeting of the Council.

Article XV

The Council shall have the power to determine its own rules of procedure.

GENERAL SECRETARIAT

Article XVI

There shall be a Secretary-General of the Organization, who shall be appointed by the Assembly of Heads of State and Government. The Secretary-General shall direct the affairs of the Secretariat.

Article XVII

There shall be one or more Assistant Secretaries-General of the Organization, who shall be appointed by the Assembly of Heads of State and Government.

Article XVIII

The functions and conditions of service of the Secretary-General, of the Assistant Secretaries-General and other employees of the Secretariat shall be governed by the provisions of this Charter and the regulations approved by the Assembly of Heads of State and Government.

1. In the performance of their duties the Secretary-General and the staff shall not seek or receive instructions from any government or from any other authority external to the Organization. They shall refrain from any action which might reflect on their position as international officials responsible only to the Organization.

2. Each member of the Organization undertakes to respect the exclusive character of the responsibilities of the Secretary-General and the staff and not to seek to influence them in the discharge of their responsibilities.

COMMISSION OF MEDIATION, CONCILIATION AND ARBITRATION

Article XIX

Member States pledge to settle all disputes among themselves by peaceful means and, to this end decide to establish a Commission of Mediation, Conciliation and Arbitration, the composition of which and conditions of service shall be defined by a separate Protocol to be approved by the Assembly of Heads of State and Government. Said Protocol shall be regarded as forming an integral part of the present Charter.

SPECIALIZED COMMISSION

Article XX

The Assembly shall establish such Specialized Commissions as it may deem necessary, including the following:

1. Economic and Social Commission.
2. Educational, Scientific, Cultural and Health Commission.
3. Defense Commission.

Article XXI

Each Specialized Commission referred to in Article XX shall be composed of the Ministers concerned or other Ministers or Plenipotentiaries designated by the Governments of the Member States.

Article XXII

The functions of the Specialized Commissions shall be carried out in accordance with the provisions of the present Charter and of the regulations approved by the Council of Ministers.

THE BUDGET

Article XXIII

The budget of the Organization prepared by the Secretary-General shall be approved by the Council of Ministers. The budget shall be provided by contribution from Member States in accordance with the scale of assessment of the United Nations; provided, however, that no Member State shall be assessed an amount exceeding twenty percent of the yearly regular budget of the Organization. The Member States agree to pay their respective contributions regularly.

SIGNATURE AND RATIFICATION OF CHARTER

Article XXIV

1. This Charter shall be open for signature to all independent sovereign African States and shall be ratified by the signatory States in accordance with their respective constitutional processes.

2. The original instrument, done, if possible in African languages, in English and French, all texts being equally authentic, shall be deposited with the Government of Ethiopia which shall transmit certified copies thereof to all independent sovereign African States.

3. Instruments of ratification shall be deposited with the Government of Ethiopia, which shall notify all signatories of each such deposit.

ENTRY INTO FORCE

Article XXV

This Charter shall enter into force immediately upon receipt by the Government of Ethiopia of the instruments of ratification from two-thirds of the signatory States.

REGISTRATION OF CHARTER

Article XXVI

This Charter shall, after due ratification, be registered with the Secretariat of the United Nations through the Government of Ethiopia in conformity with Article 102 of the Charter of the United Nations.

INTERPRETATION OF THE CHARTER

Article XXVII

Any question which may arise concerning the interpretation of this Charter shall be decided by a vote of two-thirds of the Assembly of Heads of State and Government of the Organization.

ADHESION AND ACCESSION

Article XXVIII

1. Any independent sovereign African State may at any time notify the Secretary-General of its intention to adhere or accede to this Charter.

2. The Secretary-General shall, on receipt of such notification, communicate a copy of it to all the Member States. Admission shall be decided by a simple majority of the Member States. The decision of each Member State shall be transmitted to the Secretary-General, who shall, upon receipt of the required number of votes, communicate the decision to the State concerned.

MISCELLANEOUS

Article XXIX

The working languages of the Organization and all its institutions shall be, if possible African languages, English and French, Arabic and Portuguese.

Article XXX

The Secretary-General may accept, on behalf of the Organization, gifts, bequests and other donations made to the Organization, provided that this is approved by the Council of Ministers.

Article XXXI

The Council of Ministers shall decide on the privileges and immunities to be accorded to the personnel of the Secretariat in the respective territories of the Member States.

CESSATION OF MEMBERSHIP

Article XXXII

Any State which desires to renounce its membership shall forward a written notification to the Secretary-General. At the end of one year from the date of such notification, if not withdrawn, the Charter shall cease to apply with respect to the renouncing State, which shall thereby cease to belong to the Organization.

AMENDMENT OF THE CHARTER

Article XXXIII

This Charter may be amended or revised if any Member State makes a written request to the Secretary-General to that effect; provided, however, that the proposed amendment is not submitted to the Assembly for consideration until all the Member States have been duly notified of it and a period of one year has elapsed. Such an amendment shall not be effective unless approved by at least two-thirds of all the Member States.

IN FAITH WHEREOF, We, the Heads of African States and Governments have signed this Charter. Done in the City of Addis Ababa, Ethiopia,

25th day of May, 1963

44

Responsibilities Demand Balanced, Sober Reflection: A Call to African Leaders, 1963[52]

Haile Selassie I

Ethiopia was one of the countries to retain its sovereignty when European powers began to colonize Africa in the late nineteenth century. As such, Pan-Africanists and African nationalists revered Ethiopia and its emperor, Haile Selassie I (1892–1975), for resisting colonization, particularly in 1935 when Italy invaded the country during the Second Italo-Ethiopian War. Although warfare with Italy interrupted his reign (1935–1940), Selassie's return to liberated Ethiopia in 1941 was marked by reforms, including the abolition of slavery and the strengthening of Ethiopia's role in international affairs. In spite of these accomplishments, the 1960s and early 1970s saw increased opposition to Selassie's regime from both the left and the right. The outbreak of famine in Wollo in northeastern Ethiopia led to tens of thousands of deaths and helped turn public opinion against the emperor's already weakening rule. In February 1974, escalating and violent popular and military protest led to the collapse of the Solomonic dynasty, of which Selassie was the final emperor.

Ethiopia and its regency inspired nascent African states during the initial period of decolonization in the 1960s. Selassie involved himself in these political discussions, notably serving as the chairperson at the inaugural meeting of the Organization of African Unity (OAU) in 1963. Addressing the representatives of the OAU, the following excerpt from a speech delivered by Selassie on May 25, 1963, calls for unity among African states fostered through a shared defense of sovereignty and the creation of cooperative institutions such as the African Development Bank. As he would also do in his capacity as

---

52. Haile Selassie I, "Call to African Leaders: 1963 Summit," from *Selected Speeches of His Imperial Majesty Haile Selassie I, 1918–1967* (Addis Ababa: Imperial Ethiopian Ministry of Information, 1967).

emperor, Haile Selassie encourages the OAU and its participating statesman to enhance the representation and leadership of Africa in global affairs.

Supreme Effort

Africa's victory, although proclaimed, is not yet total, and areas of resistance still remain. Today, We name as our first great task the final liberating of those Africans still dominated by foreign exploitation and control. With the goal in sight, and unqualified triumph within our grasp, let us not now falter or lag or relax. We must make one final supreme effort; now, when the struggle grows, weary when so much has been won that the thrilling sense of achievement has brought us near satiation. Our liberty is meaningless unless all Africans are free. Our brothers in the Rhodesians, in Mozambique, in Angola, in South Africa cry out in anguish for our support and assistance. We must urge on their behalf their peaceful accession to independence. We must align and identify ourselves with all aspects of their struggle. It would be betrayal were we to pay only lip service to the cause of their liberation and fail to back our words with action. To them we say, your pleas shall not go unheeded. The resources of Africa and of all freedom-loving nations are marshalled in your service. Be of good heart, for your deliverance is at hand.

As we renew our vow that all of Africa shall be free, let us also resolve that old wounds shall be healed and past scars forgotten. It was thus that Ethiopia treated the invader nearly twenty-five years ago, and Ethiopians found peace with honor in this course. Memories of past injustice should not divert us from the more pressing business at hand. We must live in peace with our former colonizers, shunning recrimination and bitterness and forswearing the luxury of vengeance and retaliation, lest the acid of hatred erode our souls and poison our hearts. Let us act as befits the dignity which we claim for ourselves as Africans, proud of our own special qualities, distinctions and abilities. Our efforts as free men must be to establish new relationships, devoid of any resentment and hostility, restored to our belief and faith in ourselves as individuals, dealing on a basis of equality with other equally free peoples.

Free and United

Today, we look to the future calmly, confidently and courageously. We look to the vision of an Africa not merely free but united. In facing this new challenge we can take comfort and encouragement from the lessons of the past. We know that there are differences among us. Africans enjoy different cultures, distinctive values, special attributes. But we also know that unity can be and has been attained among men of the most disparate origins, that differences of race, of religion, of culture, of tradition, are no insuperable obstacle to the coming together of peoples. History teaches us that unity is strength and cautions us to submerge and overcome our differences in the quest for common goals, to strive, with all our combined strength, for the path to true African brotherhood and unity.

There are those who claim that African unity is impossible, that the forces that pull us, some in this direction, others in that, are too strong to be overcome. Around us there is no lack of doubt and pessimism, no absence of critics and criticism. These speak of Africa, of Africa's future and of her position in the Twentieth Century in sepulchral tones. They predict dissension and disintegration among Africans and internecine strife and chaos on our continent. Let us confound these and, by our deeds, disperse them in confusion. There are others whose hopes for Africa are bright, who stand with faces upturned in wonder and awe at the creation of a new and happier life, who have dedicated themselves to their brothers to whom they owe the achievements of Africa's past. Let us reward their trust and merit their approval.

Accepted Goal

The road of African unity is already lined with landmarks. The last years are crowded with meetings, with conferences with declarations and pronouncements. Regional organizations have been established. Local groupings based on common interests, backgrounds and traditions have been created.

But though all that has been said and written and done in these years, there runs a common theme. Unity is the accepted goal. We argue about means; we discuss alternative paths to the same objective; we engage in debates about techniques and tactics.

But when semantics are stripped away, there is little argument among us. We are determined to create a union of Africans. In a very real sense, our continent is unmade; it still awaits creation and its creators. It is our duty and privilege to rouse the slumbering giant of Africa, not to the nationalism of Europe of the Nineteenth Century, not to regional consciousness, but to the vision of a single African brotherhood bending its united efforts toward the achievement of a greater and nobler goal.

Above all, we must avoid the pitfalls of tribalism. If we are divided among ourselves on tribal lines, we open our doors to foreign intervention and its potentially harmful consequences. The Congo is clear proof of what We say. We should not be led to complacency because of the present ameliorated situation in that country. The Congolese people have suffered untold misery, and the economic growth of the country has been retarded because of tribal strife.

Obstacles Formidable

But while we agree that the ultimate destiny of this continent lies in political union, we must at the same time recognize that the obstacles to be overcome in its achievement are at once numerous and formidable. Africa's peoples did not emerge into liberty in uniform conditions. Africans maintain different political systems; our economies are diverse; our social orders are rooted in differing cultures and traditions. Furthermore, no clear consensus exists on the "how" and the "what" of this union. Is it to be, in form, federal, confederal or unitary? Is the sovereignty of individual states to be reduced, and if so, by how much, and in what areas? On these and other questions there is no agreement, and if we wait for agreed answers, generations hence matters will be little advanced, while the debate still rages.

We should, therefore, not be concerned that complete union is not attained from one day to the next. The union of which we seek can only come gradually, as the day-to-day progress of which we achieve carries us slowly but inexorably along this course. We have before us the examples of the U.S.A. and the U.S.S.R. We must remember how long these required to achieve their union. When a solid foundation is laid, if the mason is able and his materials good, a strong house can be built.

Thus, a period of transition is inevitable. Old relations and arrangements may for a time linger. Regional organizations may fulfil legitimate functions and needs which cannot yet be otherwise satisfied. But the difference is in this: that we recognize these circumstances for what they are, temporary expedients designed to serve only until we have established the conditions which will bring total African unity within our reach.

Exploit Agreement

There is, nonetheless, much that we can do to speed this transition. There are issues on which we stand united and questions on which there is unanimity of opinion. Let us seize on these areas of agreement and exploit them to the fullest. Let us take action now, action which, while taking account of present realities, nonetheless constitutes clear and unmistakable progress along the course plotted out for us by destiny. We are all adherents, whatever our internal political systems, of the principles of democratic action. Let us apply these to the unity we seek to create. Let us work on our own programs in all fields—political, economic, social and military. The opponents of Africa's growth, whose interests would be best served by a divided and balkanized continent, would derive much satisfaction from the unhappy spectacle of thirty and more African States so split, so paralysed and immobilized by controversies over long-term measures on which there is no dispute. If we act where we may in those areas where action is possible, the inner logic of the programs which we adopt will work for us and inevitably impel us still farther in the direction of ultimate union.

What we still lack, despite the efforts of past years, is the mechanism which will enable us to speak, with one voice when we wish to do so and take and implement decisions on African problems when we are so minded. The commentators of 1963 speak in discussing Africa, of the Monrovia States, the Brazzaville Group, the Casablanca Powers, of these and many more. Let us put an end to these terms. What we require is a single African organization through which Africa's single voice may be heard, within which Africa's problems may be studied and resolved. We need an organization which will facilitate acceptable solutions to disputes among Africans and promote the study and adoption of measures for common defense and programs for co-operation in the economic and social fields. Let us, at this Conference, create a single institution to which we will all belong, based on principles to which we all subscribe, confident that in its councils our voices will carry their proper weight, secure in the knowledge that the decision there will be dictated by Africans and only by Africans and that they will take full account of all vital African considerations.

Foundation for Unity

We are meeting here today to lay the basis for African unity. Let us, here and now, agree upon the basic instrument which will constitute the foundation for the future growth in peace and harmony and oneness of this continent. Let our meetings henceforth proceed from solid accomplishments. Let us not put off, to later consideration and study, the single act, the one decision, which must emerge from this gathering if it is to have real meaning. This Conference cannot close without adopting a single African Charter. We cannot leave here without having created a single African organization possessed of the attributes We have described. If we fail in this, we will have shirked our responsibility to Africa and to the peoples we lead. If we succeed, then, and only then, will we have justified our presence here.

The organization of which We speak must possess a well-cumulated framework, having a permanent headquarters and an adequate Secretariat providing the necessary continuity between meetings of the permanent organs. It must include specialized bodies to work in particular fields of competence assigned to the organization. Unless the political liberty for which Africans have for so long struggled is complemented and bolstered by a corresponding economic and social growth, the breath of life which sustains our freedom may flicker out. In our efforts to improve the standard of life of our peoples and to flesh out the bones of our independence, we count on the assistance and support of others. But this alone will not suffice, and, alone, would only perpetuate Africa's dependence on others.

A specialized body to facilitate and co-ordinate continent-wide economic programs and to provide the mechanism for the provision of economic assistance among African nations is thus required. Prompt measures can be taken to increase trade and commerce among us. Africa's mineral wealth is great; we should co-operate in its development. An African Development Program, which will make provision for the concentration by each nation on those productive activities for which its resources and its geographic and climatic conditions best fit it is needed. We assume that each African nation has its own national development program, and it only remains for us to come together and share our experiences for the proper implementation of a continent-wide plan. Today, travel between African nations and telegraphic and telephonic communications among us are circuitous in the extreme. Road communications between two neighboring States are often difficult or even impossible. It is little wonder that trade among us has remained at a discouragingly low level. These anachronisms are the remnants of a heritage of which we must rid ourselves, the legacy of the century when Africans were isolated one from the other. These are vital areas in which efforts must be concentrated.

Development Bank

An additional project to be implemented without delay is the creation of an African Development Bank, a proposal to which all our Governments have given full support and which has already received intensive study. The meeting of our Finance Ministers to be held within the coming weeks in Khartoum should transform this proposal into fact. This same meeting could appropriately continue studies already undertaken of the impact upon Africa of existing regional economic groupings, and initiate further studies to accelerate the expansion of economic relations among us.

The nations of Africa, as is true of every continent of the world, had from time to time disputes among themselves. These quarrels must be confined to this continent and quarantined from the contamination of non-African interference. Permanent arrangements must be agreed upon to assist in the peaceful settlement of these disagreements which, however few they may are, cannot be left to languish and fester. Procedures must be established for the peaceful settlement of disputes, in order that the threat or use of force may no longer endanger the peace of our continent.

Steps must be taken to establish an African defense system. Military planning for the security of this continent must be undertaken in common within a collective framework. The responsibility for protecting this continent from armed attacks from abroad is the primary concern of Africans themselves. Provision must be made for the extension of speedy and effective assistance when any African State is threatened with military aggression. We cannot rely solely on international morality. Africa's control over her own affairs is dependent on the existence of appropriate military arrangements to assure this continent's protection against such threats. While guarding our own independence, we must at the same time determine to live peacefully with all nations of the world.

Knowing Ourselves

Africa has come to freedom under the most difficult and trying of circumstances. No small measure of the handicaps under which we labor derives from the low educational level attained by our peoples and from their lack of knowledge of their fellow Africans. Education abroad is at best an unsatisfactory substitute for education at home. A massive effort must be launched in the educational and cultural fields which will not only raise the level of literacy and provide the cadres of skilled and trained technicians requisite to our growth and development but, as well, acquaint us one with another. Ethiopia, several years ago, instituted a program of scholarships for students coming from other African lands which has proved highly rewarding and fruitful, and We urge others to adopt projects of this sort. Serious consideration should be given to the establishment of an African university, sponsored by all African States, where future leaders of Africa will be trained in an atmosphere of continental brotherhood. In this African institution, the supra-national aspects of African life would be emphasized and study would be directed toward the ultimate goal of complete African unity. Ethiopia stands prepared here and now to decide on the site of the University and to fix the financial contributions to be made to it.

This is but the merest summary of what can be accomplished. Upon these measures we are all agreed, and our agreement should now form the basis for our action.

A World Force

Africa has become an increasingly influential force in the conduct of world affairs as the combined weight of our collective opinion is brought to focus not only on matters which concern this continent exclusively, but on those pressing problems which occupy the thoughts of all men everywhere. As we have come to know one another better and grown in mutual trust and confidence, it has been possible for us to co-ordinate our policies and actions and contribute to the successful settlement of pressing and critical world issues.

This has not been easy. But co-ordinated action by all African States on common problems is imperative if our opinions are to be accorded their proper weight. We Africans occupy a different—indeed a unique—position among the nations of this Century. Having for so long known oppression, tyranny and subjugation, whose, with better right, can claim for all the opportunity and the right to live and grow as free men? Ourselves for long decades the victims of injustice, whose voices can be better raised in the demand for justice and right for all? We demand an end to colonialism because domination of one people by another is wrong. We demand an end to nuclear testing and the arms race because these activities, which pose such dreadful threats to man's existence and waste and squander humanity's material heritage, are wrong. We demand an end to racial segregation as an affront to man's dignity, which is wrong. We act in these matters in the right, as a matter of high principle. We act out of the integrity and conviction of our most deep-founded beliefs.

If we permit ourselves to be tempted by narrow self-interest and vain ambition, if we barter our beliefs for short-term advantage, who will listen when we claim to speak for conscience, and who will contend that our words deserve to be heeded? We must speak out on major world issues, courageously, openly and honestly, and in blunt terms of right and wrong. If we yield to blandishments or threats, if we compromise when no honorable compromise is possible, our influence will be sadly diminished and our prestige woefully prejudiced and weakened. Let us not deny our ideals or sacrifice our right to stand as the champions of the poor, the ignorant, the oppressed everywhere. The acts by which we live and the attitudes by which we act must be clear beyond question. Principles alone can endow our deeds with force and meaning. Let us be true to what we believe, that our beliefs may serve and honor us.

Prejudice Opposed

We reaffirm today, in the name of principle and right, our opposition to prejudice, wherever and in whatever form it may be found, and particularly do we rededicate ourselves to the eradication of racial discrimination from this continent. We can never rest content with our achievements so long as men, in any part of Africa, assert on racial grounds their superiority over the least of our brothers. Racial discrimination constitutes a negation of the spiritual and psychological equality which we have fought to achieve and a denial of the personality and dignity which we have struggled to establish for ourselves as Africans. Our political and economic liberty will be devoid of meaning for so long as the degrading spectacle of South Africa's apartheid continues to haunt our waking hours and to trouble our sleep. We must redouble our efforts to banish this evil from our land. If we persevere, discrimination will one day vanish from the earth. If we use the means available to us, South Africa's apartheid, just as colonialism, will shortly remain only as a memory. If we pool our resources and use them well, this specter will be banished forever.

In this effort, as in so many others, we stand united with our Asian friends and brothers. Africa shares with Asia a common background of colonialism, of exploitation, of discrimination, of oppression. At Bandung, African and Asian States dedicated themselves to the liberation of their two continents from foreign domination and affirmed the right of all nations to develop in their own way, free of any external interference. The Bandung Declaration and the principles enunciated at that Conference remain today valid for us all. We hope that the leaders of India and China, in the spirit of Bandung, will find the way to the peaceful resolution of the dispute between their two countries.

. . . .

Collective Security

We would not close without making mention of the United Nations. We personally, Who have throughout Our lifetime been ever guided and inspired by the principle of collective security, would not now propose measures which depart from or are inconsistent with this ideal or with the declarations of the United Nations Charter. It would be foolhardy indeed to abandon a principle which has withstood the test of time and which has proved its inherent value again and again in the past. It would be worse than folly to weaken the one effective world organization which exists today and to which each of us owes so much. It would be sheer recklessness for any of us to detract from this organization which, however imperfect, provides the best bulwark against the incursion of any forces which would deprive us of our hard-won liberty and dignity.

The African Charter of which We have spoken is wholly consistent with that of the United Nations. The African organization which We envisage is not intended in any way to replace in our national or international life the position which the United Nations has so diligently earned and so rightfully occupies. Rather, the measure which We propose would complement and round out programs undertaken by the United Nations and its specialized agencies and, hopefully, render both their activities and ours doubly meaningful and effective. What we seek will multiply many times over the contribution which our joint endeavors may make to the assurance of world peace and the promotion of human well-being and understanding.

History's Dictum

A century hence, when future generations study the pages of history, seeking to follow and fathom the growth and development of the African continent, what will they find of this Conference? Will it be remembered as an occasion on which the leaders of a liberated Africa, acting boldly and with determination, bent events to their will and shaped the future destinies of the African peoples? Will this meeting be memorialized for its solid achievements, for the intelligence and maturity which marked the decisions taken here? Or will it be recalled for its failures, for the inability of Africa's leaders to transcend local prejudices and individual differences, for the disappointment and disillusionment which followed in its train?

These questions give us all pause. The answers are within our power to dictate. The challenges and opportunities which open before us today are greater than those presented at any time in Africa's millennia of history. The risks and the danger which confront us are no less great. The immense responsibilities which history and circumstance have thrust upon us demand balanced and sober reflection. If we succeed in the tasks which lie before us, our names will be remembered and our deeds recalled by those who follow us. If we fail, history will puzzle at our failure and mourn what was lost. We approach the days ahead with the prayer that we who have assembled here may be granted the wisdom, the judgment and the inspiration which will enable us to maintain our faith with the peoples and the nations which have entrusted their fate to our hands.

45

Tribalism: A Pragmatic Instrument for National Unity, 1964[53]

Nnamdi Azikiwe

Dr. Nnamdi Azikiwe (1904–1996) was the first president of Nigeria. Azikiwe's nationalism first developed during his years as a journalist in the 1930s. His articles were instrumental in spreading nationalist ideas throughout West Africa. In 1944, he co-founded the National Council of Nigeria and the Cameroons (NCNC). In 1945, the British governor, Arthur Richards, proposed reforms that allowed for a greater number of Africans to serve in the Legislative Council. Azikiwe and other NCNC members opposed the reforms because they only permitted four elected African members, while the other members would be nominated. Nevertheless, the Richards Constitution went into effect in 1947. Azikiwe was elected to the Legislative Council of Nigeria and, in 1954, became premier of Nigeria's Eastern Region. Following independence from Britain in 1960, Azikiwe served as governor-general of Nigeria. He became president of the Nigerian First Republic from 1963 to 1966. During the 1966 coup that brought down the Republic, Azikiwe was one of the few politicians to escape assassination. Following the Civil War, he ran twice for the presidency of Nigeria, but abandoned politics after the 1983 military coup brought down Nigeria's Second Republic (1979–1983).

In this excerpt from a lecture at the University of Nigeria, Nsukka, Azikiwe affirms a positive historical role for tribal allegiances in providing security and argues for the preservation of cultural identities. Yet, he suggests that a constitution that protects individual liberties and ensures the satisfaction of basic needs contributes to the development of a national identity that would complement the cultural identities derived from tribal affiliation.

53. Nnamdi Azikiwe, "Tribalism: A Pragmatic Instrument for National Unity," in *Ideologies of Liberation in Black Africa, 1856–1970*, edited by J. Ayo Langley, (London: Rex Collings, 1979).

In its Nigerian context, our tribes which number about 400, in a population said to be fifty-five million, are really different nationalities, who united and established a political union in the form of a federation, as a result of historical circumstances. Being human, they have developed their means of communication and a way of life. So that factors of race, language and culture are responsible for the existence of tribes or nationalities.

Since tribes are so linked with human society, their existence constitutes in Nigeria, an anthropological phenomenon, and they cannot be exterminated without committing wholesale genocide to a section of the human race.

In examining this issue of tribe, from an anthropological point of view, we discover the following facts: as members of a particular race, tribes exist all over the world as individual members of the human race. They communicate with each other by speaking a common language; and they settle permanently any particular environment through the means of their culture.

We do know from anthropology that human beings with similar morphological characteristics can intermingle to produce or sustain a primary race. We know also that language can be taught to the offspring of such human beings to constitute a particular language. It is also a fact that culture can be developed as a social or material tool to enable members of such a race, who speak this particular language, to settle permanently on a geographically demarcated area and adapt themselves to such an environment. Therefore, race, language and culture constitute the essential anthropological elements which make up a tribe.

If such a tribe remains isolated it would confine itself to a primary group that would be virtually homogeneous. But if it comes into contact with another tribe or tribes then sociological problems are bound to rise, especially in respect of intermixture of races, conflict of languages and clash of cultures. It is this aspect of inter-tribal relations that I would like to examine a little closer.

. . . .

Simply stated, my thesis is to the effect that when numbers of the human race congregate in an environment to build a community, they tend to be parochial at the initial stage only to become cosmopolitan later. The factors responsible for their parochialism are mainly ethnic but those responsible for their cosmopolitanism are ethical and sociological.

I deduce from this the following position: that human beings will attach less importance to their racial, linguistic and cultural origins, so long as their individual liberties are insulated from tyranny and their group attachment is insured from want, provided that the environment in which they live is conducive to human happiness.

By individual liberties, I should be understood to mean the fundamental rights of man, to wit: the right to life, freedom from torture, right to liberty and security of person, the right to a fair trial, guarantee against retroactivity of the law, the right to privacy and to family life, freedom of expression, freedom of assembly and association, the right to marry and found a family, the right of property, the right to education, and the right to free elections. They represent the embodiment of man's quest for freedom from the earliest times to September 3, 1953, when the European Convention for the Protection of Human Rights and Fundamental Freedoms became operative. The Protocol to this Convention incorporated the right to education and to free elections. These came into force on May 18, 1954. In the light of our experience in Nigeria, we should include also freedom from discrimination.

Human happiness is an abstraction which can equally be concrete. It is abstract in the sense of the psychological, but concrete in its relation to satisfying the material needs of economic man. In case of the latter, two systems have been tried in the world, the capitalist and the socialist. Of late, a third force has emerged; it is, the welfarist.

Capitalism is an economic system characterised by private ownership of capital goods, by investments that are determined by private decision rather than by State control. It is also an instrument of private enterprise through which prices, production and the distribution of goods are determined mainly in a free market. An essential feature of capitalism is the profit motive or individual welfare.

Socialism, on the other hand, is a political and economic theory characterised by public ownership of the means of production, distribution and exchange. Its main feature is the emphasis on public welfare and its objective is that everyone should be given an equal opportunity to develop his talents, and that the wealth of the community should be fairly distributed.

Welfarism is another name for the welfare state. This is a system based upon the assumption, by a political State, of primary responsibility and for the individual social welfare of its citizens, usually by the enactment of specific policies, such as education, health, unemployment insurance, old age benefits, control of prices and rents, minimum wages, family assistance, subsidies to agriculture, housing and other segments of the economy. It is particularly concerned with their implementation directly by Government agencies.

The means of attaining human happiness and guaranteeing same for the Nigerians, who are to be insulated from tyranny and want, can be through a capitalist or socialist or welfarist framework. Whether that will be sufficient inducement to attract the allegiance of the racial, linguistic and cultural groups we are discussing will depend upon the rigidity or flexibility of such guarantees, the temperament of the people concerned, and the calibre of leadership in the country.

It is anomalous that human beings who belong to the same race, speak the same language and acquired a common culture, or those who belong to the same race and speak the same language but acquired a different culture, do not readily mix, unless circumstances force them to do so, and unless such circumstances can be made desirable and permanent.

Therefore, the key to the solution of the problem of tribalism in Nigeria is to discover the circumstances which can be superimposed on the natural chains of language and culture, which have linked the human beings who inhabit Nigeria, to enable them to develop a feeling of personal security and group preservation under changed but permanent circumstances.

The solution is purely political since the main factor in contemporary Nigerian life is based on the building of a stable nation that is founded on a common nationality. However, if loyalty to the nation must replace loyalty to the tribe, in letter and spirit, then the aim of the Nigerian nation should be to provide the diverse peoples of Nigeria with certain permanent guarantees of a constitutional, political and economic nature.

INCENTIVE FOR HIGHER LOYALTY

It is imperative that these must have both intrinsic and extrinsic values so as to modify radically, if not completely efface, the tendency to regard one's mother tongue as the only magic wand which can provide human beings with an environment where, by intermingling in their closed circle, they can obtain spiritual happiness and material prosperity under the protective umbrella of the tribal leviathan.

To me, the complete answer is the creation of a federal system of government which will concede the existence of all linguistic groups and accord them the right to co-exist, on the basis of equality, within a framework of political and constitutional warranties, that would protect their individual freedom under the rule of law and thus preserve and sustain the particular linguistic group from extinction.

Indeed, John Stuart Mill did proclaim that 'The sole aim for which mankind are warranted, individually or collectively interfering with the liberty of action of any of their number is self-protection.' After all, self-preservation is said to be the first law of nature. By preserving the linguistic groups of Nigeria and conceding to the local autonomy of some satisfactory sort, an atmosphere for respect of their customs and traditions can be created.

This simple admission of the potency of language as a vinculum of familism is a portent for preserving the corporate Nigeria as one political entity that can be worthy of admiration and respect of the world. We cannot afford to ignore this vital force in the building of our nation.

Therefore, I suggest the ultimate revision of our Republican Constitution so as to effect two changes, among others: first, to entrench adequate safeguards to buttress fundamental rights; secondly, to provide citizens of Nigeria with plentiful avenues for obtaining a balanced diet and wholesome food, a comfortable and economic shelter, a reasonable and frugal wardrobe, in addition to easy access to the necessities and amenities of contemporary life, above the minimum subsistence level.

If these constitutional and political guarantees can be underwritten in a Government-directed welfare system, such evidence of humanitarianism will work wonders in Nigerian society. The wants of human beings are few and if they are satisfied they become an insulation from subversion. History has shown that the main cause why some societies became unstable is because those who ruled failed to discover this secret yearning of humanity.

By adapting the best elements so far experienced by human beings all over the world, in the practice of capitalism or socialism or welfarism, it is my honest conviction that a Nigerian ideology, based on the eclecticism now universally appreciated as the welfare state, is the right incentive to inspire the genius that is latent in us to build an affluent society where there will be full employment for healthy, well-educated and prosperous citizens, who should be loyal and patriotic to their country.

All we need now is to produce the leaders with vision and courage to build this new society. If the leadership would be forthcoming, there can be no doubt that the followership will respond. I can see in the distant horizon a transformation of Nigeria from a developing country to a land of plenty, whose agriculture and industry are so diversified in multilateral sectors that Nigeria can literally become a world force overnight!

How can these lofty aims be realised within the context of the Nigerian situation? Are they the dreams of a visionary which exist in his fertile imagination? Are they capable of being translated to action in the foreseeable future? Are they practicable in view of our diversities of language and culture coupled with our being a developing country which depends on economic aid from external sources?

My reaction to all the above questions is that, other things being equal, dreams of a kind can come true. In this respect I find consolation in Carl Sandburg who reminisced that it was the dream of the founders of America that created it as a world's model republican state. 'The republic is a dream,' he asserted, but 'nothing happens unless first a dream.' I agree.

EMERGENCE OF NIGERIAN IDEOLOGIES

I am a realist but I can dream dreams as well. I have a deep and abiding faith in pragmatism as a safe and useful philosophy to guide the individuals of any nation to accomplish their aims. Reason, experience, and practice demonstrate the verdict of history, if we bear in mind the experiences of older countries in Europe, America and Asia.

Surely, our ancestors have survived the struggle for existence in what is now geographically identified as Nigeria. It is true that they were racially homogeneous, since they belonged to the Negroid race, on account of their skin colour, hair texture, nose structure, lip formation, facial angle, and other morphological characteristics. As a matter of fact, they were identical in appearance, and were distinct from the white and yellow races.

However, we have observed that some individual indigenes of Nigeria speak a common language and acquired a common culture. Also, we have discovered a bitter truth that many individual Nigerian indigenes speak a common language and acquired a different culture, or speak different languages and acquired a common culture.

For example, the Ibo- and Yoruba-speaking peoples, as well as other linguistic groups in Nigeria, usually identified as Sudanic-speaking or Semi-Bantu-speaking, respectively, fall in the first category. But the Hausa, Fulani, Kanuri and other linguistic groups in Nigeria usually classified as Hamitic-speaking people fall in other categories. Yet all of them have settled permanently in Nigeria and have become citizens of one country as a result of the interplay of social and economic forces.

Since only the factor of race unites the great majority of indigenous Nigerians, and the factor of language unites or disunites them only to be united or disunited further by the factor of culture, we can take comfort in knowing that, in spite of the vagaries of anthropology, our ancestors did settle permanently in certain definitely demarcated language and culture areas. They conquered the elements in the process and asserted dominance in their different environments.

The tool which enabled them to accomplish this task was an accumulation of their wisdom, proverbs, folklore and traditions. These evolved into systems of knowledge and values. As they settled permanently in their various places, after migrating from one area to another, they devised methods for maintaining law and order in their societies and they also invented ways and means for satisfying their spiritual and material needs.

My point is that our ancestors, in spite of their heterogeneous languages and cultures, have bequeathed to us a legacy of political and economic ideologies which sustained them and enabled them to survive. Now that we are confronted with welfare system, such evidence of humanitarianism problems of co-existence and we are ensconced in a wilderness of alien ideologies, which are making a terrific impact on our ways of life, the obvious move is for us, like a seaman who has drifted from salt to fresh water, without knowing it, to cast down our bucket where we are and draw fresh water to assuage our thirst. Yes, we must dig deep from our roots to discover this secret of successful co-existence.

46

A One-Party System, 1964⁵⁴

Jomo Kenyatta

> *Jomo Kenyatta (c. 1894–1978) was the first president of Kenya (for more information on Kenyatta see Document 10). On December 12, 1964, Kenya gained full independence from Britain. A month earlier, on November 10, the Kenya African Democratic Union (KADU), Kenya's leading opposition party, merged with Kenyatta's Kenya Africa National Union (KANU). Early on, Kenyatta employed the slogan "Harambee" ("Let's All Pull Together") as part of his campaign for national cooperation. Kenyatta's nationalism soon led to authoritarianism. In 1966, Kenyatta turned Kenya into a single-party state with KANU as the only legal party. Kenyatta's vice-president, Jaramogi Oginga Odinga, resigned and became a public critic of Kenyatta. He formed the opposition Kenya People's Union (KPU), but was arrested in 1969. KANU remained Kenya's only legal party until 1991.*
>
> *In the following public statement, Kenyatta attempts to defend the idea of a single-party state on the grounds that it is consistent with traditional African tribal forms of governance. He questions the notion that democracy requires a multi-party system, but he also claims that his government would not block the future development of a multi-party system.*

On my return from the recent London and Cairo Conferences, I said that from now on we will work towards a one-Party State. Events have shown not only that a one-Party system was inevitable, but also that it was the most prudent method of attaining those aims and objects which our people hold so dear.

The evils of Colonialism and Imperialism left mass poverty, illiteracy, disease and ignorance in our midst. As we embark on the historic

---

54. Jomo Kenyatta, "A One-Party System" (1964), from *Suffering without Bitterness: The Founding of the Kenya Nation* (Nairobi: East African Publishing House, 1968).

task of eradicating these evils today, neo-Colonialism in its many mani-festations has already reared its ugly head in our motherland.

Thus we have a two-fold job to do: to secure our people from aggression emanating from our enemies, and from subversion originating from some of our self-appointed friends both within and without.

Our aim in Kenya is to cultivate a social and political order which is consistent with our needs and our conditions. We will borrow what is relevant, and compatible with our aspirations, from any country of the East or West.

Africanism—which continues to gain momentum—will thereby become a powerful instrument for elevating our Continent and acceler-ating development. Nevertheless, we must be quite clear about what we mean by Africanism before we can associate it with a one-Party State.

To some, Africanism means negritude. To others, it connotes the pursuit of those ideals that are inherently African, while to yet others it implies the mixture of the African tradition with what is right, modern and progressive.

I submit that the Africanism to which we aspire in this country is the Africanism which combines the best from the past, present and future: the Africanism which seeks to fulfil what our people want to be, to do and to have.

Indeed, this is the Africanism to which I dedicated my book . . . ("Facing Mount Kenya") . . . in my early days in the political field, when I said that: 'The dead, the living and the unborn will unite to rebuild the destroyed shrines'. It is this Africanism—as opposed to chauvinistic nationalism and economic autarchy—which is becoming increasingly manifest in most one-Party States in Africa.

Why, the Western democrat asks, does the African not adopt the Western type of democracy? Why, comes the rejoinder from the other camp, does the African not go Communist and adopt our system?

We reject a blueprint of the Western model of a two-Party system of Government because we do not subscribe to the notion of the Gov-ernment and the governed being in opposition to one another, the one clamouring for duties and the other crying out for rights.

The Westminster model of Government has evolved from the tradi-tions of the people of Britain, over many hundreds of years. The irri-tating aspects of British traditions, to be discerned on some occasions in the House of Commons, have been translated into unwritten rules which embody the emotions of the Anglo-Saxon.

Yet those who are today harping on the Westminster model, trying to say that we are aspiring to a one-Party State in too much of a hurry, are themselves conscience-smitten, for they know that—having been poisoned by Imperialism and Colonialism—they are in an unenviable position. We have only just seen the leader of the so-called Opposition our beloved brother Ronald Ngala,[55] tearing up a copy of the country's Development Plan. Instead of being constructive from within, he prefers to be destructive from without.

These gentlemen have lately gone to the extent of courting what they lavishly call detention, in their alleged opposition to my recent hint about a one-Party State. In the first place, this is a cowardly reaction to a bold approach to our country's post-independence need for political stability. Secondly, everyone knows that—when some of us were tucked into detention and imprisonment—some of those who are today literally applying to be detained were warming their bellies under imperialist wings.

Nor are we prepared to justify our predilection for a one-Party system of Government by using the fragile perennial argument that Parties are the expression of social classes, and that therefore there must be only one Party. The theory of class struggle has no relevance to our particular situation here.

One of the chief gladiators of this thesis of class struggle had this to say, at the end of the last century: 'the modern labourer . . . instead of rising with the progress of industry . . . sinks deeper and deeper below the conditions of his own class . . . , there was an ever increasing mass poverty, oppression, enslavement, degeneration and exploitation . . . '.

Now there was nothing inherently foolish in these statements during the period of the Chartist movement in Britain. Laissez-faire was the catch-phrase of the times. Governments regarded capital outlay and incomes as given, and held that employment and investment were dependent only on the decisions of the entrepreneurs.

The latter thus had powers to exploit the working classes. Politics, therefore, was a superstructure erected on an economic base, and the practice of politics was therefore impotent. But in a one-Party State such as we envisage, we hold that politics is a potent instrument; it is through

---

55. Ronald Ngala (1923–1972) was the leader of the Kenya African Democratic Union (KADU), the main opposition political party. He joined KANU in 1964.

our political institutions that we influence economic trends, and not the other way round.

For instance, taking the total growth in the average earnings per worker here, the indices show a rise from 100 in 1946 to 565 in 1963. This is partial proof that trade unionists through collective bargaining, and freedom fighters through their struggle for equality of opportunity, were able to improve their lot against considerable barriers and denial of opportunity by the Colonialists.

If they could improve their lot against Colonial domination, how much more can they do so under a free Kenya Government!

The necessity for a one-Party system in most parts of Africa—including Kenya—stems from two predominant factors. First, African society traditionally revolves around the family tree, the wider pattern of blood brotherhood, and the wider network of clans and tribes. At no time did the African tribes, or groups of tribes, see the State in the same way as the Greek City States. At no time did African tribes see themselves as tinpot 'nations'. Rather, at any rate before the advent of Imperialism, they regarded themselves as responsible semi-autonomous local governments who regulated the conduct of life of the people. They continued to act independently insofar as—and to the extent to which—there was no overwhelming danger or natural catastrophe seriously threatening the existence of one or all. When catastrophes and calamities occurred, there was no doubt that many tribes acted in concert and demonstrated their community of interest. An instance is, of course, the advent of Colonialism. When the Colonisers first came to Kenya towards the end of the last century, which single tribe did not oppose them? The whole country—from the Coast to Kisumu, Masailand to Kikuyu-land, and the NFD to Abaluhya areas—is scattered with graves of our dead men and women who died at the hands of adventurous Colonialists.

Secondly, tribes in this country united in times of famine, when there was considerable movement of population from one tribe to another. By the time Imperialism, armed with all modern weapons of destruction, set upon our defenceless people and took our freedom by devious methods, inter-tribal integration had advanced so much that inter-marriage and barter trade, and other forms of co-operation between tribes, were accepted as a valuable routine.

What answer did the African have to the important question of: 'what is the State and why should I obey it?' To him, the traditional

Tribal Council—which occasionally met other Tribal Councils through nominated representatives, or in times of war through intermediaries— was at once a Government and an expression of the very personality of each and every citizen.

It may be argued by some scholars that the African took no part at all in self-government, and that government was run solely by autocratic leaders who imposed their will on their subjects. But people with such qualities of leadership are to be found in many parts of the world, and there is nothing inherently African in this.

The main point is that African leaders invariably had a number of advisers, who were selected by virtue of their logic and reasoning. They in turn elected their spokesmen by popular acclaim. The Elders thus elected were constantly in touch with families, blood brothers, clans and tribes. In this context, the rulers were to the people what the people were to them. By obeying the Tribal Councils, the people maintained that they obeyed themselves and their true will. The State—and its geo- graphical areas were immaterial—was justified on the grounds that only therein could people find peace and security.

The idea of 'constructive opposition from within' is therefore not an alien thing, so far as traditional African society is concerned. But we did not have to create Leaders of the Opposition, maintain them from public funds, and tolerate their insatiable desire for agitation, merely because they wanted to oppose for the sake of opposition.

This unity, coherence and homogeneity—although subjected to terrific pressure from close Imperialist and Colonialist rule—remained throughout most of the period of Colonial domination. In 1960, after the Constitutional Conference in London, all the Members of Parlia- ment recognised the need for and reaffirmed their faith in unity and solidarity, in keeping with this traditional African way of life.

The vanguard of the nationalist struggle for Uhuru was launched. It was only after this Party—KANU—was formed that several dissi- dents formed a splinter club which was later called KADU. It would be a sham to imagine that these self-conceited grasshopper politi- cians formed their new club because of their belief in majority rule, democracy and the rule of law. Had that been the case, the present leader of the cabal known as KADU would not have connived with a Colonial Governor in an unholy alliance to coerce the majority and delay independence.

Granted that these are valid reasons in favour of a one-Party system—either as a transient device or a permanent institution—what are the prospects for democracy in Kenya?

This depends to a large extent on the nature of the relationship between the State and the individual. It was once argued that the socialist world placed the State above the individual, and that the capitalist system placed the individual above the State. The difference between a socialist and a capitalist is that each represents a fusion of these two underlying principles in varying proportions.

Be that as it may, my Government is pledged to uphold the traditional freedoms of association, speech and assembly, and to respect the rule of law and human dignity. In case of genuine complaints, citizens have recourse to independent Courts of Law. In addition, as provided in the Constitution, machinery already exists for a change of Government through free elections when the time comes.

One question which is usually raised about one-Party States is that they do not offer a conclusive explanation about means of controlling political power. But to assume that the intrinsic desire for power will one day be eradicated is to show a very mistaken view of human nature. The desire and competition for power is a healthy thing, so long as there are effective machineries to restrain dictatorial tendencies.

It was never possible—and it never will be possible—for the human race to exist in a vacuum. In fact, progress in all walks of life has come about as the result of a conflict of ideas. It is my considered opinion that the greatest innovation in the political institutions of the world is not the one-Party State or the authoritarian regime. Dictatorships are as old as the hills. The fascinating innovation in our time is the mass Party, and the mass Party is to be found under both one-Party and two-Party systems.

It is the nature of the organisation of mass political Parties—outside the scope of this Paper—that is the real threat to the rule of law and democracy. Consequently, there are two-Party States which are tyrannical and dictatorial, and one-Party States which can be said to be democratic and liberal. In other words, all two-Party States are not necessarily democratic, and all one-Party States are not necessarily authoritarian.

Secondly, those who talk about democracy and individual freedoms must think critically about the position of democracy in the light of scientific and technological advancement, and especially in the light of the advent of mass media in communications and propaganda.

At this stage, however, we have no choice to make. Through the historical processes of the past century, we find ourselves with myriad relevant grounds and conditions for a one-Party State. It is inevitable. In our particular situation, practice will have to precede theory. But should relevant grounds for a multi-Party State evolve in the future, it is not the intention of my Government to block such a trend through any prohibitive legislation.

47
African Socialist Humanism, 1964[56]

Léopold Sédar Senghor

A major poet and politician, Léopold Sédar Senghor (1906–2001) served as the first president of Senegal and, together with Martinican poet Aimé Césaire, was a founder of the Négritude literary movement. Senghor studied in France at the Sorbonne, École Normale Supérieure, and received his Agrégation in French Grammar from the University of Paris. It was during his time in Paris and because of his contact with other colonized peoples that Senghor and others coined the term "Négritude" to refer to the celebration of the distinct cultural values and historical heritage of black people. Senghor was gradually drawn into politics under the guidance of the Senegalese socialist Lamine Guèye. In the lead-up to Senegalese independence, Senghor played an increasingly prominent role in nationalist politics. Initially, Senghor supported a federation of African states along the model of a commonwealth. Other African statesman, however, criticized this arrangement and, as a consequence, Senegal became an independent republic in 1960 with Senghor as its first president, a position he held for twenty years. In 1983, Senghor became the first African to be elected to L'Académie française. Senghor spent his remaining years in France.

Throughout his political career, Senghor was seen as a major African representative of socialist humanism—a movement that privileged Marx's more philosophical critique of alienation over his critique of economic exploitation. Like many African socialists, such as Julius Nyerere, Senghor argued that socialism was consistent with the traditional political and ethical views of African peoples. While many leaders in Africa believed in the potential benefits of socialism in newly independent African states, Senghor's socialism is strongly linked to the European social democratic political tradition and its

---

56. Léopold Sédar Senghor, "African Socialist Humanism" from *On African Socialism*, translated by Mercer Cook. Copyright © 1964 by Léopold Sédar Senghor. Reprinted with permission.

emphasis on electoral politics. The following excerpt from his book On
African Socialism *expounds upon Senghor's conception of socialist
humanism in Africa. It reflects upon the need for a political program
in Africa that takes into account the unique cultural patrimony of
Africans, a cornerstone of the Négritude movement. Senghor explains
his opposition to the East bloc in the Cold War and alliance to the
West, but also asserts the distinctiveness of an African form of socialism grounded in African values, which, nevertheless, he links with
European social democracy.*

For an African Type of Socialism

Let us recapitulate Marx's positive contributions. They are: the philosophy of humanism, economic theory, dialectical method. To these
we may add trade unionism, planning, and also federalism and cooperation, which come to us from the French idealistic socialists—Saint-
Simon, Proudhon, and Fourier, to name only the outstanding ones.

Thus, we are not *Communists*. Does this mean that we shall practice anti-Communism? Certainly not. Anti-Communism, the "witch
hunt," can have but one result: increased tension between East and
West and a continuation of the Cold War with the obvious risk of
unleashing a third global conflict from which humanity would not
recover. We are not Communists for a theoretical reason: Lenin's definition of matter proceeds from a one-sided concept, from a purely
materialistic and deterministic postulate. At the beginning of *Anar-
chism or Socialism*, Stalin goes even further: "Marxism is not only a
theory of socialism, it is a definitive view of the world, a philosophical
system."

We are not Communists for a practical reason: The anxiety for
human dignity and the need for freedom—man's freedoms and freedoms of collectivities—that animate Marx's thought and provide its
revolutionary ferment, this anxiety and this need are unknown to Communism whose major deviation is Stalinism. The "dictatorship of the
proletariat," which was to be only temporary, becomes the dictatorship
of the Party and State in self-perpetuation. "The Soviet Union," said
a Senegalese on his return from Moscow, "has succeeded in building
socialism, but at the sacrifice of religion, of the soul."

The paradox in the building of socialism in Communist countries, or at least in the Soviet Union, is that it increasingly resembles capitalistic growth in the United States, the American way of life, with high salaries, refrigerators, washing machines, and television sets, but with less art and less freedom of thought. Nevertheless, we shall not be won over to a regime of liberal capitalism and free enterprise. We cannot close our eyes to segregation, although the Federal Government combats it, nor can we accept material success as a way of life.

We stand for a middle course, for a *democratic socialism*, which goes so far as to integrate spiritual values, a socialism which ties in with the old ethical current of the French socialists. Historically and culturally we belong to this current. Besides, the French socialists—from Saint-Simon to the Léon Blum of *For All Mankind*—are not so utopian as they are reputed to be. Insofar as they are idealistic, they fulfill the requirements of the Negro-African soul, the requirements of men of all races and all countries. *Not By Bread Alone*—this is the title of a novel by Dudintsev, a Soviet writer, and the Russians read this book avidly. Khrushchev was not mistaken: De-Stalinization was imposed by the people, by the thirst for freedom, by the hunger for "spiritual nourishment."

Concluding his report on the East German Republic (Communist Germany), Michel Bosquet wrote: "When I ask [the head of a labor union] what workers demand, he replies: 'Today they want TV set and motorcycles. When they get them, they will demand a shorter work week. And then? . . . I can only answer for myself. What I should like, what I miss, is more good literature.'" This fact is not unrelated to a phenomenon observed in America; the appeal of the contemplative life as a reaction against the surrounding mechanism. Among American Catholics, the proportion of priests to laity is one of the highest in the world.

This thirst for freedom, this hunger for spiritual nourishment, strengthened by the moral tradition of French socialism, explains why numerous French Marxists in recent years have shunned Stalinism and even Communism: Henri Lefebvre, Pierre Fougeyrollas, and Edgar Morin, among others, have recently stated their reasons in sorrowful but lucid volumes. The major reason, common to them all, is that the Party has come to submerge the individual under the collectivity, the person under the class, to hide reality behind the screen of ideology. If we reflect on these various cases, we shall discover that, with the exception, perhaps, of Lefebvre, they "call into question" not only Marxism but Marx himself. For if the individual is forgotten, it is because Marx did not pay sufficient attention to the "natural determination," namely, the *Nation*, which is not effaced by class.

Marx underestimated the political and national idealism that, born in France upon the ruins of provincial fatherland, won over the world in the Revolution of 1789. "Justice," Marx writes, "humanity, liberty, equality, fraternity, independence . . . these relatively moral categories that sound so nice but in historical and political questions prove absolutely nothing." I repeat: *independence.* If the creator of scientific socialism returned to this earth, he would perceive with amazement that these "chimeras," as he called them, and above all the concept of *Nation*, are living realities in the twentieth century.

What is left of the Revolution of 1789? A political doctrine and technique, accepted nowadays even by the devout. The "worship of the Goddess Reason" was but a momentary flame. Similarly, Marxism will undergo a sifting process. Of it there will surely remain an economic doctrine and technique, inasmuch as they do not contradict the teachings of Christianity and Islam (far from it). But a third revolution is taking place: a reaction against capitalistic and Communistic materialism that will integrate moral, if not religious values with the political and economic contributions of the two great revolutions. Here the colored peoples, including the Negro African, must play their part and help construct the new planetary civilization. As Aimé Césaire says: "They will not come empty-handed to the rendezvous of give-and-take." Between two world wars, Paul Morand observed: "The Negroes have rendered a great service to America. But for them, one might have thought it impossible to live without a bank account and a bathtub." I am quoting from memory.

Our Need for a Triple Inventory

We must build our own development plan, based on European socialist contributions and also on the best of Negro-African civilization. Thus we shall merely be putting the lesson of socialism into practice. In his correspondence and even in *Capital*, Marx continued to insist that his theory is not an "open sesame to historic-philosophical theory," and that the conclusions of *Capital*, resulting from a study of the capitalist societies of Western Europe in the mid-nineteenth century, are valid only for that milieu and for that period. They were not even valid for Russia, as his letters to Mikhailovsky and Vera Zasulich indicate.

Before drawing up our development plan, we must therefore study our situation—our present situation—using the dialectical method. On a threefold level, we must prepare: (1) an inventory of our traditional civilization; (2) an inventory of the impact of colonialism and French civilization on our traditional civilization; and (3) an inventory of our economic resources, our needs and potentialities. Our development plan must not be solely economic: It must be social in the broadest sense of the word—political, economic, social, and cultural as well. We insist on this last word.

African politicians have a tendency to neglect culture, to make it an appendage of politics. This is a mistake. These two areas, like the others, are certainly closely connected, each reacting on the other. But if one stops to reflect, culture is at once the basis and the ultimate aim of politics. Remember the labor leader quoted a short while ago, "And then? What I should like, what I miss, is more good literature." He could have added, "Good theater, good painting, good music, etc." Culture is also *basic* in the socialist connotation of the word. It is "the sum of objects, ideas, symbols, beliefs, feelings, values, and social forms that are transmitted from one generation to another in a given society." We can accept this definition, though I usually call that "civilization," reserving the word "culture" for the spirit of civilization. Culture is the very texture of society.

Since the start of the century, ethnologists—not to speak of archaeologists, geographers, historians, musicologists, and linguists—have been making an *inventory of Negro-African civilization.* The Institut Français d'Afrique Noire, the University of Dakar, and Présence Africaine are continuing this research. We should all have in our libraries: *La Philosophie bantoue*, by Reverend Placide Tempels; *Dieu d'eau*, by Marcel Griaule; or simply, *Les Conttes de l'Ouest Africain*, by Roland Colin. From these volumes we would learn that Negro-African philosophy, like socialist philosophy, is existentialist and humanistic, but that it integrates spiritual values. We would learn that, for the Negro African, the "vital forces" are the texture of the world and that world is animated by a dialectical movement. We would learn that Negro-African society is collectivist or, more exactly, communal, because it is rather a *communion* of souls than an aggregate of individuals. We would learn that we had already achieved socialism before the coming of the European. We would conclude that our duty is to renew it by helping it to regain its spiritual dimensions.

The sociologists are now making an *inventory of the encounter of civilizations.* Much remains to be done in this field. The work of our African writers and artists is not negligible. They present syntheses, the elements of which must now be analyzed. For we must attain a synthesis of civilizations that retains only the fecund elements of each. The objective is a dynamic *symbiosis*—I mean a cultural blending which, like all blending or grafting, produces a more succulent fruit.

The *inventory of our economic resources* will not be the least important. We must congratulate both the governments of the federated states and the Government of Mali for having thought of it. Senegal and Sudan have, in fact, created *study committees* of competent technicians to examine our various problems and to seek the best solutions; for institutional problems, a committee whose conclusions have helped us to prepare our constitutions; a committee for social problems; another on civil service reform; still another on economic problems.

With respect to the last, it is essential that the plans for economic development be coordinated on the level of the Mali Federation. Senegal has selected Father Lebret's team. Sudan would be well advised to examine the possibility of doing likewise. The merit of Father Lebret's group is that it is affiliated with the school of economics and humanism and is motivated by an "open socialism" very similar to our own conception.

We have spoken of the Mali Federation. Needless to say, our reflections and proposals are valid for all the states of what used to be called French West Africa, for all the French-speaking Negro-African states. If we apply our reflections and proposals to Mali, it is for the simple reason that the success of the PFA[57] and of *African unity* depends on its success. If Mali succeeds, it will serve as an example and a magnet. Then we will be able to create a single federation which may extend—why not?—from Dakar to Brazzaville.

The development plan must be essentially economic and social. Nevertheless, it must be comprehensive and it must be based on the cultural inventory, so that it will flow into our political future. The economic and social choices will be made in line with our objectives. But it is in line with our point of departure—Negro-African culture—that the socialist contribution must be adapted to our realities.

---

57. *Parti de la Fédération Africaine* (Party of the African Federation) was a French West African political party founded in 1959.

48

Consciencism, 1964[58]

Kwame Nkrumah

The following excerpt comes from Kwame Nkrumah's (1909–1972) philosophical treatise, Consciencism *(1964). In it Nkrumah discusses how traditional African society had been transformed by colonialism. As a consequence, newly independent societies in Africa required new philosophical grounding. Nkrumah claimed that after attaining independence, Africans experienced a "crisis of conscience," unable to reconcile traditional African beliefs with the Islamic and Euro-Christian beliefs that had been introduced in Africa through imperial rule and conquest. To correct this bifurcation of systems of belief, Nkrumah proposes the principle of consciencism as a means of forging a new African identity that reconciles the various spiritual beliefs prevalent on the continent. Nkrumah also explains his concept of "positive action" as a form of ongoing resistance to the post-independence exploitation of Africans.*

Our attitude to the Western and Islamic experience must be purposeful. It must also be guided by thought, for practice without thought is blind. What is called for as a first step is a body of connected thought which will determine the general nature of our action in unifying the society which we have inherited, this unification to take account, at all times, of the elevated ideals underlying African society. Social revolution must therefore have, standing firmly behind it, an intellectual revolution, a revolution in which our thinking and philosophy are directed towards the redemption of our society. Our philosophy must find its weapons in the environment and living conditions of the African people. It is from those conditions that the intellectual content of our philosophy must be created. The emancipation of the African continent is the emancipation of man. This requires two aims: first, the restitution of the egalitarianism of

58. Excerpt from *Consciencism*. Copyright © 1964 by Kwame Nkrumah. Reprinted with the permission of the Monthly Review Foundation.

human society, and, second, the logistic mobilization of all our resources towards the attainment of that restitution.

The philosophy that must stand behind this social revolution is that which I have once referred to as philosophical consciencism; consciencism is the map in intellectual terms of the disposition of forces which will enable African society to digest the Western and the Islamic and the Euro-Christian elements in Africa, and develop them in such a way that they fit into the African personality. The African personality is itself defined by the cluster of humanist principles which underlie the traditional African society. Philosophical consciencism is that philosophical standpoint which, taking its start from the present content of the African conscience, indicates the way in which progress is forged out of the conflict in that conscience.

. . . In its political aspect, philosophical consciencism is faced with the realities of colonialism, imperialism, disunity and lack of development. Singly and collectively these four militate against the realization of a social justice based on ideas of true equality.

The first step is to liquidate colonialism wherever it is. In *Towards Colonial Freedom* I state that it is the aim of colonial governments to treat their colonies as producers of raw materials, and at the same time as the dumping-ground of the manufactured goods of foreign industrialists and foreign capitalists. I have always believed that the basis of colonialism is economic, but the solution of the colonial problem lies in political action, in a fierce and constant struggle for emancipation as an indispensible first step towards securing economic independence and integrity.

. . . [I]n a colonial situation positive action and negative action can be discerned. Positive action will represent the sum of those forces seeking social justice in terms of the destruction of oligarchic exploitation and oppression. Negative action will correspondingly represent the sum of those forces tending to prolong colonial subjugation and exploitation. Positive action is revolutionary and negative action is reactionary.

. . . .

In a colonial situation, negative action undoubtedly outweighs positive action. In order that true independence should be won, it is necessary that positive action should come to overwhelm negative action. Admittedly, a semblance of true independence is possible without this specific relation. When this happens, we say that neo-colonialism has set in, for neo-colonialism is a guise adopted by negative action in order to give the impression that it has been overcome by positive action. Neo-colonialism is negative action playing possum.

In order to forestall this, it is necessary for positive action to be backed by a mass party, and qualitatively to improve this mass so that by education and an increase in its degree of consciousness, its aptitude for positive action becomes heightened. We can therefore say that in a colonial territory, positive action must be backed by a mass party, complete with its instruments of education. This was why the Convention People's Party in Ghana developed from an early stage its education wing, workers' wing, farmers' wing, youth wing, women's wing, etc. In this way, the people received constant political education, their self-awareness was increased and such a self-image was formed as ruthlessly excluded colonialism in all its guises. It is also in the backing of millions of members and supporters, united by a common radical purpose, that the revolutionary character of the Convention People's Party consists, and not merely in the piquancy of its programmes. Its mass and national support made it possible to think in realistic terms of instituting changes of a fundamental nature in the social hotch-potch bequeathed by colonialism.

A people's parliamentary democracy with a one-party system is better able to express and satisfy the common aspirations of a nation as a whole, than a multiple-party parliamentary system, which is in fact only a ruse for perpetuating, and covers up, the inherent struggle between the 'haves' and the 'have-nots'.

In order that a territory should acquire the nominal attributes of independence, it is of course not necessary that positive action should exceed negative action. When a colonialist country sees the advance of positive action, it unfailingly develops a policy of containment, a policy whereby it seeks to check this advance and limit it. This policy often takes the form of conferences and protracted constitutional reforms.

Containment is, however, accepted by the colonialist country only as a second best. What it would really like to do is to roll back positive action. It is when it is assured of the impossibility of rolling back the billows of history that it applies the policy of containment, that it tries to limit the achievement of progress by devising frivolous reforms. The colonialist country seeks to divert positive action into channels which are harmless to it.

To do this it resorts to subtle means. Having abandoned direct violence, the colonialist country imparts a deceptive orientation to the negative forces in its subject territory. These negative forces become the political wolf masquerading in sheep's clothing, they join the clamour for independence, and are accepted in good faith by the people. It is then that like a wasting disease they seek from the inside to infest, corrupt, pervert and thwart the aspirations of the people.

The people, the body and the soul of the nation, the final sanction of political decisions, and the inheritors of sovereignty, cannot be fooled for long. Quick on the scent, they ferret out these Janus-faced politicians who run with the hare and hunt with the hounds. They turn away from them. Once this colonialist subterfuge is exposed, and the minion accomplices discredited, the colonial power has no option but to acknowledge the independence of the people. By its very next act, however, it seeks without grace to neutralize this same independence by fomenting discontent and disunity; and, finally, by arrant ingratiation and wheedling it attempts to disinherit the people and constitute itself their conscience and their will, if not their voice and their arm. Political decisions, just as they were before independence was won, lose their reference to the welfare of the people, and serve once again the well-being and security of the erstwhile colonial power and the clique of self-centered politicians.

Any oblique attempt of a foreign power to thwart, balk, corrupt or otherwise pervert the true independence of a sovereign people is neo-colonialist. It is neo-colonialist because it seeks, notwithstanding the acknowledged sovereignty of the people, to subordinate their interests to those of a foreign power.

A colonialist country can in fact offer independence to a people, not with the intention which such an act might be though to imply, but in the hope that the positive and progressive forces thus appeased and quietened, the people might be exploited with greater serenity and comfort.

Neo-colonialism is a greater danger to independent countries than is colonialism. Colonialism is crude, essentially overt, and apt to be overcome by a purposeful concert of national effort. In neo-colonialism, however, the people are divided from their leaders and, instead of providing true leadership and guidance which is informed at every point by the ideal of the general welfare, leaders come to neglect the very people who put them in power and incautiously become instruments of suppression on behalf of the neo-colonialists.

49

Letter from Prison to Kwame Nkrumah, 1964[59]

J. B. Danquah

J. B. Danquah (1895–1965) was a Ghanaian statesman, historian, and political rival of Kwame Nkrumah. For many years, Danquah had been a leading figure in the Gold Coast independence movement. In 1931, he founded The Times of West Africa. He helped to found the United Gold Coast Convention (UGCC) and invited Nkrumah to return to the Gold Coast in 1947 to become the party's general secretary. Danquah also helped to found the University of Ghana. Though they were former allies, Danquah ran against Nkrumah in the 1960 presidential election, but lost. In 1964, he was arrested under the Prevention Detention Act on charges of trying to overthrow the government. In the following letter from prison to Nkrumah, Danquah appeals to Nkrumah for his release from Nsawam Prison. He notes that he has never received a trial or had the charges against him explained. Danquah died in prison.

His Excellency,
Osagyefo Dr. Kwame Nkrumah, P.C., LL.D., etc.,
President of the Republic of Ghana,
Flagstaff House, Accra.

Dear Dr. Nkrumah,

I am tired of being in prison on preventive detention with no opportunity to make an original or any contribution to the progress and development of the country, and I therefore respectfully write to beg and appeal to you to make an order for my release and return home.

I am anxious to resume my contribution to the progress and development of Ghana in the field of Ghanaian literature (Twi and English), and in Ghana Research (History and Culture), and I am anxious also

59. J. B. Danquah, Letter from Prison to Kwame Nkrumah: http://www.graphic.com.gh/news/politics/j-b-danquah-s-letter-to-nkrumah-from-prison.html (accessed February 9, 2017).

to establish my wife and children in a home, to develop the education of my children (ten of them) and to restore my parental home at Kibi (Yiadom House) to a respectable dignity, worthy of my late father's own contribution to the progress of our country.

You will recall that when in 1948 we were arrested by the British Government and sent to the North for detention they treated us as gentlemen, not as galley slaves, and provided each of us with a furnished bungalow (two or three rooms) with a garden, together with opportunity for reading and writing. In fact, I took with me my typewriter and papers for the purpose, and Ako Adjei also did the same, and there was ample opportunity for correspondence.

Here at Nsawam, for the four months of my detention up to date (8th January to 9th May 1964), I have not been allowed access to my books and papers, except the Bible, and although I was told in January that my application to write to my wife, Mrs Elizabeth Danquah, could be considered if I addressed a letter to the Minister of the Interior, through the Director of Prisons, I have not, for over three months, since I wrote to the Minister as directed on the 31st January 1964, received any reply, not even a common acknowledgment from the Minister as to whether I should be allowed to write to my wife or not. As I had no opportunity to make any financial provision for my wife and children at the time of my arrest, this delay in the Minister's reply has made it impossible for me to contribute to the progress and maintenance of my wife and also for the education of my children as is my duty to the nation.

Secondly, you will recall that barely a month after our detention in the North in 1948 we were brought down to Accra and released to appear before a Commission of Enquiry set up to investigate the justice or otherwise of our arrest and detention. We duly appeared before the Watson Commission and made history for Gold Coast and Ghana. It resulted in the finding that the Burns Constitution was outmoded at birth, with a recommendation that our country should attain its independence within ten years, and that a Constitutional Committee (the Coussey Committee) should be set up to lay down the foundations of such independence and the steps to be taken towards its attainment.

In the present case, since I was arrested four months ago, I have not been asked to appear before any Judge, or Committee, or Commission, and, up to now, all I have been told is contained in a sheet of paper entitled "Grounds for Detention" in which I am accused that "in recent months" I have been actively engaged in a plan "to overthrow the Government of Ghana by unlawful means" and that I have planned thereby "to endanger the security of the State" (the Police and Armed Forces).

As no particulars of any kind were provided in the grounds for detention to indicate how the Government of Ghana came to formulate such a disgraceful charge against me, I spent in the prison here the greater part of January and February 1964 to write a review of the whole of my activities in "recent months" (roughly, from June 1962 [last release from detention] to January 1964). This writing was done by way of "Representations" in answer to the charge. . . .

I confidently assure you, Sir, that when my representations reach you, it will be realised that my contribution in the said period of "recent months" to the intellectual and cultural achievement of the country was such that what should have been sent to me on January 8, 1964, was not a hostile invasion of my home and family, like enemy territory, together with my arrest and detention, but rather a delegation of Ghanaian civil officials and other dignitaries to offer me the congratulations of the nation and the thanks of the Government. . . .

This, however was not to be, and I find myself locked up at Nsawam Prison in a cell of about six by nine feet, without a writing or reading desk, without a dining table, without a bed, or a chair or any form of seat, and compelled to eat my food squatting on the same floor where two blankets and a cover are spread for me on the hard cement to sleep on, and where a latrine pan (piss pot) without a closet, and a water jug and a cup without a locker, are all assembled in that narrow space for my use like a galley slave. . . .

I am required to sleep or keep lying down on the blankets and a small pillow for the whole 24 hours of the day and night except for a short period of about five minutes in the morning to empty and wash out my latrine pan, and of about ten to fifteen minutes at noon to go for a bath. I am occasionally allowed to do a short exercise in the sun say once a week for about half an hour. That is all I have been engaged on in four months with my talents, such as I possess, going waste and my health being undermined and my life endangered by various diseases without being allowed to be taken to the Prison Hospital for continuous observation and treatment. . . .

I am now left in a prison cell at the Special Block at the Nsawam Prison reserved for "dangerous criminals", and I am being thereby effectively prevented from making any original contribution to the intellectual and cultural progress of our country. . . .

I end as I began. I am tired of being kept in prison kicking my heels, and doing nothing worth while for the country of my birth and love, and for the great continent of Africa which was the first to give the entire world a real taste of civilisation. . . . I trust you will accept this appeal for my release from detention in the spirit of utmost confidence and cordiality in which it is written, and I look forward to my early release from prison with the greatest possible faith, expectation and confidence.

Believe me to be,

Yours Very Sincerely and Respectfully

(Sgd.) J. B. Danquah

50

Origins of the Cabinet Crisis, 1964[60]

Vera Chirwa

Born in 1932, Vera Chirwa is a Malawian human rights activist. She became the first female attorney in Nyasaland (present-day Malawi). She and her husband, Orton Chirwa (1919–1992), who was Malawi's minister of justice and attorney general, were prominent opponents of Malawi's first president, Dr. Hastings Banda (1898–1997). In 1959, the Chirwas, along with Banda, helped form the Malawi Congress Party (MCP). A lifelong women's advocate, Chirwa formed the Nyasaland African Women's League with Rose Chiwambo. Chirwa's husband was one of the ministers whose opposition to Banda's autocratic rule led to the Cabinet Crisis of 1964 (for background see the introduction to Document 51). After Banda began to persecute his opponents, the couple fled Malawi for Tanzania. They were kidnapped in Zambia in 1981 and imprisoned. Orton Chirwa died in prison, but Vera Chirwa was released in 1993 after appeals from Amnesty International. In the following excerpt from her 2007 autobiography, Chirwa recounts the public outcry against Banda's national policies. In particular, she notes her work with Chiwambo to address the crisis among pregnant women who were turned away from hospitals because they could not afford the fees that Banda's government imposed. Chirwa offers an important account of the ways Banda's policies affected everyday Malawians.

But the ministers were reacting to more than Dr Banda's style of leadership. In addition to foreign policy, they disagreed fundamentally with Dr Banda's political course on a number of points. First of all, the ministers disagreed with Dr Banda's acceptance of the recommendations of the Skinner Commission, which was set up prior to independence to look into the conditions of the civil service. Dr Banda was unwilling

60. Vera Chirwa, "Origins of the Cabinet Crisis" from *Fearless Fighter: An Autobiography*. Copyright © 2007 by Vera Chirwa. Reprinted with the permission of Zed Books.

to Africanise the civil service and replace the white civil servants after independence as many of the ministers wanted. Following the recommendations of the Skinner Report, it was decided that the salaries of white civil servants would be raised, whereas the salaries of African civil servants would remain static. The African civil servants were in uproar:

'Why are we to be paid less? We go to the same market. We go to the same shops. The whites are already getting a lot of money and now the gap is supposed to be even greater!'

Another contentious issue was the recent introduction of a three-penny charge at government hospitals. My return from London for the independence celebrations coincided with the annual nation-wide tour of the League of Malawi women and Rose Chiwambo had asked me to come along. During that tour we received a lot of complaints from the village women:

'We women have been used to giving birth at home in our villages. Then you encourage us to go to the hospital—and when we respond you decide to charge a fee!'

Three pennies was a modest fee, but it could mean all the difference to poor people, and the staff at the hospitals were taking advantage of the situation by exaggerating the fee or rejecting people who were unable to pay. After the tour we presented a list to Dr Banda of stories collected from the villages about penniless women who had been left to give birth on the roadside or been sent back from hospital in a critical situation.

People were quite upset and the ministers and the MPs sensed a general public dissatisfaction. Dr Banda had launched a self-help scheme and encouraged people to participate in building the new Malawi:

'If you want to develop the country don't leave it to the government alone. We must all work very hard because Malawi is poor. You build schools and the government will provide the teachers. You build hospitals and houses for the staff and the government will provide the doctors. You grow cabbages and tomatoes and make a road to the market, and if you need a bridge the government will build it for you.'

The League of Malawi Women, the Youth League, the ministers and the MPs had campaigned tirelessly, and the response was formidable. People built things, but where were the doctors, the teachers and the bridges? They felt that the government had failed to deliver its part of the deal; people complained that the tomatoes and cabbage were rotting in the gardens.

Many MPs approached the ministers with these complaints:

'We are getting unpopular in our own constituencies. You have to approach Dr Banda.'

The ministers decided to take all these complaints to the leader, but nobody had ever challenged his authority. He had a temper and flared up very violently; everybody, including the ministers, was afraid of him. They knew it was a critical moment for them all and decided to stand together.

'What happened to Msonthi should not be repeated', Orton said. 'If one person is sacked we should stand together.'

Orton, who was Minister of Justice, and Chipembere, who was Minister of Education, had both made arrangements to go abroad. Chipembere was going to a conference in Canada and Orton was on his way to Britain. Orton decided to cancel his trip, but Chipembere had to leave:

'I must go, but anything you decide—good or bad—I'm with you. We have made a promise to each other. Kamuzu's tactics are to divide and rule and if he expels even one of us, we'll all resign.'

At a Cabinet meeting in August 1964 the ministers presented their grievances.

'Where did you find the courage!' Dr Banda exclaimed, and started singling people out:

'You, Chiume! Since when did you become my adviser?'

The President was so shocked by the criticism that he offered to resign.

'I'm resigning and going back to my home in Britain', he said, but they rejected his resignation and, by the conclusion of the meeting, he had calmed down and seemed to have taken note of their complaints about his policies.

'I'm going to think about', he said.

The ministers had the impression that the meeting had ended amicably and that discussion on the disputed policies would now continue. In the meantime Dr Banda called in other key officials like the Speaker, the provincial governors and senior MPs, and questioned them about the situation.

'Is it true that the people are against my government?' he wanted to know, and I think he was being misled.

'No, *Ngwazi*, the ministers are conspiring against you. They just want to take over', they told him, and deliberately made mischief between the leader and his ministers to take advantage of the situation. Dr Banda then started to make new alliances and promised people seats in the government in return for their support. He sent the Speaker to win over Rose Chiwambo, but Rose was very close to Orton and Chipembere and she had listened to people's complaints during our tour with the League of Malawi Women.

'No, when people like Chirwa, Chisiza and Chipembere are pointing out these problems that I've seen with my own eyes, I'm with them. People are being oppressed here!' Rose said.

'Oh no, Rose, let's Support Kamuzu Banda. Remember he is the one who appointed you.'

'No, I'm not supporting Banda. I'm a Woman of principle.'

Rose did not even receive a proper letter of dismissal. She realised that she had been sacked at the next parliamentary session, but things had hotted up a lot more by then.

51

Appeals to the Organization of African Unity and the United Nations, 1965[61]

Kanyama Chiume and Ex-Malawian Ministers

By 1964, Malawi's prime minister, Dr. Hastings Kamuzu Banda (1898–1997), was beginning to display autocratic tendencies. Domestically, he had introduced medical fees that were extremely unpopular among the Malawian people and persecuted political opponents. Internationally, Banda had built ties with the white regimes in Ian Smith's Rhodesia and in South Africa, as well as with Portugal, which still held on to its African colonies. He publicly accused other African leaders in the region, such as Tanzania's Julius Nyerere, of trying to sabotage his rule. On August 24, 1964, Banda dismissed several ministers who criticized his policies. This was followed by the resignation of other ministers, leading to what is now known as the "Cabinet Crisis." After the resignations, Banda took the opportunity to hold a vote of confidence, which he won due to the fact that his supporters were still in government. The following excerpt comes from the autobiography of Kanyama Chiume (1929–2007) who had served as Malawi's minister of education and minister of foreign affairs. He was a leader of the opposition and fled to Tanzania after the Cabinet Crisis. In this selection, he includes two cables: one of which was sent to the Organization of African Unity (OAU) and the other to the United Nations. The cables explain the reasons behind the decision of the ministers to resign. Chiume closes by critiquing the OAU for failing to respond to the crisis in Malawi.

We ex-ministers decided to cable the secretary-general of the Organisation of African Unity at the O.A.U. conference held in Accra, Ghana, in November, 1965. This is a text of that cable: —

61.   M. W. Kanyama Chiume, *Kwacha: An Autobiography* (Nairobi: East African Publishing House, 1975).

GREETINGS:

The foundation of African unity and future continental union government must be absolute respect of individual rights and freedom and their right to choose own government, otherwise freedom in Africa loses meaning to the ordinary man who has sacrificed so much to bring it about. Banda's Malawi is a den of murder for Pan-Africanists who believe in O.A.U. for Banda is a puppet for colonialism. Banda in Smith military plane accompanied by his Finance Minister Tembo secretly visited Smith on 8th September and pledged in return for continued Rhodesian trade that will not hinder or interfere in Smith's declaring unilateral independence of Rhodesia. And that will have nothing to do with freedom fighters in Rhodesia, Banda as a tool of imperialists is trying to create hostility between the people of Malawi and their friendly neighbours of Tanzania under President Nyerere and make wild charges as a smokescreen for his anti-African activities, anti-medical treatment of his own people. Such is the unpopularity of Banda that the so called republican constitution recently imposed upon the people through his personally nominated district leaders does not provide for the election of him as President by the people but by the parliament which consists of his personal nominees. Malawi must be regarded as a political leper by the O.A.U. and the right steps taken to prevent it from drifting into a laboratory for the destruction of human lives. We wish conference great success.

Malawi ex-ministers.

A few months later we also sent the following telegramme to the Secretary General of the United Nations, drawing his attention to the plight of Malawians:—

On behalf of four million people of Malawi living in terror, murder, arson, intimidation and detention without trial, food or shelter, we respectfully request General Assembly take note Doctor Banda a puppet of Portugal and allies is a threat to Africa's stability and world peace. Doctor Banda with no support of Malawi people keeps in power by force using trigger happy youths to terrorise African people. Civil servants are murdered or beaten up for demanding decolonisation of civil service. Contrary to O.A.U. and General Assembly resolutions he has appointed top Portuguese security man as Malawi Consul in Mozambique has increased trade with Portugal and South Africa, has ordered Malawi people to obey South African government laws and is negotiating for northern portion of Mozambique in return for recognising Portuguese Mozambique to create a buffer to prevent liberation of same. In typical stooge way Doctor Banda is trying to create hostility between Malawi and Tanzania, Zambia and other African states in order aid imperialists in diverting attention of U.N. and Africa from liberating Southern Africa. Doctor Banda must be regarded as African enemy worse than Tshombe and his activities weighed against Stanleyville massacres.

Signed by Orton Chirwa, Yatuta Chisiza, Kanyama Chiume, Augustine Bwanausi and Willie Chokan, Malawi ex-ministers.

The O.A.U. does not have a human rights commission and its charter tends to help the perpetrators rather than the victims of oppression of its member states.

52

Thoughts on Nigerian Constitution, 1966[62]

Obafemi Awolowo

A leading figure in the creation of an independent Nigeria, Obafemi Awolowo (1909–1987) was one of the main supporters of a federal constitution as a means of integrating the multifarious ethnic groups within Nigeria into a single state. Prior to independence from Britain in 1960, Awolowo served as premier of Western Nigeria. Awolowo was recognized as a leader of the Yoruba—one of Nigeria's largest ethnic groups. During the civil war and the rule of the military government, Awolowo served as federal commissioner for Finance and vice-chairman of the Federal Executive Council. Awolowo left politics after the coup that brought down the Second Nigerian Republic (1979–1983) in 1983. In this excerpt from his book Thoughts on Nigerian Constitution *(1966), Awolowo contrasts unitary constitutional systems with federal constitutions. He argues that a federal constitution is necessary in Nigeria, given the country's multi-ethnic and multilingual population.*

From our study of the constitutional evolution of all the countries of the world, two things stand out quite clearly and prominently.

First, in any country where there are divergences of language and of nationality—particularly of language—a unitary constitution is always a source of bitterness and hostility on the part of linguistic or national minority groups. On the other hand, as soon as a federal constitution is introduced in which each linguistic or national group is recognized and accorded regional autonomy, any bitterness and hostility against the constitutional arrangements as such disappear. If the linguistic or national group concerned are backward, or too weak *vis-à-vis* the majority group or groups, their bitterness or hostility may be dormant or suppressed. But as soon as they become enlightened and politically

62. Obafemi Awolowo, excerpt from *Thoughts on Nigerian Constitution*. Copyright © 1966. Reprinted with permission.

conscious, and/or courageous leadership emerges amongst them, the bitterness and hostility come into the open, and remain sustained with all possible venom and rancor, until home rule is achieved.

Secondly, a federal constitution is usually a more or less dead letter in any country which lacks any of the factors conducive to federalism.

From the facts and the analysis thereof which we have given and made in this Section, the following four principles or laws can be deduced:

ONE: If a country is unilingual and uni-national, the constitution must be unitary.

TWO: If a country is unilingual or bilingual or multilingual, and also consists of communities which, over a period of years, have developed divergent nationalities, the constitution must be federal, and the constituent states must be organized on the dual basis of language and nationality.

THREE: If a country is bilingual or multilingual, the constitution must be federal, and the constituent states must be organized on a linguistic basis.

FOUR: Any experiment with a unitary constitution in a bilingual or multilingual or multinational country must fail, in the long run.

We are now in a position to asseverate, categorically and with the emphasis at our command, that, since Nigeria is a multilingual and multinational country *par excellence*, the only constitution that is suitable for its peculiar circumstances is a federal constitution.

53

African Development and Foreign Aid, 1966[63]

Kenneth Kaunda

Born in 1924, Kenneth Kaunda was the first president of Zambia (formerly Northern Rhodesia) after the country achieved independence from the United Kingdom in 1964. Originally a teacher, Kaunda entered politics in 1951 when he joined the Northern Rhodesian African National Congress (ANC). The ANC primarily opposed the Federation of Rhodesia and Nyasaland, which had been created in 1953 as a British protectorate comprised of Northern Rhodesia, Southern Rhodesia, and Nyasaland. The Federation was dominated by the white population, which benefited the most from its founding, and was unpopular among the black population. Despite the ANC's efforts to create a united front against the Federation, within seven years, Kaunda broke from the ANC and it's president, Harry Nkumbula, over Nkumbla's autocratic tendencies. Kaunda went on to form the Zambian African National Congress (ZANC) in 1958. Because of his political activism, Kaunda was imprisoned several times by colonial authorities. During one of Kaunda's terms of imprisonment, ZANC transformed into the United National Independence Party (UNIP) after other ANC members left the party.

Upon his release in 1960, Kaunda became president of UNIP. From this position he initiated a campaign of civil disobedience (the Cha-cha-cha Campaign) against British colonial authorities. In 1963, the Federation of Rhodesia and Nyasaland collapsed. In 1964, Northern Rhodesia became independent and Kaunda became the president of the Republic of Zambia. From the beginning Zambia was plagued by economic problems. Kaunda instituted a one-party state. In 1991, Kaunda, in the face of international pressure, allowed multi-party elections and fell from power. In this address, at the opening of the University of Zambia on March 18, 1966, Kaunda emphasizes the

---

63. Kenneth Kaunda, "African Development and Foreign Aid" (1966), speech made available through the Embassy of Zambia, Washington, DC: http://www.fordham.edu/halsall/mod/1966Kaunda-africadev1.html (accessed October 3, 2016).

challenges of economic development facing Zambia. In the midst of the Cold War, Kaunda resisted seeking aid from both the West and the Soviet bloc. Although Kaunda stresses the need for economic development, he warns that relying on a foreign power for aid brings with it the danger of the reassertion of foreign influence.

Recently, a very close friend of mine declared it would take us another twenty years to be really independent. Was he right? I am afraid there is a lot of truth in this. I do not know what he had in mind but I respect his intelligence and depth of analysing problems. For my own reasons, I agree with him, and here I am not talking about freeing Mozambique, Angola, Portuguese Guinea, Rhodesia, South West Africa and South Africa: I am talking now of countries like ours and many, other independent African States.

In a calm, friendly, world these problems might not have existed; our Independence might have been real. Unfortunately, we do not have the ideal world as yet; ours is a world in which the jungle law is still very much in evidence in spite of claims of civilisation, etc., etc., etc. We live in a world in which survival is for the fittest. . . .

Now we, the so called emerging countries, whether in Africa, parts of Asia or Latin America, are saddled with so many problems that to organise ourselves locally as well as internationally presents a Himalayan challenge.

Most of our weaknesses derive from lack of finance, trained personnel, etc., etc., etc.

We are left with no choice but to fall on either the east or west, or indeed, on both of them. Some of us choose to be non-aligned, believing that this might give us a breathing space to work out our own systems from which we might grow from strength to strength.

In the latter case we are not trusted by either the east or the west. When we preach the importance of man, whether he be from the east or the west, this is dismissed as a meaningless platitude from immature politicians. A very cruel world you might say, but then it is the one in which we live.

When we go to any of these big powers for help they readily will give us that help. They will say aid is being given to us without any strings because this is what they know is popular fancy with us. In fact, there is no such a thing as aid without strings.

A few examples might help to give meaning to what I say. Take training in any field—wherever you send your people they will be indoctrinated, consciously or unconsciously. They will be taught, very vigorously, to look at problems from the aid-giving country's point of view. In most cases, we like to think in terms of getting aid from various sources—that is, from both the east and west—hoping against hope that this will be a shield against interference from either. In fact we end up with a mixture of various explosive gasses in one bottle, and inevitably, explosions follow.

The question, of course, is—what are we supposed to do? We are in a hurry to reassert our Independence—it is human; it is natural. The strong beliefs we hold about the importance of man wherever be may come from lead us to believe that it is right and proper for us to mix with all our fellow men without regard to ideological differences or, indeed, any other differences.

Because of this approach and, as I have already said, we feel we are justified in sending our young people to all corners of the world to attain the necessary knowledge. This is the field in which we find ourselves helpless and yet we see it so very often that this is one of the real sources of danger to our own Independence.

At home we have got to build these extensive civil and military organisations to develop and defend our countries. We have no choice but to train our people in other countries. Some of our civil and military people arc those very ones who were used by colonising powers to suppress freedom movements. In most cases, they have been trained, again by the same powers when they colonised us.

When we make changes that do not conform to the pattern they have been used to, they take offence and the people's Government is first of all doubted, deceived and then overthrown. This often comes without the help of countries and organisations outside our own borders. The sources will depend on which side feels let down.

This is such an important subject that I do not think we should approach it from one side only. If we are honest to the cause we fought and suffered for; if we are honest to our own people, we must see that from time to time we take a critical look of self-inspection.

We are pioneers and, in a way, we are faced with more problems than a pathfinder who has no beaten track before him. The pathfinder who enters a forest has got to find his own track. This in many ways is easier, because certain things have been done in a certain way by certain people from whom we have taken over and we are trying now to redirect things in our own way. Various vested interests will not be happy with us and will naturally react and cause difficulties. We tread on a very tough road for we are not only trying to change the course of history but are also laying down a foundation. The will is there; the path is clear in our own minds; alas, the resources are limited.

I cannot help but mention, once again, that the cornerstone of our constitutions, governments and peoples must be service to man. I know this sounds so simple as to warrant no serious thought, but really when you come to think about this it is the all in all. Without man there is no constitution—there is no government—there is no law—there is no factory—there is no country. In fact, there is nothing that you can think of that would be meaningful. So those of us who are leaders of our people must not only think about the importance of man, it must be an *obsession.*

We must think and think and think again about how best we shall *serve* and *not* about how important we are as leaders of our people, or how we can safeguard our own positions as leaders. Why must we, don't we hold these in trust for our people? We must remember we are *not* elected kings, and that if we believe so much in the importance of man, we must not devise artificial methods of bottling his feelings. On the other hand, those who elected us and those who are our advisers must help their leaders by not doing things that will go to their leaders' heads so that they begin to feel that they are superhuman. . . .

Selfishness in leaders and followers inevitably leads to corruption. I cannot see, however, that uniformed men replacing elected leaders by either killing them, imprisoning them, or, indeed, sending them into exile is the answer to this problem. In some cases, Africa has witnessed the release of thousands, and in a few hours, their places were taken up by tens of thousands.

We should not, however, be over critical at this time because with the exception of one or two of those who have taken over, they have stated that they will hand power back to civil authorities. I do hope they do. If they do not do that, then I can foresee the sad growth of a second Middle East or Latin America right here on the continent. Africa cannot afford that.

To my fellow leaders on the continent of Africa I would venture to send this message—that our task and challenge is to try and help establish Governments of the people, by the people and for the people on the basis of "do unto others as you would have them do unto you"—all the time bearing in mind the application of this to the common man.

There is an obvious danger here that leaders on the continent of Africa might become so frightened of what is happening as to be preoccupied only with their own safety. I might say here that looking at the short list of my heroes I see that they have all got one thing in common, whether they were religious, philosophical, political or military, and this is that sincerely and relentlessly they served—almost without exception they were misunderstood and, indeed, all of them were misunderstood to the point where they died at the hands of the very people they served.

I am sure my heroes must be happy people because later generations understood them, worshipped them and followed them. Of course this cannot be the case with us if we suffered at the hands of our own people for corruptive practices. In other words, much as we deplore violent overthrowing of established governments, our main concern is to leave behind us stable and genuine *people's* systems of government.

54

The Arusha Declaration: On the Policy of Self-Reliance in Tanzania, 1967[64]

The Tanganyika African National Union

The Tanganyika African National Union (TANU) was formed by Julius Nyerere (1922–1999) in 1954. Under Nyerere's stewardship, the party helped lead Tanganyika to independence in 1961 after thirty-nine years of British colonization. Three years later, Tanganyika was renamed Tanzania. TANU advocated the creation of a socialist state in independent Tanzania, as outlined in the Arusha Declaration. The National Executive Committee of TANU accepted the Declaration on January 29, 1967 in the city of Arusha. The Declaration is based on a draft authored by Nyerere, which was modified and published as a document authored by the TANU party

The following excerpts from Part Three of the Arusha Declaration build off of the main principles of Nyerere's unique conception of African socialism, which blended traditional African thought on the significance of the community with a socialist critique of economic exploitation (see Document 41). Rejecting reliance on foreign financial aid, the Declaration argued that economic and industrial development would emerge from a society that embraces African socialist principles and emphasizes agricultural production. By focusing on agricultural production, Tanzania would not become overly reliant on foreign loans.

DO NOT LET US DEPEND UPON MONEY FOR DEVELOPMENT
It is stupid to rely on money as the major instrument of development when we know only too well that our country is poor. It is equally stupid, indeed it is even more stupid, for us to imagine that we shall rid

64. Tanganyika African National Union, "The Arusha Declaration: On the Policy of Self-Reliance in Tanzania" (February 5, 1967), from *Freedom and Socialism: A Selection From Writings and Speeches, 1965–1967* by Julius Nyerere (London: Oxford University Press, 1968).

ourselves of our poverty through foreign financial assistance rather than our own financial resources. It is stupid for two reasons.

Firstly, we shall not get the money. It is true that there are countries which can, and which would like to, help us. But there is no country in the world which is prepared to give us gifts or loans, or establish industries, to the extent that we would be able to achieve all our development targets. There are many needy countries in the world. And even if all the prosperous nations were willing to help the needy countries, the assistance would still not suffice. But in any case the prosperous nations have not accepted a responsibility to fight world poverty. Even within their own borders poverty still exists, and the rich individuals do not willingly give money to the government to help their poor fellow citizens.

It is only through taxation, which people have to pay whether they want to or not, that money can be extracted from the rich in order to help the masses. Even then there would not be enough money. However heavily we taxed the citizens of Tanzania and the aliens living here, the resulting revenue would not be enough to meet the costs of the development we want. And there is no World Government which can tax the prosperous nations in order to help the poor nations; nor if one did exist could it raise enough revenue to do all that is needed in the world. But in fact, such a World Government does not exist. Such money as the rich nations offer to the poor nations is given voluntarily, either through their own goodness, or for their own benefit. All this means that it is impossible for Tanzania to obtain from overseas enough money to develop our economy.

GIFTS AND LOANS WILL ENDANGER OUR INDEPENDENCE

Secondly, even if it were possible for us to get enough money for our needs from external sources, is this what we really want? Independence means self-reliance. Independence cannot be real if a nation depends upon gifts and loans from another for its development. Even if there was a nation, or nations, prepared to give us all the money we need for our development, it would be improper for us to accept such assistance without asking ourselves how this would effect our independence and our very survival as a nation. Gifts which increase, or act as a catalyst, to our own efforts are valuable. Gifts which could have the effect of weakening or distorting our own efforts should not be accepted until we have asked ourselves a number of questions.

The same applies to loans. It is true that loans are better than 'free' gifts. A loan is intended to increase our efforts or make those fruitful. One condition of a loan is that you show how you are going to repay it. This means you have to show that you intend to use the loan profitably and will therefore be able to repay it.

But even loans have their limitations. You have to give consideration to the ability to repay. When we borrow money from other countries it is the Tanzanian who pays it back. And as we have already stated, Tanzania's are poor people. To burden the people with big loans, the repayment of which will be beyond their means, is not to help them but to make them suffer. It is even worse when the loans they are asked to repay have not benefited the majority of the people but have only benefited a small minority.

How about the enterprises of foreign investors? It is true we need these enterprises. We have even passed an Act of Parliament protecting foreign investments in this country. Our aim is to make foreign investors feel that Tanzania is a good place in which to invest because investments would be safe and profitable, and the profits can be taken out of the country without difficulty. We expect to get money through this method. But we cannot get enough. And even if we were able to convince foreign investors and foreign firms to undertake all the projects and programmes of economic development that we need, is that what we actually want to happen?

Had we been able to attract investors from America and Europe to come and start all the industries and all the projects of economic development that we need in this country, could we do so without questioning ourselves? Could we agree to leave the economy of our country in the hands of foreigners who would take the profits back to their countries? Or supposing they did not insist upon taking their profits away, but decided to reinvest them in Tanzania; could we really accept this situation without asking ourselves what disadvantages our nation would suffer? Would this allow the socialism we have said it is our objective to build?

How can we depend upon gifts, loans, and investments from foreign countries and foreign companies without endangering our independence? The English people have a proverb which says, 'He who pays the piper calls the tune'. How can we depend upon foreign governments and companies for the major part of our development without giving to those governments and countries a great part of our freedom to act as we please? The truth is that we cannot.

Let us repeat. We made a mistake in choosing money—something we do not have—to be the big instrument of our development. We are making a mistake to think that we shall get the money from other countries; first, because in fact we shall not be able to get sufficient money for our economic development; and secondly, because even if we could get all that we need, such dependence upon others would endanger our independence and our ability to choose our own political policies.

WE HAVE PUT TOO MUCH EMPHASIS ON INDUSTRIES

Because of our emphasis on money, we have made another big mistake. We have put too much emphasis on industries. Just as we have said, 'Without money there can be no development', we also seem to say, 'Industries are the basis of development, without industries there is no development'. This is true. The day when we have lots of money we shall be able to say we are a developed country. We shall be able to say, 'When we began our Development Plans we did not have enough money and this situation made it difficult for us to develop as fast as we wanted. Today we are developed and we have enough money'. That is to say, our money has been brought by development. Similarly, the day we become industrialized we shall be able to say we are developed. Development would have us to have industries. The mistake we are making is to think that development begins with industries. It is a mistake because we do not have the means to establish many modern industries in our country. We do not have either the necessary finances or the technical know-how. It is not enough to say that we shall borrow the finances and the technicians from other countries to come and start the industries. The answer to this is the same one we gave earlier, that we cannot get enough money and borrow enough technicians to start all the industries we need. And even if we could get the necessary assistance, dependence on it could interfere with our policy on socialism. The policy of inviting a chain of capitalists to come and establish industries in our country might succeed in giving us all the industries we need but it would also succeed in preventing the establishment of socialism unless we believe that without first building capitalism, we cannot build socialism.

LET US PAY HEED TO THE PEASANT

Our emphasis on money and industries has made us concentrate on urban development. We recognize that we do not have enough money to bring the kind of development to each village which would benefit everybody. We also know that we cannot establish an industry in each village and through this means erect a rise in the real incomes of the people. For these reasons we spend most of our money in the urban areas and our industries are established in the towns.

Yet the greater part of this money that we spend in the towns comes from loans. Whether it is used to build schools, hospitals, houses or factories, etc., it still has to be repaid. But it is obvious that it cannot be repaid just out of money obtained from urban and industrial development. To repay the loans we have to use foreign currency which is obtained from the sale of our exports. But we do not now sell our industrial products in foreign markets, and indeed it is likely to be a long time before our industries produce for export. The main aim of our new industries is 'import substitution'—that is, to produce things which up to now we have had to import from foreign countries.

It is therefore obvious that the foreign currency we shall use to pay back the loans used in the development of the urban areas will not come from the towns or the industries. Where, then, shall we get it from? We shall get it from the villages and from agriculture. What does this mean? It means that the people who benefit directly from development which is brought about by borrowed money are not the ones who will repay the loans. The largest proportion of the loans will be spent in, or for, the urban areas, but the largest proportion of the repayment will be made through the efforts of the farmers.

This fact should always be borne in mind, for there are various forms of exploitation. We must not forget that people who live in towns can possibly become the exploiters of those who live in the rural areas. All our big hospitals are in towns and they benefit only a small section of the people of Tanzania. Yet if we have built them with loans from outside Tanzania, it is the overseas sale of the peasants' produce which provides the foreign exchanges for repayment. Those who do not get the benefit of the hospital thus carry the major responsibility for paying for them. Tarmac roads, too, are mostly found in towns and are of especial value to the motor-car owners. Yet if we have built those roads with loans, it is again the farmer who produces the goods which will pay for them. What is more, the foreign exchange with which the car was bought also came from the sale of the farmers' produce. Again, electric lights, water pipes, hotels and other aspects of modern development are mostly found in towns. Most of them have been built with loans, and most of them do not benefit the farmer directly, although they will be paid for by the foreign exchange earned by the sale of his produce. We should always bear this in mind.

Although when we talk of exploitation we usually think of capitalists, we should not forget that there are many fish in the sea. They eat each other. The large ones eat the small ones, and small ones eat those who are even smaller. There are two possible ways of dividing the people in our country. We can put the capitalists and feudalists on one side, and the farmers and workers on the other. But we can also divide the people into urban dwellers on one side and those who live in the rural areas on the other. If we are not careful we might get to the position where the real exploitation in Tanzania is that of the town dwellers exploiting the peasants.

. . . .

AGRICULTURE IS THE BASIS OF DEVELOPMENT

A great part of Tanzania's land is fertile and gets sufficient rain. Our country can produce various crops for home consumption and for export.

We can produce food crops (which can be exported if we produce in large quantities) such as maize, rice, wheat, beans, groundnuts, etc. And we can produce such cash crops as sisal, cotton, coffee, tobacco, pyrethrum, tea, etc. Our land is also good for grazing cattle, goats, sheep, and for raising chickens, etc.; we can get plenty of fish from our rivers, lakes, and from the sea. All of our farmers are in areas which can produce two or three or even more of the food and cash crops enumerated above, and each farmer could increase his production so as to get more food or more money. And because the main aim of development is to get more food, and more money for our other needs, our purpose must be to increase production of these agricultural crops. This is in fact the only road through which we can develop our country—in other words, only by increasing our production of these things can we get more food and more money for every Tanzanian.

. . . .

HARD WORK IS THE ROOT OF DEVELOPMENT

Some Plan projects which depend on money are going on well, but there are many which have stopped and others which might never be fulfilled because of lack of money. Yet still we talk about money and our search for money increases and takes nearly all our energies. We should not lessen our efforts to get the money we really need, but it would be more appropriate for us to spend time in the villages showing the people how to bring about development through their own efforts rather than going on so many long and expensive journeys abroad in search of development money. This is the real way to bring development to everybody in the country.

None of this means that from now on we will not need money or that we will not start industries or embark upon development projects which require money. Furthermore, we are not saying that we will not accept, or even that we shall not look for, money from other countries for our development. This is NOT what we are saying. We will continue to use money; and each year we will use more money for the various development projects than we used the previous year because this will be one of the signs of our development.

What we are saying, however, is that from now on we shall know what is the foundation and what is the fruit of development. Between MONEY and PEOPLE it is obvious that the people and their hard work are the foundation of development, and money is one of the fruits of that hard work.

From now on we shall stand upright and walk forward on our feet rather than look at this problem upside down. Industries will come and money will come but their foundation is THE PEOPLE and their HARD WORK, especially in AGRICULTURE. This is the meaning of self-reliance.

INDEX